W9-BRZ-300

# THE MOUNDBUILDERS

*With 153 illustrations, 20 in color*

GEORGE R. MILNER

# THE MOUNDBUILDERS
## Ancient Peoples
## of Eastern North America

Thames & Hudson

*Ancient Peoples and Places*
FOUNDING EDITOR: GLYN DANIEL

**For my parents,
George R. and Norah L. Milner**

*The Moundbuilders* © 2004 Thames & Hudson Ltd, London

All Rights Reserved. No part of this publication may be reproduced or transmitted in any form or by any means, electronic or mechanical, including photocopy, recording or any other information storage and retrieval system, without prior permission in writing from the publisher.

First published in hardcover in the United States of America in 2004 by Thames & Hudson Inc., 500 Fifth Avenue, New York, New York 10110

thamesandhudsonusa.com

First paperback edition 2005
Reprinted 2015

Library of Congress Catalog Card Number 2003101347

ISBN 978-0-500-28468-1

Printed and bound in China by C & C Offset Printing Co Ltd

# Contents

# Preface

Who built the mounds in eastern North America? In the nineteenth century, there was wild speculation about the "origin, customs, and ultimate fate of the Mound-builders."[1] These "mysterious people" supposedly had nothing to do with the Native Americans who shortly before had been decimated and pushed westward beyond the Mississippi River. In the words of one skeptic, the moundbuilder was "an illusory, mythological personage, who, in fairy-book fashion, roves through the sunny south, floats over northern lakes, traverses western prairies, wanders up and down great rivers."[2] The reality is that the mounds were indeed built by Native Americans, ancestors of the people who remain such a vibrant presence in modern America; their story is so much more interesting than fantasies about long-vanished peoples.

The great majority of the mounds have now been destroyed, flattened by plowing, or hemmed in by urban development, and the same is true of Native American villages. One can hardly imagine what it was like for the first government land surveyors who in 1808 came upon Cahokia – the largest prehistoric site in the United States – after slogging through the stagnant water and rank vegetation of the Mississippi Valley. Once reaching "the Edge of a large Prairie," there were "Twenty four or more of those mounds in Sight at one view ... All covered with Simtoms of antient ruins."[3] We now know there were about four times that number of mounds at Cahokia, along with the refuse that had accumulated over several centuries. One mound was the largest in the United States. This "most stupendous pile of earth," known as Monks Mound after some Trappist monks who once resided there, rises 100 ft (30 m) in a series of terraces and towers over all other mounds at the site.[4]

Mounds first became a subject of widespread interest about 200 years ago pl. III as Euroamerican settlers flowed inexorably westward over the Appalachian Mountains, spilling into the fertile Ohio Valley and beyond. Even Lewis and Clark's famous Corps of Discovery made a point of stopping to see a few mounds on their long journey westward to the Pacific Ocean. One of these edifices, the 62-ft (19-m) Grave Creek mound along the Ohio River in West Virginia, can still be seen today, although its immediate surroundings – downtown Moundsville – bear no resemblance to those seen by the Corps of Discovery in 1803. We are just fortunate that this "remarkable mound of earth" was not among the many that have been leveled in the name of progress.[5]

We now know that the mounds collectively span several thousand years. They were built by both hunter-gatherers and agriculturalists, some of whom lived in communities led by hereditary chiefs. Because these societies were so exceedingly diverse, it should come as no surprise that the mounds served various purposes and had different meanings for different peoples. There was a time when archaeologists dug mounds almost to the exclusion of villages, which were rightly seen as yielding fewer aesthetically pleasing artifacts. But today archaeologists direct much of their attention toward houses, storage pits, cooking hearths, personal ornaments, tools, and food debris. These remnants of everyday life tell us a great deal about how people lived long ago. Still, the mounds and what they contain provide otherwise unavailable information on life in the distant past, including which people were held in highest regard by their fellow community members.

Much of our knowledge hinges on the dating of sites and artifacts, and fortunately the means of doing so have advanced greatly in recent years. But the issue of dating is still confusing. Radiocarbon dates are not the same as calendar years because of changes over time in atmospheric carbon. Discrepancies between the two dates are far greater earlier than later in prehistory. In this book dates for the early occupation of eastern North America, from Paleoindian through Early Archaic, are given in approximate calendar years after radiocarbon dates have been adjusted, or calibrated, using the OxCal 3.4 program. Calibrated dates facilitate comparisons with climatic events that are critical in setting the stage for the peopling of the Americas. Dates based on radiocarbon are also provided because they are the ones most commonly encountered in scholarly and popular accounts of life in the distant past. The dates for later occupations – that is, from the Middle Archaic onward – are the ones that are customarily used by archaeologists. They are based on a bewildering mix of radiocarbon dates adjusted in various ways, or not at all, along with a big dose of guesswork. While they differ somewhat from calendar years, they are used to simplify the process of comparing information in this book with that found in other publications and museum exhibits. One should also be aware that the beginning and ending of the cultural periods are only estimates, some of which (especially the later ones) are more accurate than others.

When writing a book of this sort, hard choices are made in condensing innumerable archaeological facts into an account of what took place over many thousands of years. My interest here is in how people lived at different times in the past, not the many details about pottery, stone tools, and building remnants that fill technical reports. Every effort has been made to sidestep the myriad alternative ways of classifying artifacts and cultural units that form regional sequences. As this book focuses on the builders of the mounds, the temporal and geographical coverage is uneven: the last half of prehistory when the mounds were constructed receives the greatest

| CONVENTIONAL DATES | CALENDAR DATES | CULTURAL PERIODS | MOUND SITES |
|---|---|---|---|
| | | Various Late Prehistoric (Chap. 7) | *Spiro* *Moundville* *Cahokia* |
| AD 1000 | AD 1000 | Mississippian (Chap. 6) | *Toltec* |
| AD 1 | | Late Woodland (Chap. 5) | *Mound City, Hopewell* *Robbins* |
| 1000 BC | 1000 BC | Middle Woodland (Chap. 4) | *Poverty Point* |
| | | Early Woodland (Chap. 4) | |
| 2000 BC | 3000 BC | Late Archaic (Chap. 3) | *Watson Brake* |
| 3000 BC | | | |
| 4000 BC | 5000 BC | | *Read, Black Earth* |
| | | Middle Archaic (Chap. 3) | |
| 5000 BC | | | |
| 6000 BC | 7000 BC | | |
| 7000 BC | | Early Archaic (Chap. 2) | |
| 8000 BC | 9000 BC | | |
| | | Paleoindian (Chap. 2) | |
| 9000 BC | 11000 BC | | *Kimmswick* |
| 10,000 BC | | | |

— The solid lines indicate dates used in this book.
••••• The dotted lines show some of the variation in dating cultural periods that exists in the archaeological literature.

Dates for major cultural periods are debated, and new means of calibrating radiocarbon dates ("calendar dates") are forcing archaeologists to revise chronological sequences, referred to above as "conventional dates."

attention, as do the Midwest and Southeast where the mounds are most abundant. There is of course much else of interest in eastern North American prehistory, but the moundbuilding societies serve as a fine introduction to the original inhabitants of this great land.

This book could not have been completed without the assistance of many people. Several colleagues, including David Anderson, Rebecca Ferrell, Richard Jefferies, Claire McHale Milner, Lee Newsom, Michael Shott, Dean Snow, and Michael Wiant, provided insightful comments on some or all of an early draft. Scott Hammerstedt and Tim Murtha prepared the maps, and Judy Cooper and Megaera Lorenz drew several figures. Those who answered questions, provided illustrations, or rummaged through museum collections and archives for artifacts and photographs include, among others, David Anderson, Jennifer Barber, Scott Beld, Robert Brooks, James Brown, Brian Butler, Christopher Carr, Frank Cowan, George Crothers, Claudia Cummings, Richard Diehl, Ann Early, Ken Farnsworth, Russell Graham, N'omi Greber, William Green, David Hally, Judy Hamilton, Nancy Hawkins, Gwynn Henderson, Keith Jacobi, Richard Jefferies, Duryea Kemp, Jeffrey Mitchem, Steven Nash, Lee Newsom, William Marquardt, Jerald Milanich, David Pollack, Robert Riordan, Michael Russo, Martha Rolingson, Joe Saunders, Sissel Schroeder, Bruce Smith, Dean Snow, Lynne Sullivan, Michael Wiant, and Randolph Widmer. To all of these people I owe a large debt of gratitude. I also want to thank my wife and son for putting up with the many disruptions that writing a book brings about. Their understanding and support made this book possible.

1 Monks Mound is shown on this early twentieth-century postcard. The gate in front of the mound is now gone, and the road is wider.

# 1 · A Heavily Forested and Thinly Peopled Land

It is hard to imagine eastern North America covered by old-growth forest instead of by the much younger woods, plowed fields, and urban sprawl that we see today. It is equally difficult for most people to envision what life was like in the distant past. To do so we must turn to archaeology as the primary source of information about most of the lengthy period when humans were present on the continent.

## The Eastern Woodlands

Several hundred years ago a dense forest covered the land. Only the highest peaks of the Appalachians, grasslands of various sizes, and impermanent clearings for villages and gardens broke the canopy of trees. The forest extended from the Gulf Coast northward to the arctic tundra, and from the Atlantic Ocean westward to vast rolling prairies. Its western margin extended from western Minnesota southeastward into the once-glaciated part of Illinois north of the Shawnee Hills. The eastern extent of tall-grass prairie – grasses and herbaceous plants partly maintained by frequent fires, some of which were caused by humans – pushed deep into the Eastern Woodlands. This area, the Prairie Peninsula, was laced by narrow strips of woods flanking streams of various sizes, and its southern margin extended westward from southern Illinois into central Missouri. The forest and prairie transition then dropped southward through eastern Oklahoma and into Texas.

The forest and the animals that lived there were not everywhere the same. Woods rich in pines covered the Gulf and south Atlantic coastal plains where winters were mild, summers hot, and rainfall plentiful. To the north was a vast deciduous forest that varied in composition, although several different oaks were dominant. It eventually gave way to a wide band of deciduous and coniferous trees stretching from the northern Great Lakes through Ontario, New York, and into New England. Even farther north, the conifers of the boreal forest were replaced by barren tundra. Latitude, however, was not the entire story. The high peaks and plateaus of the Appalachians influenced the distributions of plants and animals, as did large bodies of water, such as the Great Lakes and, particularly, the Atlantic Ocean.

2  Eastern North America showing state boundaries along with some of the principal rivers, mountains, and prairies.

No matter how untamed the forest might have seemed to the first European explorers, it was no pristine wilderness untouched by human hands.[1] Native Americans cleared large swaths of land for villages and fields by girdling trees and lighting fires. So much underbrush was consumed by fires that it was easy for travelers to make their way through forests that in later centuries were all but impassable, such as the tangle in Virginia that so impeded troops during the Civil War's Wilderness campaign. Burning increased browse for deer and created edge zones suitable for many other edible animals and plants. Thus by accident or design, Native Americans enhanced the productivity of the land around their settlements, although any gains were transitory because game and firewood were soon exhausted, often in only a few years.

The mix of native plants and animals varied from one place to the next, as did their productivity and reliability. During late prehistoric times, many people relied heavily on maize and beans that ultimately came from Mesoamerica. Maize, which was especially important, could be depended upon where there were more than about 140 frost-free days during the growing season.[2] The northern limits of this area extended through the southern parts of Minnesota, Wisconsin, Michigan, and Ontario, and then into New England.

River valleys tended to be the best places to live in the continental interior. A wide range of plants and animals could be found as one went from river margins, through wet floodplains, to the surrounding drier uplands. People everywhere sought out white-tailed deer for their meat and hides, although the dietary contribution of venison lessened late in prehistory when human population densities rose, hunting pressure increased, and large game became locally depleted.[3]

Wetlands such as oxbow lakes from cut-off river channels were especially productive places. Abandoned channels had long shorelines relative to their

3  The Mississippi Valley in southern Illinois is quite wet during the spring. Low areas that were once swamps or lakes still fill with water at this time of the year, despite herculean efforts to drain the bottomland for agriculture. The western bluff, the Missouri side of the river, can be seen in the distance. Many edible plants and animals, along with fertile soils, made the river valleys especially good places to settle.

4 Shell heaps dot the Gulf and Atlantic coasts. This low mound, designated 3Mb°5 and excavated in 1941, was located in an Alabama marsh. Coastal wetlands, which were exceedingly rich in natural resources, were favorite places to settle throughout much of prehistory.

surface areas and were often shallow and choked with vegetation, so they were ideal fishing spots. Annual floods spread broadly across the bottomlands and, when the water receded, fish were trapped in ever-shrinking pools where they could be easily caught with nets, yielding a great return for little effort.[4] Innumerable dorsal fins creasing the surface of an almost dry pond are a memorable sight. In such situations it is possible to grab large fish by hand, if one does not mind mucking around in stagnant and foul-smelling water.

Receding floodwaters also left extensive mud flats soon covered by thick stands of pioneering plants; these included goosefoot and other weedy plants with edible greens and seeds that were part of prehistoric diets, especially in the midcontinent.[5] New sediments deposited by annual floods maintained soil fertility, and it was easy to work the silty sands of bottomland ridges and natural levees with simple stone and shell hoes.

Coastal areas were also fine places to live. They too were rich in edible plants and animals, particularly the shallow and brackish waters of estuaries, bays, and marshes. Piles of shell gradually built up where many generations of people discarded the remains of their meals. Fish were especially abundant when they swam upstream to spawn.

4

## Doing archaeology

The earliest efforts at mapping and excavating sites were focused on the contents of mounds and graves. In eastern North America, this work is usually said to have begun in the eighteenth century when Thomas Jefferson dug into a mound near his home in Virginia, although he was not the only one to do so at that time.[6] He wanted to know whether the mounds were monuments containing battlefield deaths, repositories for bones that were originally buried elsewhere, or common cemeteries. After looking at the soils and bone deposits in his mound, he decided that the disarticulated remains of many people, the old and young alike, had been buried at different times. He also said that Indians originated in Asia and came to the Americas across the Bering Strait, citing as support Captain James Cook's then-current explorations in the Pacific. Well over a century would pass before similarly sensible reports became commonplace.

Public opinion instead latched onto a singularly strange idea: the existence of a separate race of moundbuilders. Fantastic stories flourished in the near absence of solid data, which were slow in coming, and an unwillingness to pursue the little information that was available. Many thought that the moundbuilders originated in distant corners of the world. Others believed they were Native Americans, but an earlier people who had the misfortune of being pushed out by barbarians who were, in turn, displaced by waves of European settlers. Here was convenient justification – if one was really needed – to take land that was only thinly populated. After all, it seemed that better use could be made of a wilderness that had only recently come into the possession of a warlike people who had themselves displaced some superior, but otherwise unknown, folk. Little thought was given as to why mounds were no longer being built by a numerically depleted people whose societies had changed greatly during the turbulent times from the sixteenth century onward.

A direct link was made between big mounds and both enormous populations and societies likened to the world's largest ancient civilizations. Cahokia, the biggest site in the United States, exercised the imaginations of those who stood before its many mounds. It was believed that "a people capable of works requiring so much labour, must be numerous, and if numerous, somewhat advanced in the arts."[7] There existed at Cahokia "a population as numerous as that which once animated the borders of the Nile, or of the Euphrates, or of Mexico and Peru." Such wildly enthusiastic but thoroughly uninformed statements fueled speculation that the moundbuilders were not at all related to the Native Americans, who were increasingly being forced to live in squalid conditions on the worst possible land.

Toward the end of the nineteenth century, the noted archaeologist Gerard Fowke specifically addressed the problems inherent in relating mounds to the size of populations and the nature of societies. He rightly saw it as one of the "many absurd theories and notions promulgated by authors ignorant of their subject and writing only to strike the popular mind and pocket."[8] Yet his words did little to put a stop to grossly exaggerated notions of life in the past. Similar views are still being repeated today, only without the part about a separate race of moundbuilders.

The belief that moundbuilders were something other than Native Americans was finally laid to rest about a century ago, largely through the work of the Bureau of Ethnology.[9] Surveys and excavations were undertaken to provide accurate descriptions of mounds, determine how they were constructed, classify them in terms of their shape, and obtain artifacts from them. Cyrus Thomas directed this effort and wrote up the results, relying heavily on correspondence with his field workers, often quoting their descriptions verbatim. Any doubts about who built the mounds were crushed by a lengthy report published in 1894 that was packed with site descriptions and excavation details.

Many people at that time were fascinated with what could be found near their homes, and some of them corresponded with Thomas. But excavations were crude, since little in the way of even rudimentary training was available. Mound fill was stripped off as quickly as possible to unearth artifacts that were thought to be deeply buried. Much information about how mounds were constructed was thereby lost. Some objects were destined for museums or special exhibitions, including the 1893 World's Columbian Exposition in Chicago.[10] Most of them, however, were discarded in the field because only the best artifacts were considered worth saving.

5   Early archaeologists sometimes tunneled into mounds, as shown in this 1897 excavation of the Carriage Factory mound in southern Ohio. Such excavations provided little information on mound construction.

By the first half of the twentieth century, enough information had accumulated to make some sense of the distributions of certain kinds of prehistoric remains, particularly pottery and mounds. In the 1930s, the need to impose some order on the many discoveries that were being made came to a head. Innumerable artifacts were being found in large excavations sponsored by Franklin D. Roosevelt's New Deal relief programs, such as the Works Progress Administration (WPA) and the Civilian Conservation Corps (CCC).

Eventually an emphasis on description and classification gave way to an interest in learning about how societies were organized and functioned. This interest partly motivated some of the New Deal projects, but it only became a major concern in the decades immediately following World War II.

These changes in research concerns were accompanied by a shift in emphasis from individual sites to entire regions, such as certain segments of river valleys. The study of the distribution of sites relative to each other and to the natural landscape got off to a fine start with a late 1940s survey of the lower Mississippi Valley.[11] A number of regions are now well known, although the overall coverage of eastern North America is still patchy. It is, after all, a vast area.

Shifts in research direction came in no small part from new opportunities for fieldwork. Through the 1920s, inadequately funded excavations were manned by small crews that worked only for short periods of time. Yet better excavation and recording procedures were gradually introduced, most notably through work in Illinois by the University of Chicago that began in the late 1920s. The practice of archaeology changed dramatically and suddenly during the Great Depression in the 1930s. Several archaeologists – especially William S. Webb, whose nickname "Bull Neck" fitted his forceful

6

6  Large crews did an amazing amount of work at many sites during the Great Depression, particularly in the Southeast, and much of it was first rate. One such example is the 1939 excavation of a flat-topped Mississippian-period mound at the Bessemer site in Alabama.

## "Preserve these beautiful eminences"

Innumerable archaeological sites – including impressive mounds – have fallen victim to the necessities and conveniences of modern life, as well as the curiosity and cupidity of looters, commonly called "pot hunters." In fact, site destruction was one of the reasons Cyrus Thomas considered the late-nineteenth-century mound survey so pressing.[12] This is still an issue today – only there are far fewer sites than just a century ago.

The means of protecting sites were quite limited before the last few decades. Appeals could be made to civic pride, but they were rarely effectual. St. Louis, for example, was once proudly referred to as Mound City, but that did not halt the destruction of its mounds. A few lonely voices argued that they ought to be preserved for the betterment of the city's inhabitants, with one person expressing surprise that "individual taste and public spirit do not unite to preserve these beautiful eminences in their exact forms, and connect them by an enclosure, with shrubbery and walks, thus forming a promenade that might be the pride of St. Louis."[13] Sadly this was not done – land was too valuable and greed too great – and the mounds had vanished by the mid-nineteenth century. When the biggest of the St. Louis mounds was being leveled, a newspaper reported that "curiosity hunters flock there daily by the hundreds, armed with all sorts of vessels, hoping to secure and carry off some relic of the past ages."[14] Quick to capitalize on the excitement, a local business announced that "a curious two-wheeled vehicle, supposed to be an ancient velocipede" from the Big Mound was on display.[15] Velocipedes were causing quite a stir in St. Louis, and one supposedly from the Big

Mound was sure to excite credulous onlookers.

Fortunately, mounds in a number of places were incorporated into city cemeteries or public parks, and were thereby afforded some protection. One such example is a tall conical mound, the Conus, in the Mound Cemetery in Marietta, Ohio. Over a century and a half ago, Ephram Squier and Edwin Davis singled out the citizens of Marietta for special praise for preserving their mounds, while lamenting the loss of what would have been "striking ornaments" in other cities.[16] In fact, the early settlers of Marietta were so proud of their mounds that they dignified them with Latinized names. The Serpent Mound, also in southern Ohio, is another well-known site that was saved.[17] In this instance, a group of prominent Boston women raised the purchase price in the 1880s, and the earthwork was then turned over to the Peabody Museum at Harvard University. In 1900, the Serpent Mound was deeded to the Ohio Historical Society, which still maintains it as a public park.

The surviving mounds and villages are for the most part located in rural areas, but such settings do not fully protect them. Plowing soon reduces mounds to low domes, obscuring their original shapes and removing the uppermost burials and building remnants. The destruction of mounds began long ago: as early as the eighteenth century, Thomas Jefferson reported that the height of the mound he excavated was already diminished by plowing.[18] Over 200 years later, the situation is that much worse.

Pot hunters also take a tremendous toll of archaeological sites. The most notorious excavation for profit took

7   The Big Mound at St. Louis, once nicknamed Mound City, was flattened in 1869. Other mounds in the rapidly growing city were destroyed as well, despite the outcry of concerned citizens.

place in the 1930s during the height of the Great Depression. A group of men who called themselves the Pocola Mining Company tunneled deep into a large mound at the Spiro site in Oklahoma.[19] The artifacts they unearthed, including impressive engraved marine-shell cups, were then sold for a tidy profit. Public outrage fanned by newspaper articles eventually prompted efforts to halt the looting and to conduct proper excavations to make sense of this remarkable find. Today the site is fortunately preserved as the state's sole archaeological park.

The situation has now improved because of stricter laws guarding against the disturbance of sites, especially those on public land. Pot hunters can be prosecuted for looting sites.

personality – realized that Roosevelt's effort to put people back to work provided an ideal opportunity to excavate on a far grander scale than had ever before been imaginable. For the first time, big crews worked for long periods exposing large parts of many sites. In the best of excavations, the need to organize untrained laborers led to a much-needed standardization and improvement of field techniques. These innovations were in large part inspired by the University of Chicago projects.

Southeastern states were the primary beneficiaries of New Deal funding for archaeological work. Mild winters permitted long field seasons; there was high unemployment among a largely rural population; floodwaters from a major federal program, the Tennessee Valley Authority (TVA), threatened to inundate many mounds and villages; and archaeologists proved adept at obtaining federal funding. But major excavations were also conducted elsewhere, including several that exposed entire late prehistoric villages in Pennsylvania.

Since World War II, archaeologists have increasingly focused on the discovery and excavation of sites liable to be destroyed to make room for dams, highways, buildings, and the like. This work, once referred to as "salvage archaeology" but now known as Cultural Resource Management (CRM), started as surveys and excavations along rivers that the U.S. Army Corps of Engineers were turning into huge reservoirs. This salvage work was originally inspired by the great success of the 1930s and early 1940s excavations conducted as part of TVA dam projects.[20] Vastly better funding since the mid-1970s has allowed more comprehensive surveys and excavations, as well as more complete analyses of the materials from them. In fact, the current CRM work represents the second and most generous period of major public funding for archaeology – the New Deal being the first.

8    Our current understanding of life in the past is not only a result of larger areas being surveyed and more sites being excavated. Today, more different kinds of sites are dug than ever before. This shift mostly stems from the perfectly understandable CRM emphasis on areas defined by modern construction needs, which are not always the places with the biggest mounds and finest artifacts. Small sites are finally getting the attention they so richly deserve.

Many more materials are also taken from the field. This practice began with the New Deal projects, which occasionally hired specialists to deal with human skeletons, animal bones, mollusks, and ceramics. At that time it was recognized that one of the most important reasons for excavating sites was to obtain skeletons to learn about the health, particularly the nutritional status, of past peoples.[21] Regrettably, not until the late 1960s was this kind of specialized work begun in earnest.

Studies of plant and animal remains greatly improved in the 1960s and 1970s with the widespread adoption of a simple procedure, called "flotation," for extracting small items from soil. Here, dirt is washed in plenty of water to catch even the smallest animal bones and carbonized seeds in very

8  Mostly stone tools, chips of stone, and pottery (right), such as these artifacts from Kentucky, are found when walking over plowed fields. They indicate places where people once lived.

fine mesh. It was at long last possible to get the small bones and seeds needed for a fuller picture of ancient peoples' diets. Late prehistoric people who were thought to have eaten mostly maize and deer – cobs and large bones are easy to spot while digging – were found to have consumed a much wider variety of foods. Indeed, our fixation on deer as their principal quarry has more to do with Western views of the ideal game animal, which date back to the Middle Ages, than it has to do with the evidence actually at hand. Stable carbon and nitrogen isotopes in human bones also provide a direct measure of diets. Of particular importance is our ability to pinpoint when people first began to eat great quantities of maize.

If the past few decades are any guide to the future, we can soon expect many breakthroughs in our ability to extract information from old objects. Of course, all of this work depends on our being able to find and excavate sites before looters, construction projects, and modern agricultural practices destroy them. Still, the most pressing challenge that we face today is not unlike the one experienced by our Depression-era predecessors. How do we go about making the fullest use of the unprecedented amount of information that is being amassed at such great cost in time and effort?

# 2 · Mobile Hunter-Gatherers: Paleoindian and Early Archaic

When did people first find their way to the Americas? We can only be sure that it was toward the end of the Ice Age (or Pleistocene) when massive ice sheets covered much of North America. For several thousand years following their arrival in eastern North America these people practiced a mobile hunting-and-gathering way of life. They were thin on the ground, and left behind correspondingly skimpy evidence of their existence, mostly stone tools.

## Beringia and beyond

To get to the Americas hunter-gatherers had to journey across the area where the Bering Strait is now located. Here the shallow ocean floor was exposed for many thousands of years before and after the last glacial maximum around 21,000 years ago. When the sea reached its lowest point, as much as 930 miles (1,500 km) of dry land separated the Arctic and Pacific oceans.[1]

This land bridge, known as Beringia, was cold and dry, but unglaciated. It was the eastern end of the Mammoth Steppe, a vast grassland that extended largely unbroken across Siberia and into Europe.[2] Large grazing animals, most notably bison, horses, and woolly mammoths, as well as many smaller ones, roamed this grassy plain and took refuge in sheltered stream valleys filled with shrubby growth. The now-submerged coastal margin might have been particularly attractive to hunter-gatherers who ventured into this land. To the east, Beringia was bordered by two immense masses of ice in what is now Alaska and the Yukon Territory. The largest was the Laurentide Ice Sheet that covered most of Canada and extended far southward into the United States. The other was the Cordilleran Ice Sheet, a complex of glaciers that extended down from the mountainous spine of western Canada.

When did people first venture beyond the ice sheets? Excavations by Thomas Dillehay at Monte Verde in Chile may indicate that they had reached South America by 14,900 years ago (12,500 years ago in radiocarbon time).[3] While some archaeologists dispute the dating of Monte Verde, it is gaining acceptance as a truly early site after a team of specialists inspected it in the late 1990s. This early occupation of Monte Verde would mean that

9 The late Pleistocene landscape in Illinois was unlike that of more recent times.

10 Paleoindian fluted points have been found throughout the eastern United States, including this Clovis point from Virginia. Length 2.2 in (5.6 cm).

hunter-gatherers must have spread widely well before the first generally recognized signs of human occupation – distinctive projectile points known as Clovis – appear in North America south of the ice sheets.

There are two possible routes southward from Beringia, neither of which were easy going until the glacial retreat was well underway.[4] One of them passed between the massive Laurentide and Cordilleran ice sheets just east of the rugged mountains in western Canada. But even if there was an opening in full glacial times, it is unlikely that humans traveled through it until well after the ice sheets had begun to retreat. When the ice sheets were near, this so-called Ice Free Corridor would have been a forbidding landscape of newly denuded ground, sparse vegetation, and frigid lakes. The other way beyond the ice sheets involved hugging the rocky Pacific coast, skirting glaciers that filled valleys between rugged mountains. Unglaciated headlands during the glacial maximum, and for some time thereafter, were cold and sparsely vegetated places. But the glacial retreat, once begun, appears to have been relatively rapid, and there soon followed plants and animals that made the coast more attractive. If people came this way, they were perhaps

11  Selected sites mentioned in Chapters 2 and 3.

drawn forward by plentiful and vulnerable marine animals such as seals. Currently both migration routes have ardent supporters, although there is no direct evidence backing up either position. All we know for sure is that people somehow skirted the ice sheets and then colonized a new rich land.

The earliest sure signs of humans in eastern North America are the distinctive Clovis points mentioned above, which date to no more than about 13,400 years ago (the customarily used figure based on uncorrected radiocarbon dates is about 11,500 years ago).[5] They are called fluted points because, for reasons unknown to us, long flakes were removed from their sides, producing shallow channels. Any earlier occupation of the region is at present disputed.[6] Hints include a tortoise from Florida that appears to have been killed around 14,000 years ago by a wooden spear (radiocarbon date of 12,030 ± 200 years ago). The most well-known candidate, however, for an early site is Meadowcroft rockshelter, a deeply stratified site in southwestern Pennsylvania. The oldest materials there supposedly precede the Clovis sites by several thousand years. Items in the lowest artifact-bearing deposits include stone flakes and tools, as well as burnt basketry. But despite the quality of the excavation and the number of radiocarbon dates, many archaeologists remain skeptical about the early occupation at Meadowcroft. Some say the samples might have been contaminated with old carbon – the site is located in the coal-producing part of Pennsylvania. Moreover, it is puzzling that the scanty animal and plant remains from the deep levels are consistent with a temperate environment, not the tundra or boreal forest expected of a spot close to the southern edge of a vast ice sheet. At this point, evidence for a pre-Clovis occupation, while tantalizing, falls short of gaining general acceptance.

No matter when people arrived, they faced environments that were unlike 9 those experienced by their distant descendants. Although the overall trend was toward a warmer climate, the transition from full glacial to modern conditions – that is, from the late Pleistocene to Holocene – did not always proceed in the same direction or at the same rate.[7] About 14,700 years ago, based on Greenland ice core data, there was an abrupt shift to milder conditions: the Bølling Transition. There followed a cold period, the Younger Dryas, that lasted about 1,300 years before ending abruptly around 11,600 years ago. Vegetation changed accordingly, as shown by pollen cores from the Great Lakes eastward into New England.

As climate changed, a late Pleistocene mosaic of forests and grasslands – a patchy environment by today's standards – gave way to the more homogeneous vegetation cover of today.[8] Animals and plants changed their ranges individually in response to their own temperature and moisture requirements. Thus the transition to modern conditions was not a simple slow northward movement and expansion of fixed plant and animal communities. The breakup of the late Pleistocene plant cover placed new pressures on animals, and those with narrow feeding requirements were especially vulnerable. Many died off, including animals from immense mastodons and mammoths down to tiny mice and bats. While the extinction of large herbivores and the carnivores that fed on them have naturally received the most attention, they were not the only ones to disappear.

## The Paleoindians

The people who made the fluted points – collectively known as Paleoindians 10 – proved remarkably adept at surviving in diverse environmental settings. Several varieties of fluted points were made at different times and places, as were lanceolate points without the distinctive flake scars that thinned them. The dates for these people in eastern North America, once corrected, coincide reasonably well with the Younger Dryas, a return to colder conditions. Here one should keep in mind that estimates for climatic events from Greenland ice cores are more precise than those for the Paleoindian period. The latter are based on radiocarbon dates from sites identified by chance rather than by design. Moreover, changes in local plant and animal life, which would have been of supreme importance to hunter-gatherers, lagged somewhat behind the onset of new climatic conditions.

It has long been recognized that some places in eastern North America have far more than their share of Paleoindian points.[9] Early points are concentrated in several parts of the midcontinent, especially the middle Tennessee River Valley, and along the Atlantic Seaboard. The chances that old stone tools will be found, hence the overall distribution of points, is strongly affected by differences in modern land use and the archaeological attention certain places have received. While fully aware of these problems, David Anderson has argued that the hot spots reflect, however crudely, places in the continental interior favored by Paleoindians. Whatever its cause, the uneven distribution of sites continues throughout the Paleoindian period.

We do not know if Paleoindians lived in now-submerged coastal areas, although there is no reason why they would not have done so.[10] Modern sea levels were reached only several thousand years ago after a long landward movement of coastlines caused by a melting of the massive continental ice sheets. The bones and teeth of large mammals, including mastodons, have been dredged up far offshore from present beaches. Early hunter-gatherers must have been attracted to the rich plant and animal life in these places. In fact, Paleoindian points have been found in the shallow water of Tampa Bay on the west coast of Florida.

It is unusual for more than a handful of these early points to be found at any single site. In fact little, if anything, in the way of contemporaneous material accompanies the great majority of the points. Most of them were probably left behind by small and highly mobile bands, consisting of a few tens of people apiece. These tools are scattered across both river valleys and the intervening uplands, indicating that people made use of different settings as various foods became available throughout the year.[11]

A small number of Paleoindian sites yield many points and other artifacts.[12] Some of these camps are located near quarries where good stone was readily available, whereas others must have been near places that were especially rich in edible plants and animals. These repeatedly occupied spots might have been visited by somewhat larger groups of people, perhaps periodic aggregations of bands that facilitated finding marriage partners and renewing ties with long-separated kin and friends.

Much of what we would like to know about the Paleoindians – including how mobile they were, and the size and distribution of cooperating groups – is wrapped up in questions about how they got enough to eat. Rugged, brave, skin-clad hunters stalking dangerous big game dominate today's popular views of life in these distant times. Some say these hunters drove to extinction a number of large herbivores, collectively known as "megafauna."[13] Humans supposedly increased rapidly and spread across a landscape chock full of animals that were behaviorally incapable of avoiding the new predator. Hunting soon outstripped the animals' reproductive capacity, and they died out. It has even been said that the speed of this advance is why tools and bones of extinct megafauna are so rarely found together, especially in the eastern United States (a weak argument, based as it is on an absence of evidence).

As noted by David Meltzer, among others, there is little if any support for the idea that eastern Paleoindians specialized in the hunting of megafauna.[14] Hunters certainly killed mastodons and other large animals, but probably only when they were vulnerable, such as when a young, old, or sick one got mired in a watering hole. Taking advantage of opportunities as they arise is very different from tracking down and slaughtering great numbers of specially targeted prey. While hunters could have tipped the balance for animals already perched precariously on the brink of extinction, it is doubtful that they were the principal cause for the disappearance of so many species that differed widely in size and habitat preference.

The best example of tools found alongside the bones of extinct animals in the eastern United States comes from Kimmswick in east-central Missouri.[15] This site is in a hollow near its opening onto the Mississippi River floodplain. Here the bones of Pleistocene animals, including mastodons, and two intact Clovis points were discovered in pond sediments sandwiched between other deposits of soil that had washed in from the adjacent bluff and stream. Thus the context of the bones and artifacts is especially good. Several other stone tools or tool fragments, numerous chert flakes, and other animal bones were found nearby.

12 The Kimmswick excavations, Missouri, showing the level where mastodon bones and Paleoindian points were found.

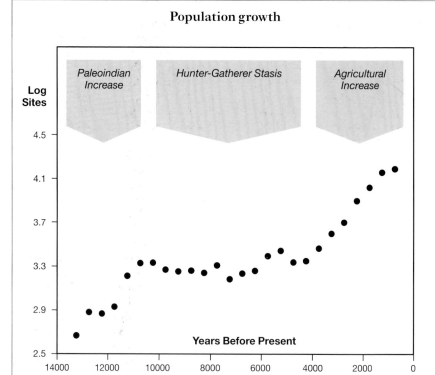

13  The sites from eight states – Alabama, Arkansas, Illinois, Kentucky, Mississippi, New York, Tennessee, Wisconsin – indicate three main stages of population growth. Periods of increase were separated by a long period of stasis.

By AD 1500, there were far more people in eastern North America than there could ever have been in Paleoindian times. But we would like to say more than that the overall population grew over time. Minimally we want to know if the rate of increase remained fixed, or whether the population grew more quickly at certain times than at others. The only way to answer such a question is to look at areas ranging from present-day states up to regions such as the Midwest and even the Eastern Woodlands as a whole. That is because the population histories of smaller areas – those that archaeologists typically study are seldom larger than a few hundred square miles – were quite varied over time, and they differed from what took place in neighboring river valleys.

An initial stab at dealing with this critical issue is made here using site files from Alabama, Arkansas, Illinois, Kentucky, Mississippi, New York, Tennessee, and Wisconsin. Different environmental settings are encompassed by these states, so it is likely that any trends detected are broadly indicative of changes that took place across much of the Eastern Woodlands, certainly the Midwest and Southeast.

There are many problems with extrapolating from numbers of sites to numbers of people. Artifact classifications and cultural phase designations can be inconsistent, vague, or inaccurate. Equal attention has not been given to all time periods, and research emphases have varied from one state to the next. Settlements differed in size and duration, mobile people produced more sites than sedentary ones, and it is harder to detect short-term hunter-gatherer camps than the permanent villages of agriculturalists. The age and location of sites influence the chances that they were either eroded away or covered by thick sediments. Some of these factors increase the number of known late sites relative to those of earlier times; others have the opposite effect. Nevertheless, the number of sites must bear some relation to the number of people, so they have value as a first approximation of population growth.

What is actually shown here are separate "components," not sites – archaeologists often refer to archaeologically distinguishable occupations as components. The time intervals assigned to the components are the ones customarily employed by regional specialists. When a component spanned two or more 500-year intervals (and most of them did so), it was divided up among the appropriate blocks of time. The resulting distribution of cultural components, which was based largely on current understandings of uncalibrated radiocarbon dates, was then converted to calendar years. This procedure had its most noticeable effect on the earliest, especially the Paleoindian, occupations. A log scale makes it easier to see periods of differential growth.

Considering the nature of these data, it is best not to be overly concerned with minor peaks and valleys in the distribution of sites. General trends, however, are a different story, and here we must be content with what happened over big chunks of time. There appear to have been three general

stages of population growth: early and late increases, about 0.06 percent per year, were separated by an almost stationary period. One should keep in mind that long-term trends across a broad region mask periods of population increase, stagnation, or perhaps even decline that might have taken place over several centuries in part or all of the eight-state area.

Whatever caused these changes in population growth across the Eastern Woodlands had to act through increasing fertility, decreasing mortality, or both. Much attention has been directed toward this issue as it pertains to the transition to agriculture. The range of fertility for modern hunter-gatherers overlaps with that of agriculturalists who rely on primitive tools and frequently shift their fields.[16] As far as mortality is concerned, death from starvation was surely never too distant for people forced to rely on their own efforts in inherently risky environments. Social groups of all sizes, and as large as entire communities, must have gone extinct with appalling regularity throughout prehistory. But with the greater control over production that came with agricultural economies, the magnitude or frequency of mortality crises perhaps decreased ever so slightly. Many millennia of efforts to reduce the risk of severe hardships from food shortfalls contributed to population growth through the adoption of increasingly labor-intensive means of production that yielded a greater and more stable return from a given amount of land. Over the long run, populations and new means of food production ratcheted upwards together. Whatever happened, shifts in fertility or mortality at the aggregate level need only to have been slight – imperceptible from the perspective of a human lifetime – as shown by the site data.

There is only a little additional direct evidence from the eastern United States that humans hunted megafauna or scavenged their carcasses.[17] The skull of a late Pleistocene bison with a fragment of a stone point lodged in it has been found in a river in Florida. Other wet sites in Florida have yielded tools made from the bones and ivory of now-extinct proboscideans. But humans need not have killed these large animals. Bones subsequently fashioned into tools – and not all claims of purposefully worked bone are convincing – might have been scavenged from animals that had died from natural causes.

The Paleoindians cannot have had the same diet in all places because they lived in very different natural settings that changed as the climate warmed.[18] They inhabited everything from periglacial tundra and spruce parklands to a more southerly mosaic of boreal and deciduous forests and grasslands. Species diversity was certainly low in the bleak landscape immediately south of the retreating ice sheets, but some animals could have been present in great numbers, such as caribou that travel in herds. If specialized hunters lived anywhere, they would have been here. But the evidence for what people ate is so thin that we know only that the northern Paleoindians hunted caribou along with smaller animals including hares. Farther south, a wider array of edible plants and animals would have favored generalized, and typically more reliable, hunting-and-gathering practices. Fish bones as well as fruit and weed seeds from Shawnee-Minisink in eastern Pennsylvania are evidence of this dietary breadth. As we have seen, a now-extinct tortoise was hunted in Florida, and possibly elsewhere as well. These animals were easy prey, precisely the kind of creature – slow, defenseless against spears, and edible – that people could have pushed to extinction. Yet even here climate change cannot be eliminated as the principal reason for the tortoise's demise.

Each year Paleoindians crossed long distances, as indicated by widely scattered sites, most of which were occupied only briefly. It is not unusual to find projectile points and other tools fashioned from high-quality stone, usually chert, that outcropped as much as 200 or more miles away from where the artifacts were found.[19] People apparently visited sources of good stone, made their tools there, and took away just what they were likely to need. It made no sense to carry large amounts of rock across long distances if most of it was going to be discarded when fashioning tools. Group mobility is also indicated by the extensive reworking of the edges of tools made from good stone.[20] As might be expected, people were thrifty with their use of high-quality stone when they were camped far from where it outcropped. Spear points and knives were resharpened when dull, and when they got too small they were often turned into scrapers, awls, and other tools.

At late Paleoindian sites we find decreasing amounts of stone from distant sources, indicating that people routinely tended to travel shorter distances.[21] Regional traditions marked by different projectile point styles also become more apparent as time wore on. These changes were a natural outcome of an increase in population that inevitably restricted the distances over which people could freely travel in their quest for food.

We only have a crude notion of population change based on counts of sites, although it appears that over the long run periods of early and late growth were separated by a time of relative stasis (see box p. 28). With a 0.06 percent annual increase in sites, Paleoindian population growth was quite likely far lower than the figures used by researchers who argue that rapid expansion ended in megafaunal extinction. Interestingly, the rate of increase in Paleoindian sites is similar to that which occurred during the last few thousand years of prehistory. Early hunter-gatherers accommodated their greater numbers by spreading out to a wider range of environmental settings and switching to a broader array of foods. But they still managed to maintain a foraging way of life. Their distant descendants, in contrast, solved the dilemma of too many mouths to feed by intensifying food production through the development of agricultural economies. But that is a story best left for later chapters.

## Mobile Archaic foragers

The following period, the Early Archaic, is thought to have lasted 2,000 or more years and to have ended about 8,900 years ago (the customarily used figure based on radiocarbon dates is 8,000 years ago). Throughout this period population densities remained low. Population growth had slowed, presumably because the land was essentially full of people who continued to practice a mobile way of life.

Early Archaic camps were distributed across both river valleys and the intervening uplands, with the largest tending to be near rivers.[22] Many of the Early Archaic sites were visited on one or more occasions by people whose

14

14 Deep archaeological deposits have been uncovered at several sites in eastern Tennessee, including Icehouse Bottom where they date back to Early Archaic times.

stay must have been short, perhaps no more than a few days. The diversity of artifacts is low, consistent with a rather narrow range of tasks, such as killing and butchering an animal. Yet there are sites that show evidence of a broader array of activities and longer occupations. Here shallow pits, piles of rock, hearths, postmolds that once held wooden posts for shelters or drying racks, dog burials, and even debris-filled deposits (or middens) have been found. They yield many chipped stone tools, including points and scrapers, as well as hammerstones and grinding slabs made from cobbles. Some blocks of stone had shallow depressions pecked into them to hold nuts while they were cracked open with rocks. Perishable materials were certainly present as well. Impressions of woven objects, both mats and bags, have been seen in clay hearths from sites in Illinois and Tennessee. Although we know little about mortuary customs because skeletons are rarely found, it seems that people were occasionally buried in the vicinity of their camps.

Based on what is known about hunter-gatherers from recent times, people probably lived in small bands of only a few dozen members. Contacts between groups were absolutely essential for gaining access to neighbors' territories during times of hardship and ensuring there were sufficient eligible marriage partners. There is little direct evidence for such contacts, although a bead made from a marginella shell, a marine snail, dating to the end of the Early Archaic has been found at Modoc rockshelter in southwestern Illinois.[23] Such unusual objects were passed from one person to the next and, after a lengthy period perhaps spanning several generations, they ended up far from their points of origin.

The food debris found in Early Archaic sites indicates the use of both closed canopy forests and more open places, including brushy edge zones.[24] Hickory nuts and, to a lesser extent, acorns are found, as are the bones of white-tailed deer, rabbits, squirrels, raccoons, and other animals. We do not know a lot about regional and temporal variation in diets, although people ate different animals and plants depending on what was available nearby.

Thus a continuation of a well-established mobile life characterizes the Early Archaic reasonably well. More accurately, there is strong continuity with Paleoindian times if the early people are not regarded as specialized big-game hunters. Of particular importance is an aspect of early Holocene foraging practices that is difficult to appreciate because of poor preservation: the collection of plant foods. The use of plants – a reliable and expandable source of food – sets the stage for what happened later when larger populations put greater pressures on local resources.

15 Early Archaic objects were discovered in the early 1950s beneath a limestone overhang known as the Modoc rockshelter in southwestern Illinois. The sequence of soil layers helped archaeologists work out the long history of hunter-gatherer occupation in this part of the Mississippi Valley.

# 3 · Sedentary Hunter-Gatherers: Middle to Late Archaic

The next several thousand years spanned a time when people in many places began to live for longer periods in repeatedly occupied camps. Great deposits of garbage gradually built up in resource-rich places. The "involuntary builders of such refuse heaps" – as New Deal archaeologist William S. Webb called them – produced sites with numerous artifacts, features, and burials.[1] They give us a much fuller view of life than is available for earlier times. Most importantly, the first halting steps toward agriculture were taken. The cultivation of crops was related to a more sedentary existence, at least during part of the year. But it is clear that people began to settle in more or less permanent camps long before they made significant use of any cultivated plants. This period also saw the first purposeful construction of mounds for ceremonial purposes.

The 3,000 years following 6000 BC is referred to as the Middle Archaic. The dates customarily assigned to archaeological periods and sites are not the same as calendar years estimated by the most recent calibration methods. In this instance, the actual date for the beginning of the Middle Archaic period is about 900 years earlier than the customarily used figure of 6000 BC. From this chapter onward, the dates for sites and culture periods usually correspond to those that for better or worse are deeply entrenched in the archaeological literature. The period that follows is rather predictably called the Late Archaic, extending to the opening centuries of the first millennium BC.

Much of this lengthy span of time coincided with the warmest part of the Holocene, the Climatic Optimum from about 8,000 to 4,000 calendar years ago.[2] Pollen sequences indicate that warmer and more arid conditions caused an expansion of tall-grass prairie or a shift to drier woodlands in the Midwest. Elsewhere, such as in northeastern Arkansas and the Missouri Bootheel, drought-tolerant plants became more common in both upland and floodplain settings. By this time the productivity of valleys had been enhanced by the development of meandering streams that created narrow oxbow lakes.[3] They were ideal habitats for fish, waterfowl, and mammals such as beaver and muskrat, and quite naturally attracted people as well.

The long inland movement of the shoreline, which started at the end of the Ice Age, was essentially completed by the early Late Archaic, although it

16 Many of the coastal shell heaps have been destroyed, as shown in this picture from a century-old postcard. Here, shell is being carted off from a mound at New Smyrna, Florida.

has continued to change somewhat since then.[4] Coastlines dotted with shell 16 heaps indicate where camps were occupied for many generations. It is not known whether people in earlier times lived along now-drowned shorelines. Nonetheless, the settled existence indicated by these coastal sites was contemporaneous with the shift to a more sedentary life in the continental interior, where deep middens also formed alongside rivers and wetlands.

## Containers and camps

Stone points that were hafted to make spears and knives are the most distinctive chipped stone tools to have survived.[5] Tools made by pecking and grinding stone – instead of by chipping off flakes – also became relatively common. They included axes, net weights, and atlatl weights fashioned from banded slate, basalt, quartz, and hematite, among other rocks. Atlatls 17 were short sticks used for hurling spears more forcefully, the butt ends of the spears being held in place by hooks that were often made of antler. The atlatl weights were small, polished stones of various shapes, each one perforated by a hole laboriously drilled through it. When found with skeletons,

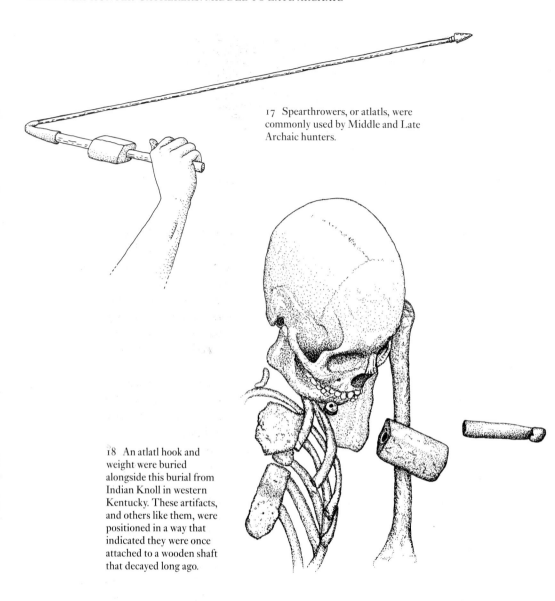

17  Spearthrowers, or atlatls, were commonly used by Middle and Late Archaic hunters.

18  An atlatl hook and weight were buried alongside this burial from Indian Knoll in western Kentucky. These artifacts, and others like them, were positioned in a way that indicated they were once attached to a wooden shaft that decayed long ago.

18  the weights and hooks are often positioned as if they had once been attached to wooden shafts. Tools and ornaments made of materials that often fail to survive, such as bone awls and shell beads, were also used, much as they were during other times in prehistory.

Some of the most important innovations in the Middle and Late Archaic were new kinds of containers for storing and cooking food.[6] While it had little immediate impact, this development ultimately had such profound consequences that Bruce Smith has dubbed it the "Container Revolution." First on the list were the cucurbits: squash and the bottle gourd, which at the outset were quite possibly more highly valued as containers or net floats

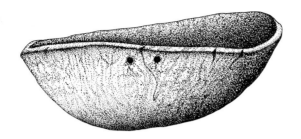

19 Bowls were sometimes carved from steatite, such as this one from Flint River in northern Alabama. Height 7 in (17.8 cm).

than as food. They date back as early as 5000 BC in the midcontinent, and an equally old gourd has been found alongside a burial in Florida. Around 2000 BC there appeared tub-like vessels carved from steatite, or soapstone, that 19 outcrops in the Appalachians.[7] For the most part these vessels, along with some made from other kinds of relatively soft stone, are found at sites in the Appalachian and Atlantic states. Soot on their exteriors indicates that they were often nestled amongst the coals of campfires, but presumably they were also used for "stone boiling," where water is heated by placing hot rocks into the container.

The first pottery was made in the southern Atlantic coastal plain around 2500 BC; more than a thousand years would pass before people west of the Appalachians began to use it.[8] We do not know why pottery-making initially spread so slowly and irregularly – it must have had something to do with the availability of other suitable containers such as light and durable baskets, which are in many situations superior to heavy and fragile pots. Only early in the first millennium BC did pottery become common across a broad area, making it a convenient marker for the subsequent Early Woodland period.

Mobile ways of life began to give way around 4500 BC to the repeated use of base camps occupied for longer periods of time, probably by larger numbers of people.[9] This shift, which occurred earlier in some places than in others, is most widely recognized in the form of large shell and midden heaps in the southern Midwest and Southeast, mostly along rivers. The 20 Read site overlooking the Green River in western Kentucky is a good example. It was not particularly large when compared to the biggest middens, but still consisted about 130,000 cu. ft (3,700 cu. m) of debris-laden soil and shell, in equal measures. Many pits, usually shallow basins, as well as hearths, postmolds, human and dog burials, and house floors, have been discovered when excavating these sites. Piles of rock, much of it scorched and badly cracked, have also been found, used either in earth ovens or for heating water.

It is clear that wetlands attracted people.[10] At Koster and Modoc rockshelter, both in Illinois, thick deposits laden with artifacts developed at the foot of bluffs bordering the Illinois and Mississippi river floodplains. Animal

20 Several shell heaps along the Green River in western Kentucky, such as the Carlston Annis site, were excavated by WPA crews during the Great Depression.

bones indicate the use of not only the river but especially the abundant nearby backwater lakes and swamps. Farther south in Illinois, deep middens at Black Earth were located alongside a shallow lake and swamp, all that remained of a much larger late Pleistocene lake. In western Kentucky, another deep midden known as the Ward site was perched on the edge of a steep bluff overlooking a broad bottomland where a sluggish creek disappeared into an extensive swamp. All of these sites were located where edible plants and small animals were abundant, dependable, and easily obtained. Because of the concentrated nature of these resources and the high reproductive potential of heavily harvested species, people found it possible to settle down for long periods without exhausting local food sources.

Not all of the attention on resource-rich places resulted in large piles of debris. Several Late Archaic sites in the Mississippi River floodplain near East St. Louis, Illinois, consist of numerous features, primarily shallow pits often clustered together, alongside abandoned river channels.[11] Digging pits through the hard clay at some of these sites was no easy task with simple tools (the clay at one of them so resisted modern steel shovels that exhausted excavators nicknamed it Devil's Island). These campsites must have been occupied by small groups who repeatedly visited the lake shores, but did not return often enough to precisely the same spot to produce deep middens. The Mississippi River folk were presented with a wide choice of potential campsites scattered along the banks of the long oxbow lakes and swamps that criss-crossed the broad floodplain.

People also buried their dead in the heavily used midden and shell mounds.[12] Judging from the skeletons, these campsites were visited by

21, 23

22

21   Middens in plowed fields at Black Earth in southern Illinois were easily visible from the air; they are the dark blotches in the light soil in the background. The area in the foreground was once a swamp.

22   The most experienced WPA excavators, called "trowel men," performed the exacting work of digging burials in the western Kentucky shell heaps.

groups comprising people of all ages and both sexes. Funerary artifacts indicate that what people did in life and how they treated each other was mostly determined by age, gender, and ability. At the Middle to Late Archaic Read site, infants had the fewest artifacts, and atlatl weights and hooks were mostly found with adult males; those over forty-five were buried with fewer artifacts than younger adults. Old adults at the contemporaneous Black Earth site likewise had a narrower range of artifacts. During Middle Archaic times at Koster, a few people with debilitating conditions were buried amidst habitation debris, not elsewhere with other group members. All of this shows that people possessing great productive and reproductive potential were more highly regarded than the elderly, weak, and unfit.

So in contrast to commonly held, but overly romanticized, notions of hunter-gatherer life, a person's worth was measured by his or her contributions to group survival. The situation was apparently similar to that observed by the early nineteenth-century Lewis and Clark expedition. In Lewis' words: "Those nations treat their old people and women with most difference [deference] and rispect where they subsist principally on such articles that these can participate with the men in obtaining them; and that, that part of the community are treated with least attention, when the act of procuring subsistence devolves intirely on the men in the vigor of life."[13]

Despite the move toward a more settled existence, people in the Middle and Late Archaic still pursued mobile lives. Christopher Ruff has shown that skeletons from Tennessee River shell heaps conform to a hunter-gatherer, not agriculturalist, pattern for differences between the sexes in femoral bending rigidity, or leg strength.[14] Male mobility was greater than that for females, presumably because they spent more of their time away from the main camps taking part in arduous hunting trips over rough terrain.

The large shell and midden heaps have naturally attracted the greatest attention, but they are not the only sites to have been excavated.[15] Widely scattered artifacts and other debris indicate the existence of short-term camps, many of which were located in the uplands between river valleys. These camps would have been used by people attracted to groves of nut trees, dense stands of berry- and seed-producing plants, and good hunting spots.

The midcontinent was not the only place where people settled down in especially favorable places. Far to the south, Middle to Late Archaic people living along the tributaries of the lower Mississippi River focused much of their attention on rich wetlands that were home to fish, waterfowl, and several mammals.[16]

The Atlantic and Gulf coasts are dotted with deposits of shell that mostly postdate 2000 BC.[17] They were located in places where food was especially plentiful, such as backwater bays and estuaries. Many of these shell heaps formed crescents or even complete rings, so it appears that when people settled down for lengthy periods they tended to arrange themselves in a circle. Old shell heaps were obvious landmarks in rather flat and marshy places –

23 People during Middle to Late Archaic times were attracted to wetlands with their abundant game and edible plants. A diverse mix of resources provided a measure of security to the hunting-and-gathering way of life.

they still are today. It is therefore not surprising that later generations interested in keeping their feet dry would have chosen to settle down at precisely the same spot as their predecessors, as long as it continued to be favorably located. The shell deposits thus grew over time, some reaching enormous proportions. While the most commonly eaten shellfish varied from one place to another, those from brackish water were quite abundant, underscoring the fundamental importance of marshy areas. Excavators have found that the deposits of shell are also loaded with animal bones, particularly those from fish.

Accumulations of shell are not the only signs of a heavy use of coastal settings. At the Boylston Street Fish Weir in Boston, Massachusetts, many fish weirs were constructed of closely spaced stakes.[18] These Late Archaic weirs, designed to trap fish as the tide receded, were built and replaced over at least 1,500 years. Collectively they covered an area that exceeded 5 acres (2 ha).

There was not a unidirectional and steady progression during the Middle and Late Archaic toward increasingly sedentary ways of life; in some areas people never really settled down in long-occupied camps. The Black Earth site in Illinois is a fine example of how people adapted to alterations in their immediate surroundings brought about by climatic change.[19] The Late Archaic people here were not as tightly tethered to the wetlands as their predecessors. They were able to disperse to take advantage of a wider distribution of reliable food sources as forests expanded at the expense of grasslands after the mid-Holocene warm and dry period. A reduced emphasis on wetland and river-edge settings at that time is also apparent elsewhere in the midcontinent.

### Growing native plants

Studies of plant remains over the past quarter-century have greatly altered ideas about Middle to Late Archaic ways of life. In fact, Bruce Smith among others has argued that eastern North America – more precisely, the southern Midwest and northern Southeast – was one of the few places in the world where plants were independently domesticated.[20] This work is surely one of the most important of the recent developments in our understanding of eastern North American prehistory.

The long road to agricultural economies began with the frequent creation of clearings.[21] By repeatedly occupying the same campsite, people broke the forest canopy, thereby producing sun-drenched open spaces, and enriched the soil with everyday waste. The first steps toward agriculture presumably involved no more than tolerating useful plants that grew in these clearings, or even encouraging them through occasional weeding and watering. Today we are all familiar with sunflowers and the descendants of Late Archaic thick-walled gourds, the acorn and scallop squashes, crooknecks, and fordhooks. The other cultigens that were such an important part of diets for several thousand years are not as widely known. They include goosefoot, marsh elder, maygrass, erect knotweed, and little barley.

Cultivated plants first appeared across a broad area stretching from central Illinois southward to northern Alabama, and from Missouri and Arkansas eastward to the western Appalachians.[22] Cucurbits also extended into the Northeast. While people spread these plants beyond their natural ranges, the mix of species that they grew was not always the same. At least four of the plants had become domesticated by the second millennium BC, with the earliest appearing just over 4,000 years ago. The morphological changes said to mark their domesticated status are "testa" (seed coat) thickness for goosefoot; "achene" (seed) size for marsh elder and sunflower; and rind thickness for cucurbits. The changes in the seeds are thought to encourage quicker germination and seedling growth, characteristics that gave them a selective advantage in the dense stands of plants that grew around settlements and in gardens. It is noteworthy that the first domesticated plants appeared at the same time as overall population growth picked up slightly after thousands of years of stagnation. Considering the fuzziness of our dating of both the earliest domesticated plants and change over time in numbers of sites, the convergence of these events is remarkable.

Such hardy plants, which quickly invaded old campsites, were an additional reason to return repeatedly to spots where other essential foods were plentiful. Seeds could have been stored for use during the late winter months, a lean time of the year when a little extra food might mean the difference between life and death. These seeds must have been highly valued when shortfalls occurred in the food usually offered by the rivers and wetlands. Like traditional householders everywhere, the people who grew these plants were undoubtedly more concerned with minimizing risk than maximizing yields.

Over many thousands of years these plants became increasingly important in many parts of the Eastern Woodlands, the lengthy move toward agriculture spurred on by pressing local needs each step of the way. Having tasted a goosefoot-based porridge, I am at a loss to see what would have attracted people to such a mixture other than sheer necessity! More to the point, actively caring for gardens would have taken more work than simply collecting wild plants. But the availability of a convenient and nutritious source of food eventually offset any drawbacks with growing these weedy plants.

Agricultural economies were not a foreseeable end toward which generations of prescient hunters-and-gatherers unerringly headed. These people could not have anticipated, nor would they have cared about, any benefit that crops might provide some distant generation. Instead they used imperfect knowledge to make choices about how best to satisfy their immediate needs. Humans are remarkably adept at dealing with short-term problems, such as working out how to get enough to eat. They are, however, largely blind to the long-term consequences, either good or bad, of their actions.

## Alliances and antagonisms

By about 4000 BC, the exchange of non-local materials, among them copper, marine shell, steatite, banded slate, and colorful cherts, had taken off.[23] If the variety and number of non-local artifacts bear any relation to the level of communication among different bands of people, the groups must have had more contact with their neighbors than previously.

Artifacts made from non-local materials were circulated for long periods as they were passed from one person to the next before ending up far from where they originated. Judging from what generally took place in more recent small-scale societies elsewhere in the world, the social significance of these objects outweighed any value that stemmed from their rarity, beauty, or utility. The people who ended up with items such as copper and marine shell would have been unaware of their origins. Even the most widely traveled people could have had only limited, and quite likely fanciful, knowledge about what lay beyond their direct experience or that of their elders and the members of neighboring groups. In that regard they were much like the natives of Highland New Guinea who, when first contacted in the early

# Moving earth at Poverty Point

Until recently, Poverty Point and related sites that were in use about three millennia ago were thought to be the first examples of moundbuilding. Poverty Point's temporal priority – it was occupied for many centuries beginning at least 3,500 years ago – has now been lost to Watson Brake, but that does little to diminish its importance.

Poverty Point is located about 15.5 miles (25 km) west of the present Mississippi River channel in northeastern Louisiana.[24] It sits on the edge of Maçon Ridge overlooking swampy land to the east. The main part of the site consists of six curved earthen ridges and several mounds. Of the five mounds near the ridges, one has been likened to a bird, another is conical, and the rest are platforms. An additional bird mound, the Motley mound, is located north of the main group. The bird mounds – one must have a vivid imagination to see them as such – are elongated and have ramps jutting from one of the long sides. They are big mounds: one is 69 ft (21 m) high and the other 51 ft (15.5 m). The conical

24 In this computer-generated view of Poverty Point, Louisiana, the large mound is shown next to the low, curved ridges that end at the bayou. The ramp that extends toward the ridges is lower than the rest of the mound. One of the smaller mounds is clearly visible in the upper left-hand corner.

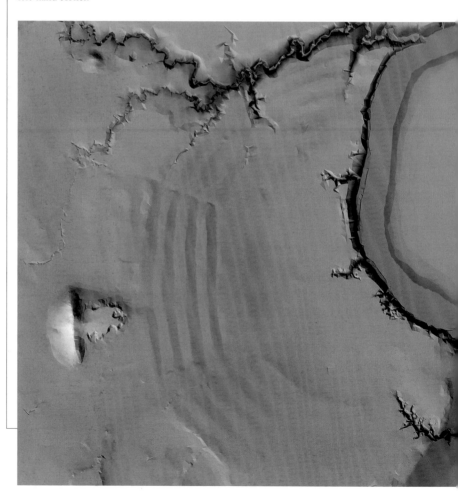

25 The largest mound at Poverty Point is located adjacent to low earthen ridges (upper left).

mound is also a respectable 24.5 ft (7.5 m). South of the main group is a seventh mound, Lower Jackson, that recent work suggests was built before the rest of the site.

The six nested arcs of debris-laden soil are each about a meter high. The outside diameter of the set of ridges is about three-quarters of a mile (1.2 km); the inside diameter defined by the innermost ridge is about half that distance. The ridges are interrupted by narrow gaps forming openings that radiate outward from the innermost part of the site. Just beyond the open ends of the curved ridges is a steep slope that drops to Bayou Maçon. The largest mound is situated midway along the ridges, and its elongated ramp points toward them. Recent detailed topographic mapping of the site has shown that the general layout of the ridges is not quite as symmetrical as once thought. Hearths, postmolds, and other features have been discovered in the ridges, although why the ridges were built remains a mystery.

Exactly what went on at Poverty Point is likewise unknown. People lived there, but how many of them did so, how long they stayed, and what they did while there are questions that require much more work to answer. It is likely, however, that people from the surrounding area periodically assembled at the site for the kinds of social interactions common to all groups of people, such as finding marriage partners and renewing bonds of kinship and friendship. But why haul dirt to build mounds and ridges? All we can say for sure is that it was necessary to create a space within which socially and ritually significant events could be conducted.

The site has given its name to small lumps of baked clay of various shapes. Great numbers of these so-called Poverty Point objects have been found, and it is thought they were used for cooking in this stone-starved part of the valley. The lumps could have been heated and put in earth ovens or dropped in water to heat it.

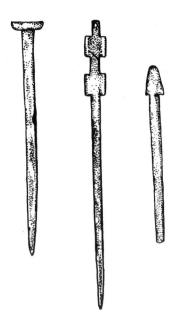

26 Carved bone pins, such as these pins from Black Earth, Illinois, have come from a number of Middle Archaic sites. Longest pin is 6.5 in (16.5 cm).

1930s, had no idea that their highly valued shells came from the sea, or indeed that the sea even existed.

Neighboring groups in Middle to Late Archaic times maintained regular communication with one another, at least enough to share symbols that must have had some mutually recognized meaning. Distinctive carved bone pins dating from 4000 to 3000 BC, for example, have been found in sites scattered across the southern Midwest.[25] Other shared artifacts include certain more or less contemporaneous stone points, which are large and often found in caches, from northeastern Mississippi and adjacent states. Perhaps the pins and points marked a common kin affiliation, individually negotiated trade partnerships, or some form of shared ritual knowledge.

Greater numbers of items moving among neighboring groups, perhaps with changes in what those interactions signified, coincided with the shift to a more settled way of life.[26] Social mechanisms facilitating cooperation in times of need greatly benefited increasingly sedentary people. Anything that lessened the dire consequences of food shortages enhanced the chances of long-term survival. After all, everybody must have experienced lean years at some point, especially in the midcontinent during the mid-Holocene warm and dry period.

Contact between neighboring groups during late Middle to Late Archaic times occasionally resulted in bloodshed.[27] Stone and antler-tip projectile points have been found lodged in bones, and some of these unfortunate people were scalped or decapitated. People also fought one another in earlier times – one Early Archaic skeleton from Kentucky also has a projectile point embedded in a bone – but little is known about these conflicts because there are so few early human remains. It is difficult to say how widespread or common fighting was in the Middle and Late Archaic. Many victims of violence were buried in the midcontinental shell and midden mounds, but these are the sites that yield most of the best-preserved skeletons. The connection, therefore, between large campsites and conflict may be more apparent than real.

All that can really be said is that the people who frequented the big debris heaps were occasionally picked off by their enemies. Tensions would have been likely to erupt into outright violence when people were unwilling or unable to relinquish claims to favorable places; that is, when they could not easily resolve their differences by simply walking away. Conflicts probably broadened and intensified when neighboring groups fell on hard times, making it more difficult for people to move or expand their territories in search of desperately needed food.

It is perhaps significant that worsening intergroup relations coincided with a greater exchange in items from distant places. Uncertainty over what would happen when separate bands met encouraged customs that allayed suspicion and fear. Gift-giving is always a good means of smoothing social interactions.

## Early mounds

Middle and Late Archaic people rarely set out to build mounds, but when they did they made some impressive ones, even when compared with those built much later. The small mounds that first appeared at this time are also important: they are among the earliest examples of formally organized and permanently marked cemeteries maintained by increasingly sedentary people.

The most impressive mounds were built in the lower Mississippi Valley.[28] One of the earliest mound complexes – it also happens to be one of the biggest and most elaborate – is Watson Brake. Recent work by Joe Saunders and his colleagues has done much to clarify when it was built. Eleven mounds are connected by a low ridge about 3.5 ft (1 m) high, and together

27

27  This computer-generated view of Watson Brake in northeastern Louisiana shows the ring of mounds.

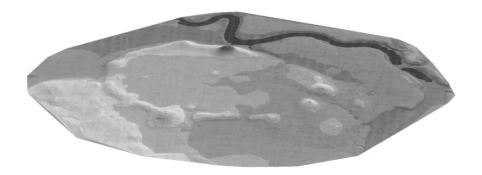

28 Mound A is the largest of the mounds at Watson Brake in Louisiana.

28     they form an oval about 919 ft (280 m) in diameter. They are from 3.5 ft to 15 ft high (1 to 4.5 m), except for one that reaches up to 24.5 ft (7.5 m). These mounds were built on a low terrace near the Ouachita River in northeastern Louisiana, and the surrounding swamps provided the inhabitants of Watson Brake with much of their food.

Watson Brake has been known for a long time – the number of mounds and their large size ensured that the site could not be missed. But its significance was only recently recognized when calibrated radiocarbon dates showed that mound construction began as early as 3400 BC (calendar years). This surprisingly early date serves as a fine example of a single discovery that has had a great effect on our perceptions of prehistory.

Watson Brake makes it clear that the tradition of moundbuilding started well before the larger and much better known Poverty Point site, also located in northeastern Louisiana, which is for the most part a terminal Late Archaic mound complex.[29] At Poverty Point there are six nested and curved ridges of soil accompanied by several mounds (see box p. 44). The tallest mound at 69 ft (21 m) is remarkable for any prehistoric time horizon. Excavations have shown that several mounds were built in separate stages, and postmolds along with other features indicate that each platform was used for an unknown amount of time before being covered with yet more earth.

Numerous artifacts have been found at Poverty Point, including small stone tools, or microliths, used for cutting, drilling, and scraping. Most noteworthy are an unusually large number of beads and small animal-like figures made from various materials. Much of this material, such as galena and copper, originated in distant places, so contact of one sort or another was maintained among widely scattered groups.

Poverty Point was not the only site with mounds in the lower Mississippi Valley and adjacent Gulf Coast during the period from approximately 1600 to 600 BC, although it was the largest of them.[30] As one might expect, the big mounds and fancy artifacts at Poverty Point have prompted considerable speculation about the nature of this society. Whatever took place must have been rooted in what happened much earlier at sites such as Watson Brake. Perhaps people who were scattered around these sites periodically gathered there for various reasons. They could have taken part in all sorts of commonplace, but essential, social interactions such as arranging marriages, reinforcing kin ties, establishing trade partnerships, and forging intergroup alliances. The aggregation of people was made possible by the proximity of rich, reliable, and easily harvested resources, especially those from nearby wetlands. The mere presence of a mound – a prominent landmark built through sustained collective effort – may have been enough to draw people back to a traditional meeting place imbued with social and perhaps super-

24, 25

29

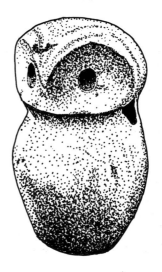

29  Many small figures, such as this jasper owl bead, have been found at Poverty Point, Louisiana, and related sites. Height 1.1 in (2.8 cm).

natural significance. A sense of community was underscored by the combined work of generations of people to move enough earth to make a coherent and readily visible site plan.

While big mounds can be impressive, they alone do not indicate organizationally complex societies and large populations. Mound construction requires only modest investments of effort if it is stretched out over a sufficiently long period. The occupations of Watson Brake and Poverty Point spanned several centuries, if not longer, and it is reasonable to suppose that moundbuilding took place, at least intermittently, over much of these periods.

A century ago Gerard Fowke – an eminently practical man who was forever skeptical about enthusiastic but ill-informed claims about mounds – addressed the labor issue by noting that it took only a day for a crew of 40 to load 10,000 bushels of maize onto a steamboat.[31] He went on to say that if these men carried the same weight of dry soil, they would have produced a mound about 40 ft (12.2 m) in diameter and 10 ft (3 m) tall. He did not say how far the grain was carried, nor does his figure include the effort needed to dig dirt. Fortunately, labor estimates can be used that are based on observations of Mexican peasants who, in a five-hour workday, excavated dirt with a digging stick and carried it over known distances. If 40 of these men were to carry enough dirt to build Fowke's mound over distances of 164 ft (50 m) and 328 ft (100 m), it would take them about 3.5 and 5 days respectively.

Turning now to Poverty Point, the Mexican figures for digging and carrying earth can be used to provide a rough idea about what was involved in building the mounds and ridges, as long as we also know the amount of earth that was moved and the length of the moundbuilding period. Fortunately, Jon Gibson has presented low and high estimates of the earth in Poverty Point's mounds and ridges.[32] He also believes that most of the construction took place over a period of no more than 300 years, although information on this point is sketchy. Most of the soil could have been scraped up near the mounds and ridges, so the lower distance in the Mexican study, 164 ft, is used here in estimating the labor needed at Poverty Point. Putting this information together, if 100 people worked for three centuries, they would have had to dig and carry dirt for 16 to 18 days each year, depending on whether the low or high volume estimates are used. The point of this exercise, and others like it, is not to determine the number of laborers who were available or the duration of the work. It is simply to show that moundbuilding does not create onerous demands on local households except when construction periods are short and populations are small.

Much has been made of the fancy ornaments and other objects found at Poverty Point, but their mere presence means little. Craft specialists, a hallmark of complex societies, are not needed to produce nice objects with commonly available tools. Members of small-scale societies around the world make aesthetically pleasing objects requiring great perseverance and considerable skill. More interesting is what the beads and tiny figures, as well as many varieties of chert, might indicate about exchange networks. In terms of what has survived, it seems that a great many more unusual materials and objects ended up at the site than left it.[33] In this regard, Poverty Point is much like the mound and earthwork complexes in Ohio that were built about a thousand years later. Something seems to have been at work other than the simple reciprocal exchanges between people that were typical of that time. Perhaps periodic aggregations of people, many bearing easily portable gifts essential for various social and ritual activities, resulted in an imbalance in the movement of non-local items that, over numerous generations, accumulated at Poverty Point.

Other southeastern mounds dating to this period, most of which are located in Louisiana and Florida, tend to be poorly known.[34] One such site is Horr's Island on Florida's southwestern coast where there are mounds along with deep shell middens. Excavations into Mound A revealed a sequence of separate building episodes that eventually produced a 19.5-ft (6-m) pile of sand and shell. First, a low sand mound covered by shell was built on a dune; later, more sand and shell was added to make it bigger, finally ending in a thick shell cap. Other mounds at Horr's Island were from 5 to 13 ft (1.5 to 4 m) high. Two of them consisted of both sand and shell, whereas a fourth was made up of just shell. Easily distinguished strata indicate separate sources of fill, and these layers were probably added at different times. While we do not know exactly how the mounds were used, these piles of shell and sand were deliberately built – they were not mere

30

30  One of the earth and shell mounds at Horr's Island in Florida is Mound D.

heaps of waste shell. Presumably the mounds were ritually significant structures related to a nearby settlement.

Mounds in the Midwest were quite small in comparison to the largest ones that dot the lower Mississippi Valley and Gulf Coast. Middle to Late Archaic people in west-central Illinois and adjoining Missouri commonly buried their dead in natural knolls or low mounds, typically only a few feet high, perched on high bluffs overlooking adjacent floodplains.[35] The knoll and mound distinction is of little consequence because the two look so much alike. Moreover, the addition of soil often did nothing more than accentuate a natural rise on a ridge crest.

By pulling together information from Late Archaic cemeteries, including mounds, in west-central Illinois and neighboring Missouri, Jane Buikstra and Douglas Charles have argued that some groups were more mobile than others.[36] Most of the human remains found in cemeteries along the Illinois and Mississippi rivers were from burials of intact bodies. These people lived near resource-rich parts of the floodplain – a relatively settled existence meant that it was a simple matter to bury a corpse in a nearby cemetery. Conspicuous cemeteries could have marked claims to the best segments of the

31   The move toward a more sedentary way of life involved the occupation of places where resources were especially plentiful and reliable. These places were typically alongside rivers, lakes, and swamps, or on the edges of coastal bays, estuaries, and marshes.

valley. Formal burial grounds are used by many people around the world to signal control over valued, but limited, resources such as land.

The situation was different in contemporaneous cemeteries along the smaller streams that creased the surrounding uplands, where piles of disarticulated bones were commonly buried. The people who lived between the major rivers were probably more mobile than the valley folk. Here, the most productive patches of land were smaller and more widely distributed than they were in the big river floodplains. Bundles of defleshed bones were easier to carry over long distances to burial grounds than heavy, smelly bodies.

Whatever the specific meanings attached to mounds and exchanges of rare items, they must have stemmed from a desire to claim rights over particular places and to foster cooperation among groups that focused on smaller territories. Such changes were related to the greater numbers of people who occupied the Eastern Woodlands. More people, on average, increased the chances that any single group might impinge on the hunting ground of its neighbor. Regular communication, which involved exchanges of items of symbolic or personal significance, presumably eased tensions before they spun out of control. These efforts at maintaining peaceful relations, however, were not always successful, as shown by the remains of people killed and mutilated by their enemies.

Over the long run, the transformation from a hunting-and-gathering way of life to one based partly on cultivated plants – a move toward the more intensive use of smaller areas by increasingly sedentary people – was irreversible. Population growth, which accelerated during Late Archaic times when domesticated plants first appeared, ensured that for their distant descendants there could be no return to a purely hunting-and-gathering existence. That would only have been possible with a drastic reduction in the numbers of people, and it did not even take place several thousands of years later in the wake of horrifying losses from the Old World diseases introduced by Europeans.

# 4 · Builders of Burial Mounds and Earthworks: Early to Middle Woodland

Several important changes in how people lived were taking place as much as 3,000 years ago. A rich ceremonial life, which had undoubtedly been present all along, took a new and dramatic turn with the construction of elaborate burial mounds. Certain community members were often singled out when the time came for burial. In some places geometric earthworks, the largest of which enclosed many acres of ground, were also built. In the midcontinent, native cultigens, several of which had been domesticated earlier, were consumed in much larger quantities than ever before. Pottery was acquired where it was previously absent, and it became more common in the Southeast where it dated back to the Late Archaic period. In fact, the appearance of pottery across much of eastern North America is used as a convenient marker for the beginning of the Early Woodland period. The overall population was increasing at a greater rate than during much of Archaic times, and contacts among neighboring groups broadened and deepened.

Societies classified as Early Woodland had appeared by the opening centuries of the first millennium BC, and they lasted for the next 500 or more years. In the Midwest and Southeast, the next half-millennium or so ending around AD 400 is referred to as Middle Woodland. In the Northeast and along the Eastern Seaboard, Middle Woodland is said to continue longer, to as late as AD 1000. As usual, regional differences in when cultural units are said to begin and end are related to the quality and quantity of radiocarbon dates, as well as the somewhat arbitrary business of dividing up continuous technological and social change. But there was also true variation in local cultural sequences.

Two additional terms – "Adena" and "Hopewell" – are often used when referring to Early and Middle Woodland artifacts and sites, particularly mounds. The name Adena comes from an estate in Ohio where a large mound was dug about a century ago. For the most part it refers to Early Woodland sites in the middle Ohio River Valley, including southern Ohio, northern Kentucky, southeastern Indiana, and western West Virginia. But there is some uncertainty over the age of these sites because many mounds were excavated long before radiocarbon dating was a possibility. For example, Adena mounds in Kentucky are said to date as late as the first few centuries of the first millennium AD, which falls squarely within Middle

33

32 Selected sites mentioned in Chapters 4 and 5.

33 The name Adena comes from a large mound in Ohio that was dug in 1901.

Woodland times. Middle Woodland sites and artifacts, especially those from Ohio, are sometimes also labeled Hopewell. This term refers to a group of mounds where numerous extraordinary artifacts were found, many of which were dug up for the 1893 World's Columbian Exposition in Chicago.

## Burial mounds

pl. IV

One of the most notable aspects of Early to Middle Woodland societies is their tendency to construct mounds, most of which are referred to as "conical" mounds. Not all people at that time built them, but it was nonetheless a common practice, especially in the Midwest and Southeast. While the burial of the dead has for obvious reasons dominated studies of mounds – after all, there are plenty of skeletons – it has become clear that they were much more than simply burial places.

34 Some Adena mounds covered areas where a long sequence of structures once stood, such as at the C&O site in Kentucky. The postmolds for four circular structures are shown in black.

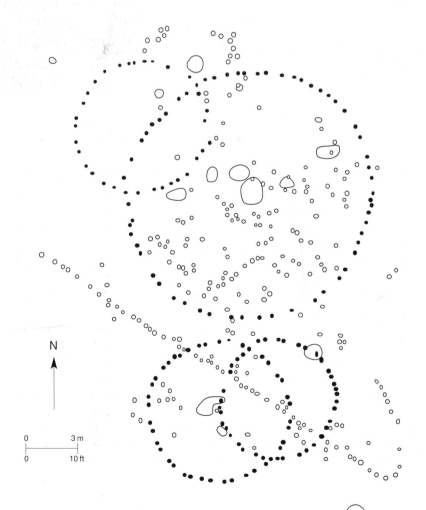

N

| 0 | 3 m |
| 0 | 10 ft |

35 Soil stains for paired posts and four internal supports, which supported a structure, were found by excavators when they dug the Crigler mound in Kentucky during the Great Depression. By this point in the excavation only a small part of the mound remained standing.

Mounds dating to Early Woodland times varied greatly in size and in how they were constructed.[1] Some were rather unimposing piles of earth with simple construction histories like those associated with so-called Red Ochre burials that date from terminal Archaic through Early Woodland times in the upper Midwest. Far to the south, mounds that tended to be no taller than a person were also thinly scattered along the Gulf Coast and Florida's Atlantic Coast. The biggest of the mounds played a prominent role in the now-discredited moundbuilder myth. They include the 62-ft (19-m) high Grave Creek mound in West Virginia. It was enough of a local landmark 200 years ago that the men of Lewis and Clark's Corps of Discovery felt compelled to stop and admire it on their long journey westward to the Pacific.

Of the mounds dating to Early Woodland times, by far the most impressive are those referred to as Adena in the middle Ohio River Valley. Many of them were built over places where large wooden structures once stood.[2] Sometimes these areas had been used for a long time, as indicated by rows of postmolds for many structures beneath the C&O, Riley, and Wright mounds in Kentucky. Elsewhere the mounds covered only single structures, such as at Crigler, Morgan Stone, and Robbins, also in Kentucky. Here the

34

35

57

## Stacked cemeteries at Robbins mounds

36  The large Robbins mound in Kentucky was dug in 1939 and 1940 by a WPA crew.

The two Robbins mounds in northern Kentucky were excavated during the Great Depression.[3] The largest – about 130 ft (39.6 m) in diameter and 20.5 ft (6.2 m) high – is an excellent example of how an Adena mound eventually reached its final size. Fortunately, the WPA excavators were so skillful at drawing mound cross-sections that many decades later it is possible to reconstruct the mound's appearance at different points in its long history.

The first step in building this large mound involved dumping earth over a cremation within a circular wooden structure, and then a small heap of soil was deposited to cover the spot where the structure once stood. Further soil was later added to create new graves and to cap earlier groups of them, enlarging the mound. Individual graves, typically log tombs, were added separately to the margins and top of the mound, expanding its girth and increasing its height. Many graves, particularly the rectangular log-lined tombs, were bordered by earth on all four sides. When tombs were located on the sides of the mound, one or more edges of the graves required little additional soil. Much of the effort in making these tombs was spent on chopping down big trees for the logs that lined them.

The addition of graves stopped several times during the mound's construction, at which point the cemetery was partially or completely covered by a layer of earth. New graves were then added as before, until they too were capped by more soil. Eventually old graves settled and log roofs collapsed, creating low spots in the mound's surface. These depressions were used for new tombs or were filled when more soil was laid down for additional graves. The mound was sometimes more peaked than it was at other times, and its apex shifted somewhat laterally. So when construction was complete, the highest point was no longer perfectly centered over the original wooden structure.

37 Many log-lined tombs were found superimposed on one another in the Robbins mound.

mounds – at least their initial construction episodes – conformed closely to the locations of the earlier buildings. Thus there was continuity in the use of ceremonial space, even if these spots were used for distinctly different purposes.

The buildings and enclosures covered by the mounds were mostly circular, although some were rectangular. Frequently their postmolds defined areas so big that the structures could not have been roofed over. The roofed buildings were often constructed in a style unique to Adena sites: their circular walls consisted of pairs of outwardly slanting posts. Their size and contents make it clear that they were not regular domestic structures. Some of them played a part in mortuary ceremonies before they were destroyed and covered completely by earth. Ashes and charred wood at the Morgan Stone mound show that the building and the body within it were burned before being buried. The situation was somewhat different at the largest of the Robbins mounds, where a small pile of dirt was put over a cremation within the building, and only later was it burned down and covered by still more earth.

Adena mounds also contained graves, often large numbers of them that had accumulated over time. At Robbins, the sequence of burials was occasionally interrupted by caps of soil that covered much or all of the mound.[4] These soil layers created new and somewhat smoother surfaces, so the enlargement of this mound involved more than the addition of new graves to an ever-expanding pile of earth.

An Adena mound might contain bodies buried in very different ways. The most impressive graves were the log-lined tombs, which consisted of logs stacked against low earthen walls, and sometimes also distributed across the floors. Impressions in the soil reveal that bark was often left

36

37

38 This stone platform pipe was from the Crigler mound in Kentucky. Part of it has been restored. Many platform pipes, some more ornate than others, have been found with Adena burials and, especially, in Middle Woodland graves from Ohio, Illinois, and other states. Length 6.6 in (16.7 cm).

on the tree trunks. Additional logs must have been used to form the roofs. Cross-sections through the tombs show that dirt eventually settled into them from above, presumably after the roof supports had decayed. The eventual collapse of tomb roofs contributed to the irregular contours of the mounds. Each tomb contained the remains of no more than a few individuals, mostly completely articulated skeletons stretched out on their backs. Highly valued objects were often worn by these people or lay beside them. Among the most notable objects discovered, mainly in graves, are stone platform pipes, small carved stone tablets, copper bracelets and breastplates, pieces of cut mica, and marine shell beads.[5] Broken pottery has also been found, and Berle Clay has pointed out that the distributions of sherds in a few mounds could indicate some kind of graveside ritual.[6]

While many Adena mounds were quite large, the work required of any single family was probably not very great if stretched out over many years. Moundbuilding involved the addition of numerous small deposits of soil, many of them associated with the construction of individual graves, that took place over a long time. The labor needed was well within the capacity of even small communities whose members worked only infrequently on the mounds.

The periodic renewal of mound surfaces, which was so apparent at Robbins, was presumably related to ceremonies that reconsecrated the ground. Perhaps such events took place at a fixed interval or were held when something unusual took place in the local social group. Whatever happened, people repeatedly came back to the mounds after earlier graves had been sealed by new layers of earth.

Outside of the middle Ohio Valley, mounds were generally small and infrequent before about 2,200 years ago. But by Middle Woodland times mounds of earth or stone had become common across the Midwest and Southeast. The majority of these Middle Woodland mounds were circular to oval piles of earth and were rarely more than a few yards high, although some were much larger. The biggest include the elongated ones over mortuary structures associated with some of the Ohio geometric earthworks. Yet however similar the mounds might appear from the outside, they differed greatly in how they were built, the ways in which graves were constructed, and the number of people they contained.

The Middle Woodland mounds in Ohio often covered the remains of structures that had walls consisting of rows of upright poles and roofs frequently supported by additional posts.[7] These structures were filled with bones and artifacts indicating lengthy use; for example, frequent fires in crematory basins. Often there was only a single room, although occasionally several rooms were joined by short and narrow passageways. Inside lay cremations, piles of disarticulated bones, and intact skeletons, but it is difficult to tell how many people ended up in them. Despite poor preservation and wretched early excavation techniques, it is nonetheless clear that

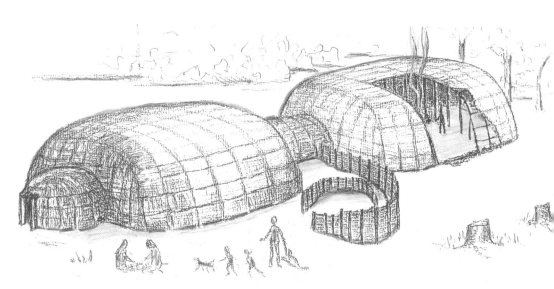

39 (*above left*)  Postmolds for a large structure were exposed during the 1977 excavation of the Edwin Harness mound in Ohio. The postmolds are shown in white.

40 (*left*)  The main part of the Edwin Harness structure, which was filled with burials and artifacts, was made up of two large rooms connected by a narrow passage.

41 (*above*)  The large mound at Seip in Ohio is open to the public.

the largest structures held many people. Seip Mound 1, the Edwin Harness mound, and Mound 25 at Hopewell, all in Ohio, contained the remains of at least 132, 178, and 102 people respectively. These figures certainly underestimate the true number of burials, though by how much we do not know.

39–41

Artifacts were also placed in these buildings, although not always along with human remains. Some objects have survived intact, whereas others were destroyed during the activities that took place in the buildings or when bodies were burned. Occasionally great hoards of artifacts have been unearthed, including those made from copper, mica, and obsidian. Some objects were carefully wrapped before being placed in the structures because

57

42 Remnants of paint, as well as two suspension holes, are visible on this breastplate from Seip in Ohio. Length 11.1 in (28.2 cm).

42   certain copper artifacts, especially breastplates and axes, are covered by impressions of textiles and, more rarely, scraps of woven materials.[8] Both vegetable fibers and rabbit fur were used to make the fabric found at Seip, and some of it was painted.

A carefully studied rectangular building in Mound 13 at Mound City in central Ohio serves as a good example of one of these structures.[9] Some of the mound, which had a diameter of about 70 ft (21.3 m) and a height of 3 ft (0.9 m), was dug in the 1920s after it and nearby mounds were damaged or
43   destroyed by the army's Camp Sherman. Mound 13 was partly covered by a barracks, which made the hard work of digging that much more difficult. Further excavations were undertaken about 40 years later when the National Park Service developed the site (it is now a fine park that is well worth visiting). James Brown combined information from both excavations, allowing him to identify two sequential structures. The later one, a square building defined by soil stains where vertical posts once stood, measured about 40 by 42.5 ft (12.2 by 13 m). The floor in the middle of the building was littered with bits of mica, pieces of artifacts, and burned bones that heavy use had trampled into the floor before it was sealed with a thin layer of sand. The floor next to a specially prepared crematory basin, which was just over 4 ft wide and 6 ft long (1.3 by 1.8 m), was burned by hot fires. There were also four low earthen platforms with the burned bones from several people and pieces of artifacts; 13 piles of burned bones, some with ornaments; and a shallow burial, also with broken artifacts. Most remarkable of
44   all was the Great Mica Grave, which the original excavators found. It was a shallow depression with a raised rim that measured 6.5 by 7 ft (2 m) on a

43 Mounds within the army's Camp Sherman in Ohio – a site now known as Mound City – were excavated in the 1920s. Excavations were conducted alongside, and even under, barracks.

44 The Great Mica Grave was found in Mound 13 at Mound City.

side. The soil of the rim was mixed with beads, perforated animal teeth, pieces of galena, and broken pipes, among other items. The grave was lined with mica, and it contained the cremated bones of four people, a copper headdress, and a mica circle. It was covered by a low pile of earth, some sand, and still more mica. While burials such as the Great Mica Grave dominate our impression of Hopewell mortuary customs, few if any artifacts accompanied the overwhelming majority of the people whose remains were placed in these structures.

Despite the impressive contents of many of Ohio's Middle Woodland mounds, not all of them covered structures, numerous bodies, and extraordinary objects. One such mound, Armitage, was about 6.5 ft (2 m) high with a diameter of 80.5 ft (24.6 m), and contained human bones, hearths, postmolds, and impressions of logs.[10] One skeleton was surrounded by bark, the other burials consisted of 14 piles of cremated bones. The posts predated the mound, and they were taken down before the human remains were deposited. People returned to Armitage several times before the mound reached its final dimensions; during these visits small fires were lit and more earth was added.

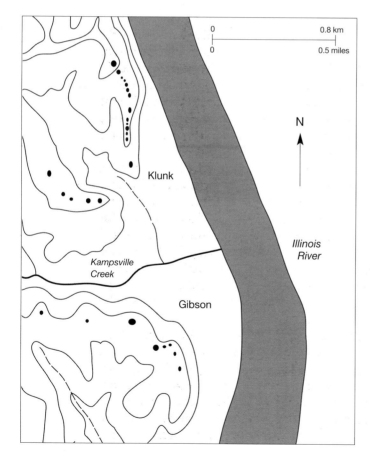

45 The Gibson and Klunk mounds in Illinois are strung out along the crests of steep bluffs that line the Illinois River floodplain. The mounds are on the north and south sides of a small hollow where the town of Kampsville is located. The contour lines are at 100-ft (30-m) intervals.

46  Log-lined central tombs in Middle Woodland mounds in Illinois were surrounded by simpler graves.

Of the Middle Woodland mounds elsewhere in the Eastern Woodlands, the ones along the central and lower Illinois River and adjacent Mississippi River in western Illinois are particularly well known. They are commonly lined up along narrow fingers of steep bluffs that border the valleys, although some are located in the floodplain, including several of the largest ones. The bluff-top mounds are wonderful places to excavate – nice views, cool breezes, and easily dug loess soils – as long as one keeps an eye out for the rattlesnakes that infest these places.  45

The contents of the western Illinois mounds differ from one another, although many had central tombs surrounded by simple graves.[11] Before  46 moundbuilding commenced, the upper dark soil horizon was sometimes removed. The mound fill that was subsequently deposited often consisted of small lenses of earth corresponding to separate basket loads. Blocks of sod were also stacked up, generally with the grassy side facing downward. It is commonly said that caps of clay-rich soil were added to finish the mounds. While such deposits occasionally appear to have been laid down, the supposed caps are usually no more than soil horizons that developed naturally over the many centuries since the mounds were finished.

The central crypts typically held the remains of only a few people. Occasionally these tombs were replaced, resulting in deposits of soil from separate construction episodes that are difficult to tease apart. The log-lined tombs were surrounded by low ridges of earth, which were sometimes covered with thin layers of brightly colored clay. Under favorable conditions the impressions of decayed grass or mats can still be seen on these surfaces, as well as bone pins that once held the coverings in place. The log-lined tombs often contained intact skeletons as well as disarticulated bones that were pushed to one side to make way for new bodies. Some tombs held only scattered human remains, indicating that most of the bones were picked up after the flesh had rotted off them. After they were taken from the tombs, individual bones and small parts of skeletons, presumably held together by desiccated soft tissue, were placed on the earthen ridges along the edges of the deep rectangular pits. Burial in one of these tombs was likely as important for reaffirming group identity through a sense of shared experience as it was a means of commemorating a person's life and disposing of a corpse.

Fine objects were often buried with the people in the log-lined tombs.[12] Among them were stone platform pipes, chipped stone blades and tools, freshwater pearl beads, perforated bear canines, cut and polished pieces of bone from carnivore and human jaws, sheets of mica, marine shell cups and beads, and copper earspools, panpipes, and celts. Well-made pots with decorated and polished surfaces were also buried. They include a group of 20 vessels placed alongside an infant in a deep pit that initiated the construction of Mound 7 at the Elizabeth site in west-central Illinois.

Arranged around the central tombs were simple graves. Usually the pits were barely large enough to hold a single body, which was generally stretched out on its back. These people were often buried with artifacts, but they were a rather unimpressive lot when compared to the items from the nearby central tombs.

Mounds in other areas might share some but not all of these features, as shown by mounds along the Mississippi River near Trempealeau in southwestern Wisconsin.[13] Several rectangular tombs from 6.5 to 11.2 ft (2 to 3.4 m) long and from 0.9 to 2.3 ft (0.3 to 0.7 m) deep were found when digging these mounds. The tombs were surrounded by low ridges composed of soil removed from the pits. Strips of bark from several kinds of trees were occasionally preserved where they lined the tombs and extended out to cover the adjacent ridges – in one tomb the bark was still several inches thick, despite decay and compaction over many centuries. Each tomb contained the remains of two to several dozen people represented by extended skeletons and bundles of disarticulated bones. In one of the tombs, small piles of bones, including both skulls and long bones, were placed on a narrow ledge between the central pit, which held additional skeletons, and the surrounding ridge of soil. Presumably these bones were pulled out of the main pit to make room for later burials. Many fine objects, including those made from copper, accompanied the Trempealeau burials. But despite the presence of central crypts, the numerous peripheral graves so typical of the Illinois mounds were lacking at Trempealeau.

Several rectangular tombs were excavated at Helena Crossing in east-central Arkansas in mounds that were located on the heavily eroded edge of Crowley's Ridge above the flat Mississippi River bottomland.[14] These tombs differed somewhat from one another, although they were built with large

47

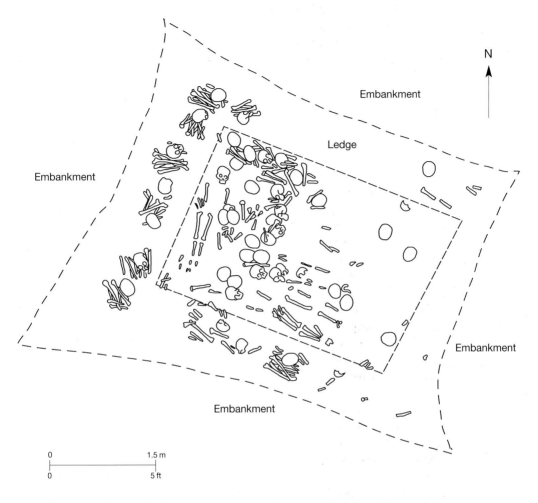

47 Human remains were found in the central pit and on the surrounding ledges in Schwert Mound 18 at Trempealeau, Wisconsin.

logs and one had earthen embankments along two of its sides. At Helena Crossing – in contrast to the classic Illinois situation – the tombs were located in various parts of the mounds. Much like Middle Woodland sites elsewhere, fancy burial artifacts included those made from copper, marine shell, and mica.

Other arrangements of graves have also been found in Middle Woodland mounds. Returning to Trempealeau, dirt was sometimes merely piled on human remains that had been placed on the ground.[15] Both fully extended skeletons and groups of disarticulated bones were laid down on surfaces that were prepared by removing as much as 1 ft (0.3 m) of the original topsoil.

In many places there are mounds that contain burials scattered through-out their fill. They include the well-known Copena mounds, which averaged

48 Many Copena mounds were rather small, such as this one at the Walling site in Alabama photographed in 1941.

48 about 6 ft (1.8 m) in height, in the middle Tennessee River Valley of northern Alabama.[16] Excavators have found intact skeletons, some in puddled clay graves or wooden canoe-like troughs, as well as cremations and bundles of bones. Much like what occurred elsewhere, various objects were buried with the dead, and it was the *cop*per along with gal*ena* that gave Copena its name.

49 Four low mounds at Tunacunnhee at the base of Lookout Mountain in northwestern Georgia show how differently bodies could be handled at a single site.[17] Three earthen mounds were covered with stone slabs, a fourth was composed almost entirely of rock. Some bodies were laid out in extended and flexed positions, while others were cremated or defleshed before burial. The artifacts were a diverse lot, particularly considering the small number of burials in each mound. They included rather plain stone tools, but also bear canine ornaments and, rarer still, panpipes covered with copper and silver, copper breastplates, and shark teeth, among other objects.

Two of the Tunacunnhee graves are worthy of special mention because they were located beyond the outer limits of the mounds (a similarly located pit has been excavated at Elizabeth).[18] These sites make it clear that mortuary-related activities were not restricted to mounds, but signs of them are rarely uncovered because few archaeologists bother to look for them.

Elizabeth is instructive for two other reasons. A deposit of debris that included obsidian flakes was located on a steep hillside no more than 164 ft (50 m) away from the mounds – a remarkable find because obsidian is rarely found in Illinois.[19] The flakes must have been buried during ceremonies that

49 Mound C at Tunacunnhee was covered with stone slabs.

took place around the Elizabeth mounds. Excavations were also undertaken at a nearby campsite known as Napoleon Hollow, which is situated below the mounds. Michael Wiant and Chip McGimsey found that the materials from Napoleon Hollow differed from normal habitation debris; many more fancy Hopewell pots, blades, and unusual kinds of stone, including obsidian, came from the site than expected. There seemed to be too few ordinary hunting and agricultural tools and the best cuts of meat were brought to the camp, judging from a disproportionately large number of bones from the fleshy parts of deer. The Napoleon Hollow findings are consistent with those of an excavation of a habitation area near the Tunacunnhee mounds that yielded pieces of copper and mica. Thus it appears that people periodically assembled at special camps to conduct ceremonies that included, but were not restricted to, the burial of the dead in nearby mounds.

## Ceremonial platforms

While most Middle Woodland mounds were low to high domes of earth, flat-topped rectangular and circular mounds were also built in the Midwest and Southeast.[20] Several decades ago, archaeologists were reluctant to accept the possibility that earthen platforms were built at this time, but that is not true today. Studies of old field notes and collections along with new excavations have clearly shown that the platforms were widely, if thinly, distributed during the Middle Woodland period.

One platform used for burial purposes was excavated at the Crooks site along a Louisiana bayou.[21] Within Mound A, which measured 83 to 86 ft (25.8 m) at its base and 17.3 ft (5.3 m) high, there was a low platform later covered by two major episodes of mound construction. The initial platform had a 45 by 70-ft (13.7 by 21.3-m) flat top that was as much as 2 ft (0.6 m) high, on which several pits, lenses of charred material and ash, and three hearths were found. There were also well over a thousand burials, both intact skeletons and disarticulated bones, in the mound. Almost 400 of them were in the upper part of the platform and on its surface, the rest in deposits that covered the platform. Often the bodies were buried in shallow graves, at least some of which were lined with mats. For the most part these people were adults, but poor preservation presumably reduced the number of juveniles that could be identified. Only a few skeletons had artifacts with them, including pottery, chipped stone tools, and copper earspools and beads.

Mound A at McKeithen in northern Florida is another burial platform – it was low and rectangular, and later covered with a mantle of sand.[22] Graves were dug into the platform, and empty pits show that bones were removed

50   The Ozier mound at Pinson is a large Middle Woodland mound.

once bodies had decomposed, which would not have taken long in shallow graves in this hot, humid climate. Hearths and posts were also present, as were two small piles of animal bones. The bones – most of the meat eaten was venison – were presumably all that remained of feasts that took place on or near this mound.

Some platforms were used for something other than the burial of the dead. They include the Capitolium mound at Marietta, Ma°50 at Walling in northern Alabama, the Ozier mound at Pinson in western Tennessee, and Mound A at Cold Springs in north-central Georgia.[23] Recently it became necessary to dig part of the Capitolium during a renovation of the public library that sits on the mound. When that was done, it was discovered that the builders of the mound had removed the original topsoil before they added thin horizontal layers of sand and gravel. These deposits were in turn covered by more earth that enlarged the mound upward and outward. Patches of burned soil show that fires were lit on the various construction stages. At Walling, a few layers of fill were laid over an earlier debris-laden midden. Pits, hearths, and postmolds were found when the mound was excavated, but there were no obvious patterns to the posts that would indicate the presence of substantial structures. At one point, small amounts of colorful clays were laid down, seemingly intentionally. At the Ozier mound, at least six building episodes, each covered by a thin layer of sand, were identified in soil cores. Hearths were found in excavations of the uppermost sand layer. The Cold Springs mound was built in at least five stages. The maximum horizontal dimensions of the mound were essentially established by the first construction episode, so each new deposit raised it upward, not outward. Numerous features, mostly scattered postmolds, were found on these surfaces.

It is unlikely that whatever took place on these four platforms was exactly the same. After all, they were used by different and widely separated groups of people. But these events all involved the use of carefully prepared surfaces that were periodically renewed by the addition of more soil. Sometimes these layers were of different colors. Moreover, the ceremonies held on these surfaces, regardless of their specific form or purpose, involved lighting fires and erecting posts.

## Geometric and irregular earthworks

In addition to mounds, there are many Adena and Middle Woodland earthworks, particularly in central Ohio southward into central Kentucky. Some also lie farther afield, such as Pinson in western Tennessee, Mann in southwestern Indiana, Golden Eagle in west-central Illinois, 15FU37 in western Kentucky, 20IA37 in central Michigan, Little Spanish Fort in west-central Mississippi, and Marksville in east-central Louisiana.[24] Often the only evidence of their existence comes from old maps because many were flattened long ago. Yet a number of them have survived. Sometimes they have done so

51 The huge earthwork complex at Newark, Ohio, includes this octagon and circle. Mounds are located inside gaps in the octagon's walls.

51     in peculiar ways, such as a part of the Newark earthworks in central Ohio that is in the Moundbuilders Country Club golf course.

One way to provide a taste of the rich diversity in earthwork shapes and sizes is to discuss them in terms of three categories: small circles; large circles, squares, and other shapes; and hilltop enclosures conforming to local topography. But before going any further, one must realize that any such classification masks a great deal of variation in size, shape, layout, and construction details.

Small enclosures usually consisted of circular embankments up to about 6 ft (1.8 m) high, often with internal shallow ditches and gaps for easy entry.[25] The sizes of 58 of these circles in Ohio, Kentucky, and Indiana, mostly from Ephraim Squier and Edwin Davis' rough estimates, range from 0.2 to 2.7 acres (<0.1 to 1.1 ha), averaging 0.8 acres (0.3 ha). There were smaller ones as well, but these attracted scant attention so little is known about them. Often several small circles were built close to one another, and at least some of them surrounded wooden structures or mounds, including the well-known Mount Horeb earthwork and the Marietta Conus.

Mount Horeb, which sits on the crest of a hill in the beautiful horse-farm country of central Kentucky, consists of a circular shallow ditch surrounded by a low embankment.[26] The WPA excavators of this Adena site uncovered a row of postmolds along the ditch's inner edge. This wall of posts, assuming it was high enough, screened the earthwork's interior from view – the embankment was not sufficient to do so. The ridge, ditch, and wall arrangement makes no sense from a defensive point of view: the low embankment was outermost, and the ditch and wooden wall, in that order, came next. So the earthwork must have been of ceremonial importance. The excavators did not find the refuse normally present on village sites, suggesting no significant occupation near the circle.

Mount Horeb was probably not the only circular embankment with a wooden wall. Recently a large circle of postmolds similar to the one at Mount Horeb was discovered while Frank Cowan and his colleagues

52, pl. v

52 The Mount Horeb earthwork has been partially excavated (shaded area), and a circle of postmolds was discovered just inside the ditch.

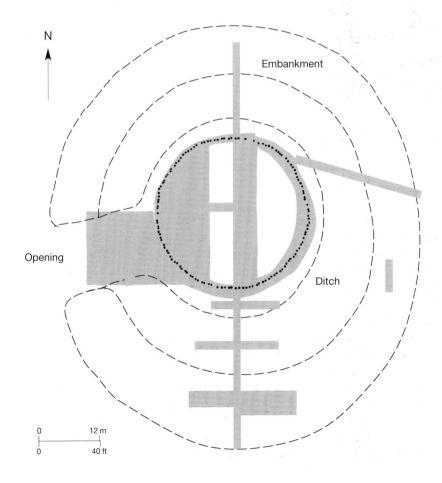

75

conducted excavations at the Stubbs earthwork in southwestern Ohio.[27] These postmolds are thought to be located where a low circular earthwork, which is no longer visible, was mapped in the early nineteenth century. It appears as if the posts were taken down before they rotted, and the empty holes were filled with earth that often contrasted strongly with the surrounding natural soil. The careful work at Stubbs is especially exciting because it shows that it is still possible to identify the positions and sizes of earthworks that disappeared long ago.

Another fine example of a circular embankment and ditch can be seen in the city of Marietta's Mound Cemetery.[28] Here a low ridge and corresponding-

pl. II

ingly shallow ditch surround a high conical mound called the Conus. Just like Mount Horeb and many other circles, the low earthen ring is located immediately outside the shallow ditch.

The Conus fills much of the space within the embankment and ditch, but that is not true of all of the mounds within small circular earthworks. Several examples of the latter include Spruce Run and Wright in central Ohio,

53, 54

the Anderson Great Mound in east-central Indiana, and the Biggs mound in northeastern Kentucky.[29] Fires and cremations were an important part of the rituals that took place at these sites. Sequentially built clay platforms, each blanketed by ash, were found in the Anderson Great Mound. Ash, charcoal, and burned bones were spread across the surface covered by the Biggs mound. A few features, including postmolds, were also noted in excavations at Anderson and Biggs. Little is known about Spruce Run because it was dug well over a century ago, yet it too covered a layer of ash. The Wright Mound contained two cremations and three other burials.

Much larger geometric earthen enclosures were also built.[30] They include the roughly oval Adena earthwork known as Peter Village that is within sight of Mount Horeb – its low embankment and exterior ditch enclosed about 23 acres (9.2 ha). But most of the large earthworks were constructed in central and southern Ohio during Middle Woodland times. These embankments, often with adjacent ditches, usually formed reasonably regular shapes such as circles, squares, octagons, and parallel lines. The great majority of the geometric earthworks – at least those mapped by Ephraim Squier and Edwin Davis in the mid-nineteenth century before many were flattened – enclosed areas of several acres up to about 50 acres (20 ha), although a few were much larger. The embankments were often joined together, enclosing correspondingly larger areas.

The shapes of the geometric earthworks contrast strongly with those of the highly irregular hilltop enclosures.[31] Many of them have been found in Ohio, although they also occur in the Southeast. Walls of earth and stone were put along the edges of hills or slightly downslope from them, and sometimes they ringed entire hilltops, including the huge Fort Ancient earthwork in southwestern Ohio that enclosed about 125 acres (51 ha). Embankments at other sites, such as at Pollock in southwestern Ohio, merely cut across places that provided easy access to the tops of hills.

53 A ditch and embankment surrounded the small Biggs mound in Kentucky.

54 The Great Mound at Anderson in Indiana consists of a well-preserved embankment and ditch, which are shown here. The mound itself is not as large as its name implies.

At least some of the Middle Woodland sites had wooden walls that enhanced the visual effect of the earthen embankments.[32] Parts of such walls have been traced in Robert Riordan's excavations of the Pollock earthwork. He found that one wall segment consisted of a wooden framework that was once thickly plastered with mud. It burned, producing considerable amounts of distinctive reddish soil, and toppled over, eventually being covered to form a low embankment. Elsewhere a wooden fence lacking a daub covering was built on a low earthen ridge – it too was later covered by still more earth.

Features that survived long enough to be recorded often blocked the openings in embankments. Obvious obstructions include mounds put just inside breaks in the walls of a number of the large regular squares and octagons.[33] Gaps in the hilltop embankment at Fort Ancient are an especially good example of the importance of partially occluded openings in an earthwork's overall layout. Here mounds, stone circles, ponds, and specially prepared walkways were put in or near the openings. Apparently, the gaps in the Fort Ancient earthwork were more important than the earthen embankments. The walls forced people to pass through openings filled with symbolically significant obstacles and paths.

Nobody knows how long it took to build an earthwork. N'omi Greber has pointed out that this work, if stretched out over many generations, did not require a particularly large number of people.[34] Two or more embankment construction stages have indeed been identified at several sites. But not all excavations of embankments have revealed discrete construction episodes. This does not necessarily discount the possibility that the enclosures were built over many years. They could have been made by gradually lengthening incomplete walls rather than by adding new soil to increase the height of low, but already fully formed, enclosures. Only the latter method would show up as separate building episodes in cross-sections of the earthen ridges. This way of constructing an enclosure meant that its ultimate shape and size had to be known in advance and possibly marked out on the ground. But despite claims to the contrary, it would have been no great feat to lay out a geometric earthwork, as the ever-practical Gerard Fowke noted a century ago. At least some of the earthworks were located in pocket prairies where they would have been more visible than if surrounded by trees. Just such a setting is indicated by a buried soil horizon beneath the Great Circle earthwork at Newark.

An effort was made to keep the work to a manageable level.[35] Soil came from nearby borrow pits and the ditches alongside embankments, or it was simply scraped up from the ground next to the enclosures. Anyone who has moved loads of dirt or large rocks knows from first-hand experience that the work of carrying them over anything more than short distances far exceeds the effort spent digging soil or grubbing stones out of the ground. So whatever the symbolic significance, if any, of paired embankments and ditches, there was a practical reason why they lay next to one another. For example,

55

55 Part of the Newark earthwork complex was preserved in a park, as shown in this picture from an early twentieth-century postcard.

the 16.5-ft (5-m) high embankment of the 1,201-ft (366-m) wide Great Circle at Newark was located next to a correspondingly deep ditch. The easiest soil to dig was also used to make up the bulk of the earthworks. Hard clay at Marksville was avoided in favor of overlying looser soil, lessening the problems faced by people who had only simple digging tools at their disposal. Debris-laden surface soil was similarly used in at least some of the embankments in Ohio.

The Serpent Mound in southern Ohio does not fit comfortably into any of the three categories noted above, although it is worth mentioning here because this deservedly famous earthwork is commonly said to be an Adena site.[36] This long, low embankment snakes its way down a narrow ridge. The tail forms a tight spiral, and the other end widens to join an oval embankment, commonly interpreted as the head, although some have thought the snake is swallowing an egg. Surprisingly little work has been done at the Serpent considering the attention the earthwork has received. Recently even the dating of the site has been brought into question. Long thought to be an Adena site based on slim evidence, a couple of radiocarbon dates from a small excavation raise the possibility that the earthwork might be no more than a thousand years old. Middle Ohio Valley people at that time are not known for building large earthworks – only a few mounds – although they had a high regard for snakes, as shown by small pieces of copper shaped into sinuous serpents. In short, earthworks are hard to date, and more work must

56, pl. VI

56 The Serpent Mound in Ohio is one of the best-known earthworks, but there are questions about when it was actually built.

be done at the Serpent Mound. Fortunately, well over a century ago a few enterprising people had the good sense to preserve it.

All these earthworks surely served ritual instead of defensive purposes. The embankments were often penetrated by many more openings than would be prudent if they were meant to keep enemies at bay – the hilltop embankment at Fort Ancient, for example, had as many as 67 of them.[37] Furthermore, the perimeters of many earthworks were much too long to be manned by the people who lived nearby. Saying that the earthworks had some ritual significance, however, is not very revealing. It is clear that many of the Ohio Middle Woodland earthworks enclosed spaces used for the burial of the dead, but this function alone would not have required such large enclosures. So it is not surprising that excavations within and near the earthworks, although limited, have turned up evidence of other activities. For example, postmolds for several big rectangular wooden structures have been discovered within a large circular earthwork at Seip.[38] These buildings contained numerous stone blades as well as mica and other non-local materials.

58

## A remarkable site: Hopewell

Hopewell in central Ohio, originally known as Clark's Works, is noteworthy because some of the most impressive artifacts from the Eastern Woodlands were found there.[39] Many of them were uncovered while digging for objects to include in the 1893 World's Columbian Exposition; others were discovered during further excavations in the early 1920s.

The site consisted of a square embankment adjacent to the much larger Great Enclosure. The Great Enclosure was a roughly rectangular ridge and exterior ditch that encompassed more than 100 acres (40 ha). In the mid-nineteenth century the embankment was still about 4 to 6 ft (1.2 to 1.8 m) high. Within the larger of the enclosures were two additional embankments, one of which surrounded the largest mound at the site, Mound 25. This slightly irregular mound measured as much as 189 by 550 ft (57.6 by 167.6 m), and it was

about 21 ft (6.4 m) tall. It is not known exactly how many mounds were originally present at the site, but there were probably about 40, most of which were small.

Excavations in the mounds yielded impressive artifacts, often buried together in single deposits. Mound 25 contained a great number of them, including well over 100 finely made obsidian bifaces and a large cache of copper artifacts such as axes and breastplates. The obsidian points were clearly intended for display – many were so large they had no practical value, and they were often rather oddly shaped. Over 500 copper earspools were found elsewhere in this mound, including a considerable number stuck together in a large mass. The other mounds also produced precious objects: Mound 11, for example, had about 300 pounds (136 kg) of obsidian, and several thousand sheets of mica were buried in Mound 17.

57 A large cache of copper artifacts (bottom center) was found in Mound 25 at Hopewell when it was excavated over a century ago.

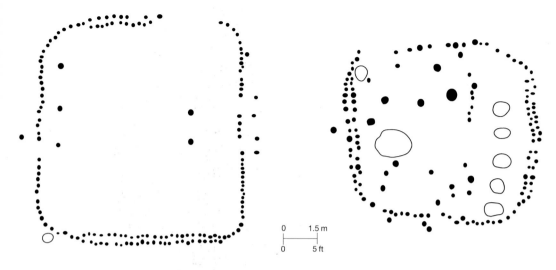

58 These two large structures within the Seip earthwork in Ohio had roughly square floor plans (they are shown side-by-side for comparative purposes). The postmolds are black and pits are open ovals.

Small flakes of mica, a mineral that breaks apart easily when worked, presumably came from attempts to fashion artifacts for special ceremonies, including funerals.

Postmolds for large rectangular and circular structures have also been found in excavations immediately outside the Stubbs earthwork.[40] Domestic refuse was notably sparse near the wooden buildings, and there were few features other than the postmolds. Thus the buildings appear to have been special-function structures that were perhaps occupied by people who congregated at the earthwork during one or more times of the year.

## Precious objects

The Adena and Middle Woodland societies are also noteworthy for their exchange of non-local raw materials and artifacts that had some long-forgotten symbolic significance. The people buried in the Adena mounds possessed numerous items fashioned from copper, such as bracelets, as well as mica cut into various shapes. Trade increased during Middle Woodland times, judging from the numbers of artifacts, the distances covered, and the range of societies that participated in these interactions. Among these materials were copper from the Lake Superior deposits; silver from Lake Superior and especially Ontario; galena from Missouri and Illinois; mica from the southern Appalachians; chert from various places including Ohio, Indiana, and Illinois; pipestone from Ohio and Illinois; alligator teeth from the lower Mississippi Valley eastward to Florida; marine shells, especially

59, pl. xiii,
pl. xvii

59 This head cut from sheet mica was found at the Turner site in Ohio. Length 6.9 in (17.5 cm).

whelks, from the south Atlantic and Gulf coasts; Knife River chalcedony from North Dakota; and obsidian from Yellowstone in Wyoming.[41] The distance over which the obsidian had to be carried is remarkable – Yellowstone and the main concentration of Ohio earthworks are separated by about 1,430 miles (2,300 km). At this point we do not know if the obsidian was carried overland or in canoes along rivers. If by water, the longest stretch being the Missouri, the journey along meandering rivers was more than twice the straight-line distance.

60

60 Many large obsidian bifaces were found in Mound 25 at the Hopewell site in Ohio. The longest specimen is 9.6 in (24.3 cm).

61  Chert bifaces from Mound 2 were piled up in the early 1890s field camp at the Hopewell site in Ohio.

For some unknown reason, many more objects made of non-local materials ended up in Ohio than elsewhere.[42] The uneven distribution of obsidian artifacts and debris is particularly apparent. The overwhelming majority of all the obsidian from sites east of Mississippi came from only two of the Hopewell site mounds. Excavations at Hopewell also yielded large caches of copper objects and mica. Impressive hoards have been found at other sites as well. At Fort Ancient, for example, more than 50 copper artifacts, mostly breastplates and earspools, were accompanied by about twice as many from cut mica. Over 100 pieces of cut mica were taken from a grave in the Edwin Harness mound. Deposits of chipped stone artifacts made from high-quality non-local chert have also been unearthed. The most impressive cache – from Hopewell's Mound 2 – consisted of over 8,000 large oval bifaces, small groups of which were covered with earth as if laid down as separate bundles. And these were not the only sites in central and southern Ohio that yielded great quantities of artifacts fashioned from non-local materials.

Several other places in the Eastern Woodlands also have an unusually large number of non-local items.[43] Many fine objects, such as worked copper and marine shells, were buried in the Illinois mounds. One of two deposits of chert bifaces at the Baehr site contained over 6,000 of these artifacts. Small piles of bifaces were placed on the ground, and then they were each covered with a little dirt, just like those found in Hopewell Mound 2. Each bundle might have been a separate contribution by a family or other social group. Turning to the Southeast, more Hopewell-style copper artifacts have been found in the Copena sites than anywhere else in the South. Yet individual sites, such as Tunacunnhee, have also produced unusually large numbers of Hopewell-related artifacts.

Most of the non-local items must have been passed from one individual to the next, presumably as part of ceremonies that required displays of wealth or generosity. There is reason to believe, however, that a down-the-line movement of goods was not the only way precious items crossed long distances in the Middle Woodland period. It is difficult to see how such exchanges could account for the huge deposits of non-local objects, such as the hoards of obsidian, copper, and mica at some of the Ohio sites. The obsidian is especially interesting: the two great hoards at Hopewell reached Ohio without much of it, if any at all, being left behind along the way. As James B. Griffin pointed out almost 40 years ago, a few people might have traveled long distances to get the obsidian, among other raw materials.[44] Such trips need not have occurred often, no more than once a generation or so, and some might never have been repeated. Once finished, they must have become the stuff of legend.

Nobody knows what the inhabitants of Ohio and a few other key places gave in return for the unusual objects. Nor do we have any idea about what could have motivated people to head off into unknown lands and permitted safe travel with heavy loads of valuables. Perhaps it had something to do with the esoteric knowledge that the builders of the greatest mounds and earthworks were thought to possess.

What we can say is that the Middle Woodland period was a time of unusual harmony.[45] The numerous skeletons unearthed at many sites show few signs of the kinds of injuries that occur when people fight each other. A lessening of conflicts is consistent with more permeable social boundaries that allowed some people to travel unscathed across long distances with ritually significant and highly unusual objects.

## Where they lived

While much remains to be learned about the mounds and what they contain, we know more about them than about ordinary settlements. Sparse habitation debris makes most campsites hard to find. Moreover, much of the early pottery quickly breaks apart in plowed fields, especially in the north where repeated freezing during long winters takes a great toll on exposed sherds.

Soil stains from posts that supported buildings, screens, and drying racks have been found in many excavations.[46] Houses were usually circular to oval, varying widely in size, and were rather flimsy structures that could be thrown up without too much effort. Other features included hearths and shallow basins. Most of the pits must have been used for storage purposes, although some contained fire-cracked rock consistent with their use as earth ovens.

Sites tend to be small: debris rarely covers more than several acres, and often much less.[47] Where structure remnants have been uncovered, there are usually only a few buildings arranged in no apparent order. So it seems that many people, perhaps the great majority, lived in relative isolation in dispersed communities where houses were strung out along the banks of lakes and creeks, or other especially favorable spots. Clusters of structures lacking any evidence of superpositioning indicate that there were also compact villages. But for the most part these settlements did not consist of many households, nor did people live there for a long time, based on the scanty refuse they left behind. At a few sites, however, heavy scatters of debris along with numerous features and dark middens indicate occupation by larger numbers of people for longer periods of time. Scattered around the

## The move toward agriculture

Recently there has been an explosion of information about ancient diets that has come about through the use of water screening, or flotation, to extract bones, seeds, and nutshells from sediments. It is now possible to use the botanical information to illustrate the overall trend in the intensification of food production.

In the two graphs shown here, each dot represents plant remains from separate sites. Some sites were occupied at different times, so each occupation gets its own dot. The plants include nuts, mostly hickories; introduced crops, both maize and beans; and the native cultigens squash, goosefoot, marsh elder, erect knotweed, maygrass, little barley, and sunflower. All sites have more than 100 identifiable fragments. The horizontal axes show the approximate ages of the samples, while the vertical axes indicate the proportions of different kinds of plants.

Most sites are from the midcontinent, which is where botanical specialists have been especially active. The sites are unsorted according to geographical location, amount sampled, season of use, or length of occupation. Thus any patterns in these data will be muddier than if sites could be reliably separated according to their function and season of use.

The upper graph shows the proportion of each sample that consists of the carbonized remains of plants grown in gardens. Nutshells serve as a crude measure of wild plant food; the inclusion of plant remains such as berry or grape seeds has no noticeable effect on general patterns.

The lower graph is organized much like the upper one, except that the dots indicate the abundance of introduced cultigens (maize and beans) relative to all cultivated plants (maize and beans, plus the native cultigens). Beans are poorly represented in the samples, so what is shown is essentially the representation of maize in the samples of cultivated plants.

It is far simpler to identify the range of foods in diets than it is to estimate the amounts that were eaten. Yet despite an inability to go directly from preserved materials to the composition of prehistoric meals, it is reasonable to suppose that major shifts in the proportions of food remains – for example, plants that were cultivated instead of merely gathered – mark a significant change in how people went about getting enough to eat. If these data accurately reflect past reality, then native cultigens were first used heavily in many places about 2,000 years ago, and maize began to make a major contribution to diets about 1,000 years later.

more permanent settlements were short-term camps used when hunting, fishing, or collecting wild plants.

Settlements were often clustered in the vicinity of the big Ohio earthworks, which comes as no surprise because earthworks were often situated in the widest stretches of river valleys, the most attractive places to live.[48] Here again households were usually widely scattered, as indicated by bits of pottery and stone distributed thinly across farmers' fields.

Coastal sites likewise vary in size, and many of them are composed largely of the discarded shell from innumerable meals.[49] Judith Bense has found that shell deposits along the Gulf Coast range from amorphous

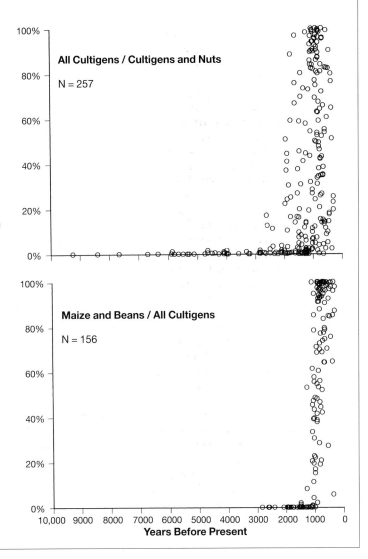

62 The road to agricultural economies was long but not smooth. The dots in the upper graph show the proportion of carbonized cultigens, both native and introduced plants, relative to nutshell at many sites. An upward jump occurred as early as 2,000 years ago in some parts of the midcontinent. The lower graph shows the proportion of maize and beans, mostly the former, relative to all cultigens, including the native crops. The shift to maize took place about 1,000 years ago. The graphs are based on published data, and each occupation (the dots) consists of at least 100 identifiable plant fragments.

**All Cultigens / Cultigens and Nuts**

N = 257

**Maize and Beans / All Cultigens**

N = 156

Years Before Present

dumps to large rings and long ridges conforming to the nearby shorelines. Pits, hearths, and postmolds have been identified in them. These sites, including many shell middens, seem to be distributed in clusters along the coast. So here too people were unevenly distributed across the land. Each group of sites includes one large midden, some of them accompanied by mounds.

## Cultivating gardens

About 2,000 years ago there was a major change in what people ate in the midcontinent.[50] From that point onward, many of them relied heavily on plants grown in their gardens, including goosefoot and erect knotweed. Productivity near settlements correspondingly increased, most importantly through the addition of a readily storable harvest of nutritious seeds. The heavy reliance on a mix of native cultigens was not the first change in diets that took place, nor would it be the last. It was nonetheless important because it signaled a departure from long-established ways of life that focused largely, if not exclusively, on hunting game, fishing, and gathering wild plants.

For several decades it has been widely recognized that the move toward agriculture spanned several thousand years. As we have already seen, Middle to Late Archaic people had begun to direct more of their attention toward plants and animals that were locally abundant and rapidly replaced through high reproductive rates. They included weedy plants that produced starchy and oily seeds that could be eaten immediately or stored for lean times of the year.

While there can be no question that the transition to agriculture was lengthy, it does not necessarily follow that it was as gradual as commonly thought (see box p. 86). Archaeologists typically favor interpretations featuring slow and steady change over those involving abrupt discontinuities. That is because most of the latter have been shown to result from significant gaps in cultural sequences, so intermediate stages are missing. Yet here is an instance where it could be argued that major shifts in food production took place in a few sharp and widely spaced steps – meaning in human terms that each transition might have spanned several lifetimes.

In the midcontinent, native plant seeds increase dramatically in samples of carbonized plant remains from sites that are as much as 2,000 years old, sometimes virtually replacing nutshells. This shift in food use occurred when the overall population was growing; in fact, this was the second major period of increase (the first took place much earlier in Paleoindian times). A little maize also made its appearance almost 2,000 years ago, but it would only become a dietary staple after many more centuries had passed.[51] Thus both native cultigens and maize were around long before they rather suddenly became major components of diets over the space of only a handful of generations.

A step-wise shift to a heavy reliance on native cultigens suggests that a point was eventually reached where major social and technological innovations were required if further increases in yields were to be realized. Such a pattern makes sense if we take into account the close links between the different elements of human cultures. Throughout most of prehistory, the slow overall rate of population growth meant that innumerable incremental changes in how people structured their lives were enough to satisfy additional demands for food. When one's existence hangs in the balance, people tend to opt for the familiar, as long as it works sufficiently well, rather than to experiment with something that by its very novelty is inherently risky. But particular ways of life are not infinitely adjustable – there inevitably comes a time when tweaking an existing strategy for survival is no longer sufficient. Any further reliance on native cultigens had to involve a major restructuring of the annual cycle and the means through which workers were organized for critical tasks, so group mobility and size, gender roles, social institutions, and the like had to change more or less in tandem. But once committed to a new way of life, the proportion of seeds in diets skyrocketed. For hundreds of years thereafter, further incremental changes in how people lived once again resulted in sufficient increases in yields whenever they were needed.

The use of indigenous cultigens seems to have been much less to the north, east, and south of the midcontinent. It was not as if these plants were totally absent – cucurbits, for example, have been found at archaeological sites dating back to the mid-Holocene in the Northeast – but people do not appear to have relied nearly so heavily on them. In areas peripheral to the midcontinent, another thousand years would pass before people shifted from wild plants to those grown in gardens, in this instance largely maize. We cannot expect that dietary practices changed in lockstep across the length and breadth of such an environmentally and culturally diverse region.

People everywhere continued to eat whatever they could get from gathering wild plants such as nuts and berries, as well as from hunting and fishing.    63

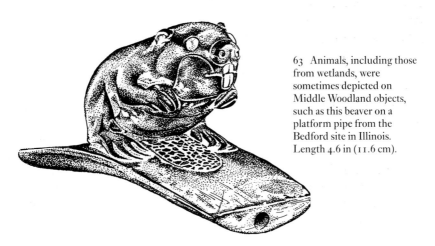

63 Animals, including those from wetlands, were sometimes depicted on Middle Woodland objects, such as this beaver on a platform pipe from the Bedford site in Illinois. Length 4.6 in (11.6 cm).

64 This large conical mound is one of many Middle Woodland mounds in the Mississippi Valley in Jackson County, Illinois. Midwesterners at that time favored marshy places where food was plentiful.

Meat from white-tailed deer and other mammals added much to diets, but so too did fish in the wet river valleys.[52] The essential role of fish in many diets had a great influence on decisions about where to settle. For example, the Early to Middle Woodland sites along the Mississippi River in southwestern Illinois tended to be located near extensive backwater lakes and swamps. Shellfish and fish quite naturally made up a large part of the diets of coastal people. Shell heaps, however, can be deceiving. Judith Bense has pointed out that fish were actually more important than shellfish as a source of food along the Gulf Coast – their bones are just not as noticeable as the shells.[53]

Changes in diets are commonly believed to have resulted in the much more widespread use of pottery midway through the first millennium BC. The crude Early Woodland vessels must have satisfied some demand that did not exist before, presumably a desire to cook seeds to make a thick porridge. While a reasonable enough explanation for the adoption of pottery in the midcontinent, people elsewhere did not eat nearly so many seeds. Perhaps these people, some of them at least, also shifted to foods such as acorns that required greater preparation time, including prolonged cooking. Whatever happened, the earliest pots were unlikely to have been a great improvement over the cooking or storage containers that had been around for a long time. The tilt toward pottery must have been related to some combination of cooking and storage requirements, the durability and portability of various kinds of containers, the labor costs in making them, the contexts within which they were used, and the degree of group mobility.

It is possible that new food-production strategies played a big part in what we see as most unusual about this period of time: great ceremonies, extraordinary symbolically charged objects, and generally harmonious relations. When people switched to a heavy reliance on plants, it became possible to produce surpluses with little additional work, making this a time of relative plenty. The extra food could be deployed to sponsor ceremonies involving the construction of mounds and earthworks. A greater reliance on plants grown in gardens also provided a cushion that blunted the dire effects of shortfalls in wild foods. Correspondingly fewer periods of great hunger meant that people did not have as many reasons to trespass on land claimed by their neighbors, who might also be experiencing hardship. A relaxation of tensions could explain why some individuals, even if only a few of them, seem to have been able to travel long distances carrying precious artifacts through the territories controlled by many different people.

## The nature of these societies

Mounds provide a few clues about how these societies were organized. Often only some community members were singled out for special mortuary treatment. These people were buried with the finest objects then available, many of which were fashioned from rare or non-local materials.

While most of the mounds held only a tiny fraction of the nearby population, access to mounds was not as restricted as archaeologists once thought.[54] When many of the sites were dug during the Great Depression, it was believed that many Adena mounds contained mostly young men. But better means of estimating age and sex are available today: when examining the Robbins skeletons, I found that a wide range of ages and both sexes were well represented in the collection. Yet it is still true that at Robbins and elsewhere, mostly adults were buried in the Adena mounds. The situation for the Ohio Hopewell mounds is similar – at one point it was thought that males greatly outnumbered females. Lyle Konigsberg, however, found a roughly equal representation of the two sexes in his study of the surviving bones from Seip Mound 1. There were also individuals of all ages, although fewer infants than expected. Having too few infants is common in archaeological samples because ancient mortuary customs sometimes excluded the very young from burial grounds, bone preservation is frequently poor, and excavation methods are often inadequate for finding small bones.

The people in the central tombs of the Illinois Middle Woodland mounds provide some information on the segments of communities that enjoyed the highest social standing. These particular tombs held juveniles and adults, both men and women.[55] At some sites, such as the Gibson and Klunk mounds in the lower Illinois Valley, a disproportionate number of adults and males were buried in these crypts and on the surrounding earthen ridges. Women seemed to have been granted access to the tombs only when men were already present. But this pattern does not hold true everywhere in west-central Illinois, such as at Elizabeth. The men buried in central tombs at Gibson were somewhat taller, on average, than those in the nearby simple graves. So it seems that an imposing physical presence had something to do with the chances of achieving high status in some communities.

The people who received special treatment upon their deaths must have held positions of great respect and influence in their lineages or communities. Many of these individuals played a part in rituals critical to the well-being of their groups, judging from the fragments of ceremonial costumes that have survived.[56] They include a few cut wolf palates retaining the anterior teeth, including sharp canines, from Kentucky and Ohio sites. One of the cut palates was buried with someone whose upper front teeth had been knocked out long before death – the wolf palate was probably held in the mouth as part of a mask. It was perhaps similar to the bear's head and skin worn by a person depicted on a figurine found at the Newark earthworks. Other cut maxillae and mandibles, complete with teeth, from both carnivores and humans have been unearthed from sites scattered across the

65

65  This stone figurine found in Newark, Ohio – in the vicinity of one of the largest geometric earthwork complexes – depicts a man, perhaps a shaman, whose head is covered by a bear mask. Height 6.3 in (16 cm).

Midwest. At least some of them must have been attached to masks or other articles of clothing. Antlers from deer headdresses have also been found, such as one made of copper from a mound at the Hopewell site. Deer costumes might have been associated with hunting magic, which was so commonly employed around the world by people who had no control over the whereabouts of elusive game. It is even possible that deer symbolism had a distant descendant in the use of antlers to signify leadership positions among the historic-period Iroquois, although there is no reason to believe that the precise meaning of these symbols was the same.

Local leaders probably played a critical role in maintaining contacts among neighboring but essentially autonomous communities. Key people at Tunacunnhee no doubt owed much of their success at acquiring Hopewell-style objects to their location along an important communication route.[57] A historic trail passed by the site, and the use of that trail may have extended far back into prehistory because it is a natural route through rough country.

In addition to being a conspicuous display of wealth, the objects that ended up in mounds must have been potent and widely recognized symbols that underscored connections between different groups of people and their relations with the supernatural. Many of the artifacts and the designs on them, such as depictions of raptorial birds and waterfowl found on pottery, occur at sites scattered across the Midwest and Southeast. So we know that by this time, if not earlier, certain beliefs had found currency throughout much of the Eastern Woodlands. Some of these objects probably played an integral part in the rituals that took place around the mounds, such as the copper-covered panpipes that were perhaps played before being buried.

Especially influential members of prominent kin groups probably orchestrated the construction of mounds to enhance their prestige in local communities, much like what happened with the erection of megaliths among a very few Southeast Asian peoples into the twentieth century.[58] These were the individuals who possessed the wherewithal to mobilize the resources required for festivals where dirt was moved to make permanent monuments. Once the organizational changes permitting a heavier reliance on native cultigens were in place, people probably had the capacity to produce surpluses with little additional effort, and this food could have been used to support periodic aggregations of people. Preparations for special occasions can be impressive, as I have seen myself on a Micronesian island where numerous participants in a funeral laid out vast quantities of food, far in excess of what could have been immediately consumed.

Whatever went on around the mounds, it involved much more than the preparation of a suitable burial ground. The situation was perhaps similar to that found among the Mapuche of Chile, where moundbuilding had more to do with the use of certain spots for key ceremonies than with the necessities of burial.[59] The eventual size of a Mapuche mound was related to the number of people who took part in these events and how often they got together, not the importance of the person buried in it.

67

Perhaps rival kin groups participated in competitive displays near the mounds and earthworks to enhance their local reputations. Such events would account for the great numbers of precious items that were destroyed or buried. Ersatz objects were even used when real ones were in short supply, including mica-covered clay beads mixed with pearl beads from the Edwin Harness mound, and large points from black cannel coal instead of obsidian from the GE mound in southwestern Indiana.[60] The necessity of putting on the greatest show possible with whatever was at hand meant that mortuary conventions were forever being reinterpreted to meet the demands of the moment. So the particular ways bodies were handled and the artifacts found with them varied greatly, even within single burial contexts such as the structures in Ohio.

The most elaborate mortuary facilities – among others, the Adena log-lined graves, the Illinois Middle Woodland central tombs, and the Ohio Hopewell structures – all seem to have been used by some form of social group ranging from single families to extended kin groups. Common burial in elaborate tombs or structures served to reaffirm group affiliation while

66 Impressions of logs were clearly visible in Adena log-lined tombs when they were excavated by WPA crews in the Great Depression. One such example is this tomb in the Wright mound, Kentucky.

67  Middle Woodland pottery was sometimes very well made, especially vessels used in funerals and other ritual events.  This pot with a bird design is from west-central Illinois.

reinforcing the social standing of key lineages within local communities. The most influential people were the ones who were able to marshal the resources needed to organize impressive displays related to funerals and celebrations of ancestors. These events must have involved the active participation of large kin groups, considering the work involved in building or refurbishing burial structures, platforms, and earthworks, and in collecting the various materials – including rare objects – consumed in the ceremonies. Work is often lightened by making it part of socially and ritually significant occasions that attract willing participants, and it is even possible that gift-giving, commonly practiced during the historic period as part of significant events, put people in the debt of their hosts. Such presentations, if they occurred, would have contributed to the wide circulation of fancy goods at that time. One is reminded of the potlatches of the Northwest Coast where large quantities of items, many of which had symbolic significance, were presented, distributed, and destroyed on occasions calculated to enhance the prestige of the individuals who sponsored them.

Once built, the mounds served as major landmarks that marked long-standing connections to particular areas. For example, many Adena mounds in the rolling country of central Kentucky sit on locally high spots. They would 68 have been a clear reminder that many generations had preceded the people that currently lived nearby. Thus the Adena mounds and associated wooden structures were quite likely highly visible symbols of rights to particular territories; after all, survival rested squarely on undisputed access to land.

68  The large Wright mound was located on a high hill in the rolling Kentucky Bluegrass. This photograph shows the mound in 1937 before it was excavated.

Despite all the pomp and ceremony that accompanied the burial of key people, evidence for special treatment during their lives is lacking. Judging from the burials, they possessed more precious objects, mostly ornaments, that were displayed on special occasions and marked ritually and socially significant positions. But nothing indicates that the most influential community members lived very differently than anybody else. A lack of distinction among people during their lifetimes in terms of the layouts of sites and the kinds of features and objects within them distinguishes these societies from the chiefdoms with strong hereditary leaders that arose hundreds of years later.

Eventually the construction of elaborate burial mounds and the exchange of non-local objects virtually ceased. Years ago it was thought that people simply "gave up the habit of building Mounds, for some reason or other," as if this practice was simply one of preference that was unrelated to other aspects of these cultures.[6] We would now say that transformations in how societies were organized, and hence how key people were treated upon their deaths, lie at the root of why the construction of mounds and the ceremonial events that went with it were much less important in Late Woodland times. Changes in social organization were closely related to alterations in population size, technology, subsistence practices, and intergroup relations. But precisely what happened and why it did so are hotly debated.

I  Mounds, such as this one composed of shell in St. Petersburg, Florida, are occasionally shown on old postcards. While it is now gone, the mound was at one point an attractive centerpiece for the grounds of a hospital.

II  The Conus in the Mound Cemetery at Marietta, Ohio, is shown in this photograph from an early twentieth–century postcard.

**III** The Moundbuilders – their place of origin was hotly debated – were the subject of great attention in the nineteenth century. This fanciful depiction of an excavation, complete with strata and various kinds of burials, was painted by I. J. Egan to illustrate popular public lectures by M. W. Dickeson, a medical doctor. This mound cross-section was part of a larger canvas in several parts: the Monumental Grandeur of the Mississippi Valley, advertised as covering 15,000 sq. ft.

**IV** One of the most impressive of the conical Adena mounds is located in a park at Miamisburg, Ohio.

**V** (*opposite above*) Mount Horeb in Kentucky consists of a shallow ditch and low embankment, part of which is shown here. Snow fills the ditch, the embankment is on the left, and the middle of the earthwork is to the right.

**VI** One of the most celebrated sites in the Eastern Woodlands, the Serpent Mound snakes its way down a ridge in Ohio.

**VII**  There are three large mounds at the Etowah site in Georgia, in a park that is open to the public.

**VIII**  One of the biggest mounds at Moundville was located within the plaza.

**IX** Ritually significant constructions, such as this so-called "woodhenge," were located along with earthen mounds and residential buildings on relatively high ground beside a swamp at Cahokia in Illinois. Large posts were erected by sliding them into deep pits with a slanted side ("Cahokia Bathtubs") and then pushing them upright.

**X** Monks Mound at Cahokia is by far the largest mound in the Eastern Woodlands. Today an interstate highway passes immediately north of the mound where there was once a swamp in an abandoned Mississippi River channel.

**XI** For part of its history, the central area of Cahokia in Illinois consisted of mounds (including Monks Mound) and a huge plaza that were surrounded by a strong wooden wall. The floodplain was actually much wetter than shown here.

**XII** In some parts of the Cahokia site there were closely placed, thatch-covered houses. Many everyday activities took place nearby, as indicated by broken stone tools, pottery, bones, and other garbage.

# 5 · Villagers Facing Great Change: Late Woodland

Mounds continued to be built during the period from AD 400 to 1000, although they were for the most part smaller and less elaborate than those erected just a few centuries earlier. Nor did they contain as many fancy objects. Daily pottery was also rather drab, especially in comparison to the finest of the Middle Woodland vessels. The lack of artifacts that appeal to modern aesthetic tastes is a fatal shortcoming in the eyes of those interested in museum-quality objects. Thus it comes as no surprise that archaeologists once paid scant attention to this "slightly murky interval" dominated by "gray" cultures: the Late Woodland period.[1]

This lack of attention was misguided because it missed the fact that critical changes in Native American societies took place in Late Woodland times. Populations grew while settlement locations and their configurations changed. Communication among separate groups of people broke down,

69  This Late Woodland cooking pot from southwestern Illinois has its exterior surface roughened by cordmarks. It was found sitting upright with another pot in a storage pit at the Mund site. Height 8.9 in (22.5 cm).

and relations deteriorated to the point of outright warfare. Late in the first millennium AD maize became an essential part of the diets of many people. Why that occurred and how it set the stage for the widespread development of the hierarchically organized societies known as chiefdoms are two of the most important questions facing archaeologists today. The chiefdoms that first appeared at this time became much more common and widespread after AD 1000, and are the subject of the next chapter.

### Small mounds

70 Some of the best-known earthen constructions are the strangely shaped "effigy mounds" scattered across southern Wisconsin and neighboring parts of Illinois, Iowa, and Minnesota.[2] These mounds are for the most part poorly dated, although many if not all of them were built between the eighth

70 Many Late Woodland effigy mounds have been partially or completely destroyed, such as the Wehmhoff mound in Wisconsin that was cut in half by a road. This photograph dates to the 1920s.

71 Moundbuilding involved many people, perhaps entire communities, as shown in the above reconstruction of such work on a high spot overlooking the upper Mississippi River valley.

and the eleventh or twelfth centuries. Often they have animal-like shapes – they are customarily referred to as birds, bears, panthers, turtles, and lizards – while others take on more fanciful forms or are simple linear ridges or domes of earth.

The effigy mounds tend to be low, but they can be as long as several tens of yards.[3] They were usually built in one flurry of activity that involved scraping up soil and carrying it over short distances. Often the original topsoil was dug away before earth was added to form a mound. A few shallow depressions that were never filled even survived to historic times, so instead of mounds we have depressions, referred to as "intaglios." The mounds usually contained only a few features, including the burials of juveniles and adults that consisted of complete skeletons, piles of disarticulated bones, and cremated bones. Often the features and burials were put in the head and heart areas of the animal-shaped mounds. But only a few individuals were buried in each mound, a tiny fraction of the people who lived nearby.

Effigy mounds are unevenly distributed across the upper Midwest, and the most commonly occurring shapes are not the same in all places.[4] Lynne Goldstein has noticed what seems to be a relationship between the distribu-

71

72 This long-tailed shape – commonly called a panther or "water spirit" – can be found among other effigy mounds near Lake Koskhonong in Wisconsin.

tions of various kinds of mounds and particular resources. Bird mounds were commonly built in the vicinity of the Mississippi Flyway, and turtles 72 were often put where wetlands were abundant. Such a linkage should not be surprising because the lives of these people were centered on making do with whatever was locally available. These mounds were typically built near 73, 74 one another to form groups that ranged from a few mounds to several dozen of them, arranged in no particular order.

The builders of these mounds seemingly followed a hunting-and-gathering existence.[5] Pieces of pottery, stone tools, and other kinds of debris have been found near many mounds, and it is likely they were left by individuals who congregated at these spots to hold ceremonies that involved moving earth and burying a few people. These events would have provided opportunities to arrange marriages and to establish cooperative relations with the members of other groups. A few dozen people working for several days could have thrown up a mound while participating in the festivities that accompanied such gatherings. Perhaps social groups identified by totemic markers built the mounds to establish claims to particular areas. If so, then several such groups lived in close proximity, perhaps in single communities, because different kinds of mounds were commonly mixed together at single sites.

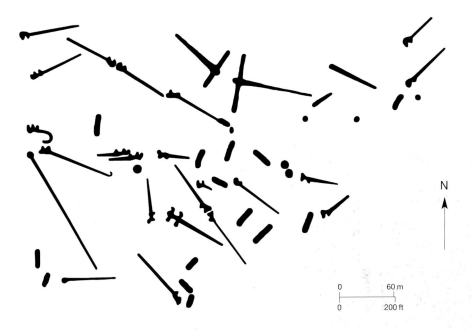

N
↑

0 ⊢─────── 60 m

0        200 ft

73  The above diagram of the Lizard group, Wisconsin, illustrates the often clustered spacing of effigy mounds.

74  Effigy mounds are often lined up in rows on high ground, such as these animal shapes near Lake Waubesa in Wisconsin.

Oval to circular burial mounds were also built at this time in other parts of the Eastern Woodlands.[6] Often more earth was added as new bodies were placed in the mounds, so these low piles gradually grew larger. In the mid-continent – from the Ozarks to the Ohio Valley – it was not at all uncommon for the mounds to be associated with great amounts of stone. In some places, rough rocks were simply piled up. Elsewhere, stone platforms or simple structures made of stacked rocks were built, often covered by earth. It is likely that there were once many more of these low piles or pavements of stone; the ones that survive occur in places such as narrow forested ridges that were difficult or impossible to plow.

Mounds dating to this period have been excavated in west-central Illinois on high bluffs overlooking river floodplains.[7] For the most part they were simple piles of earth for graves that held single bodies. Even when used for long periods, as indicated by numerous burials, these low mounds remained rather inconspicuous. They often appear much like natural knolls, which can also contain burials. Little consideration was seemingly given to the lay-out of these cemeteries: later graves cut through earlier ones, and old bones were tossed into the new graves or discarded in the soil that was added to enlarge the mounds. In short, the locations of burials were soon forgotten, and little attention was paid to what was in earlier, and presumably unmarked, graves.

The Illinois mounds contain both juveniles and adults, as well as both males and females. While there is little, if any, discernible evidence for status differences among the burials, not all people were treated alike. Dispropor-tionately large numbers of artifacts accompanied some of them, children as well as adults. But unlike their Middle Woodland predecessors, these people were not as well endowed with rich grave goods, and they were not otherwise singled out for special treatment when they died.

Late in the first millennium AD, new kinds of mounds were increasingly incorporated into village layouts in parts of the southern Eastern Wood-lands, especially in the central to lower Mississippi Valley. They were not the first mounds to be built near habitation areas. But they do represent the beginning of a site plan that consisted of a centrally located plaza sur-rounded by mounds and domestic buildings. This plaza-and-mound arrangement eventually became common during the subsequent Mississip-pian period.

Of particular importance are platform mounds, such as those at sites in the lower Mississippi Valley collectively referred to as Coles Creek.[8] Considerable work, including mound excavation, has been done at one of these sites, Lake George, in western Mississippi. Moundbuilding began here somewhat before AD 800, but it greatly increased after that time. The Lake George mounds were constructed in several stages, at least some of which supported buildings. The largest mound, known as Mound C, contained both burials and structures, consistent with the use of the latter as charnel houses. Buildings on mounds that contained the bones of

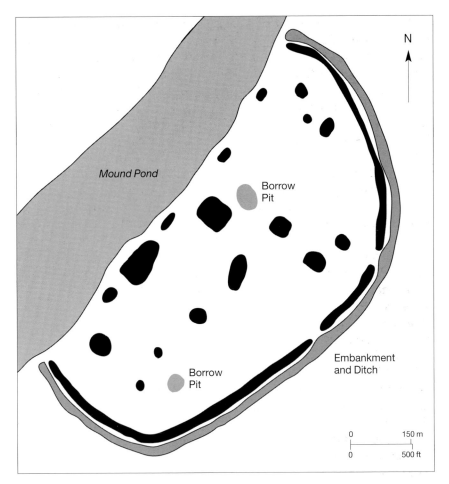

75   At Toltec in Arkansas the mounds (black) were arranged around two plazas, and they were in
turn surrounded by an embankment (black) and ditch (shaded). The site is located alongside an
abandoned Arkansas River channel known locally as Mound Pond.

important ancestors would become a regular feature of major Mississippian
settlements.

The Mississippi Valley, however, was not the only place where these
mounds were built – in fact, the single most impressive mound center is
Toltec in the heart of Arkansas.[9] Here, 18 mounds were accompanied by two          75
plazas, habitation areas, and a defensive embankment and ditch. The
mounds included rectangular platforms, alongside which were sometimes          76
the discarded remains of feasts, including many white-tailed deer bones. So
at least some of the earthen platforms were used for ceremonies that
involved the distribution of food, presumably during events orchestrated by
leading figures in this society (see box p. 112).

Perhaps these feasts bore some resemblance to one that the late eighteenth-
century naturalist William Bartram took part in while traveling through

northern Florida. On this occasion the warriors and most important men, along with Bartram and other visitors, were served choice cuts of meat from "three great fat bears already well barbecued or broiled," along with other food, while seated in a "banqueting house" in the "public square."[10] Whatever remained of the meal was later distributed to less notable people, the "families of the town." The dignitaries then retired to a "council house," discussed weighty matters, smoked tobacco, and drank the "black drink," a stimulant made from holly that could induce vomiting and was thought to have a cleansing effect. The square was then used by villagers for a "frolick [that] continued all night."

## Feasts at Toltec

Over 100 years ago Cyrus Thomas called Toltec, which dates from AD 700 to 1000, "the most interesting group in the state" of Arkansas.[11] Thomas' warm enthusiasm about the site, then known as Knapp Mounds, has been fully justified by Martha Rolingson's recent work.

Toltec is located alongside an old river channel, fittingly named Mound Pond, that was left behind by the meandering Arkansas River. Its location alongside a backwater lake was one that would be seen time and again throughout the subsequent Mississippian period.

Eighteen mounds along with habitation areas surrounded two plazas, and they were enclosed by a ditch located immediately outside an 8-ft (2.4-m) high embankment. The ends of the curved ditch and embankment met the shores of Mound Pond – together, the roughly straight bank and curved defensive work define a D-shaped area of 104 acres (42 ha). The site area is fairly flat, although the largest plaza is located on its highest point. Ten mounds, including the two biggest ones, surrounded this 623 by 1247-ft (190 by 380-m) plaza. Excavations in the plaza have yielded little in the way of artifacts; it must have been kept clean, presumably in preparation for important ceremonies.

Plowing and erosion have reduced many of Toltec's mounds, but the two largest ones are still 37.5 ft (11.5 m) and 49 ft (15 m) high. They towered over all the others, most of which were no taller than the height of an adult. Excavations in several low mounds show that they were constructed of nearby soil – these particular mounds were built in a few brief bursts of effort. In contrast, excavations into one of the two large mounds show that it was built in at least five stages.

Martha Rolingson's excavations have provided a remarkable view of at least one of the activities that took place on or around Toltec's mounds. She dug into a low square platform known as Mound S, which was located on one edge of the plaza bordered by ten mounds. It was roughly 52.5 ft (16 m) in each direction, although the back of it was slightly longer than the front. Unfortunately the upper portion of the mound was not intact, but it did not appear to have ever supported a building. More importantly, the excavators uncovered a deposit of many bones, mostly from white-tailed deer, at the rear of the mound – that is, on the side opposite the plaza. The bones were scattered over an area of about 3,660 sq. ft (340 sq. m). They became less

## Scattered enclosures

Mounds were not the only large construction projects undertaken in the Late Woodland period. In some places low walls were put up that partially or completely encircled the crests of hills. At least some of the hilltop enclosures in northern Ohio date to this period, on the evidence of excavations at Greenwood Village.[12] Here several low embankments and shallow ditches cut across points of easy access to a high flat area otherwise bordered by steep slopes. Little in the way of ordinary features and trash was found, so this hilltop was most likely used for a ceremonial purpose.

common as one got further from the mound, indicating that the debris came from events that took place on the low earthen platform. This trash was not exposed for very long before it was buried – the bones lacked signs of weathering, and there is little evidence of damage from village dogs. Thus this small pile of earth was built for special use during feasts that must have attracted enough people to leave behind great amounts of refuse. Once the feasts were completed, the discarded bones were covered with soil – a sensible move if we consider the overpowering stench any meat residue would have produced in the heart of the site.

Excavators also found debris when they worked on Mound D, another low mound that fronted the same plaza as Mound S. This platform was enlarged at least twice, and perhaps three times; the earliest platform measured 42.5 by 62.5 ft (13 by 19 m) and the second at least 105 by 125 ft (32 by 38 m). Debris-rich middens containing the bones of white-tailed deer were found along the sides of these two mound stages. Once again, the refuse was hidden out of sight of the plaza and soon buried. A final layer of soil covered the 5-ft (1.5-m) high second platform, although not much of this deposit has survived. The final layer might have capped the mound to signal its termination as a ceremonial platform. It is also possible that it was only added to bury smelly garbage that had accumulated behind the mound.

76  The Toltec site in Arkansas encompassed a number of mounds, including these two large ones. The site is open to the public.

Farther south, low rock walls (popularly referred to as stone forts) are thinly scattered from southern Illinois eastward into Kentucky.[13] They were often built in remote places far from major population concentrations in the river valleys. These long piles of stones took no special skills to build, and rocks were carried over short distances, lessening the most labor-intensive part of the work. Often the rocks only blocked off places where access was easiest, and small stone mounds were built near many of them. Ordinary debris can be found nearby, but usually it is scarce and widely scattered.

The stone enclosures are often thought to have been defensive structures solely because of their locations on hills. Yet it is hard to see that large forts were necessary in areas that were apparently sparsely populated. These were places where dispersal to remote spots would have been an effective response to threats from enemies. Even if there was a need to build forts, it is doubtful that nearby populations were sufficient to man the walls. It is more likely that the walls and steep slopes delineated ritually important places much like the earlier Middle Woodland hilltop enclosures. The principal elements of traditions passed down through frequent repetition could have been retained over the several centuries that separated these people from their Middle Woodland predecessors. But if there was such a connection, it is puzzling that the distributions of the Middle and Late Woodland hilltop enclosures are not the same. Until further work is done, the Late Woodland stone walls remain a mystery.

## Villages become commonplace

The remains of structures are often an easily observed part of archaeological sites dating to the Late Woodland period, a marked contrast to earlier settlements. Isolated houses have been found, as have small groups of them that presumably belonged to a few closely related families. Clusters of a dozen or more structures have also been identified. Here buildings share similar alignments or are arranged in some regular fashion, indicating coherent community layouts. One gets the impression that most villages were occupied for only several years by no more than a few dozen people.

In some places middens mark spots used for lengthier periods. They include partial or complete ovals of dark, organic-rich soil where houses and other features were arranged around multi-purpose open spaces. Examples of such sites include Jamestown in southern Illinois and Pyles in northeastern Kentucky.[14] The Jamestown and Pyles middens measured 197 by 262 ft (60 by 80 m) and 722 by 833 ft (220 by 254 m) respectively. Their sizes were typical of villages dating to this period.

77    Lines of small postmolds mark the locations of walls of structures, most of which are rather small oval to rectangular houses. Individual structures cannot have been occupied for more than a few years before they began to fall apart, because they were built with small rot-prone posts and few serious attempts were made to repair them. Other features at these sites include

77 Excavators at Robinson's Lake in Illinois are using trowels to clean a house floor to identify stains where wall posts once stood (dark spots). In southwestern Illinois, the floors of houses at this time were commonly dug into the ground so the surrounding earth could provide some insulation.

commodious and often numerous storage pits. They underscore the importance to relatively sedentary people of storing food for lean times of the year.

We have a good idea of what villages and smaller sites were like in the Mississippi Valley near present-day St. Louis because many large-scale excavations have been conducted there.[15] Structures dating to the end of the first millennium AD tended to surround small open areas. Some of these open spaces were completely devoid of features, whereas others contained central posts, several large pits laid out in a square, or a big structure used for some unknown purpose. The overall village layout – domestic buildings encircling public spaces that might contain special features – presages elements of later Mississippian mound centers. Scattered around these villages

78 Several communities were identified at the Range site in southwestern Illinois. Here small houses (shaded) and pits (open) surrounded an open area that enclosed a large structure marked by postmolds (shaded).

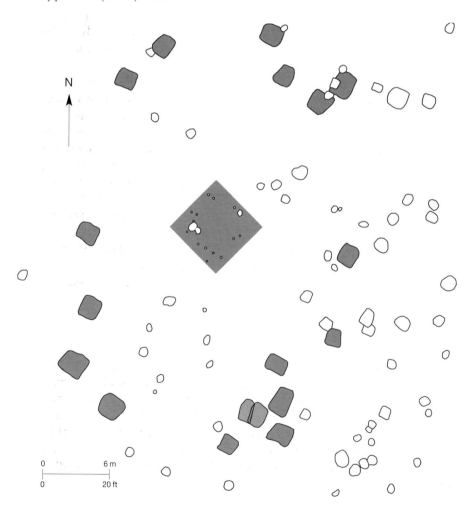

N

0        6 m
0        20 ft

were camps in both floodplain and upland settings that were used for only days or weeks at a time.

In most places neighboring villages tended to be roughly the same size, and were usually occupied by only a few dozen people. But that situation began to change toward the end of the first millennium AD, especially along the central and lower stretches of the Mississippi River and its principal tributaries.[16] Here, permanently occupied sites included locally important centers as well as outlying settlements, both villages and isolated houses. The principal sites with mounds tended to be inhabited by larger numbers of people for several generations or even centuries, much longer than the surrounding small settlements. Toltec and Lake George are fine examples of these mound centers. The mounds at the major sites were built at different times, and seem not to have been used for the entire period these settlements were occupied. But even abandoned mounds fixed the basic structure of a site because they were such prominent features. The mounds, used or not, might have been linked to stories about important events or specific ancestors or lineages, much like the monuments of more recent societies elsewhere in the world. If this were so, then the mounds – in fact, the entire settlement layout – served as a visual representation of the history and structure of these societies.

Populations in many parts of the Eastern Woodlands continued to grow during the Late Woodland period. Many more sites, often with greater amounts of debris, signify larger groups of people, longer occupations, or both. In addition to being scattered thickly along major rivers, sites were often distributed far up smaller streams. This occupation of areas away from major rivers has been noted in several parts of the Midwest and Southeast, although it is difficult to measure the degree to which the overall distribution of settlements had changed from earlier times.[17] In the midcontinent, the movement from river valleys was facilitated by a greater reliance on native cultigens: because it was possible to increase the productivity and reliability of food from less desirable places, people were not as tightly tethered to the richest settings. But this solution only worked for several centuries. Eventually population growth caught up with agricultural output, and something else had to be done.

## The switch to maize

By Late Woodland times the starchy and oily seeds of several native cultigens had become essential parts of diets in many places.[18] While the most intensive use of these cultigens was in the midcontinent, the most heavily used seeds were not always the same. After the seeds were harvested, they were probably parched in pots placed over open fires, if they were to be stored for hard times. Mistakes made while doing so probably account for the large clumps of charred seeds occasionally thrown away along with other trash.

In west-central Illinois, and presumably elsewhere as well, a greater emphasis on these weedy plants was accompanied by an increase in work-load, especially for women.[19] Women in small-scale agricultural societies are often heavily involved in the strenuous work of planting, tending, and har-vesting crops, as well as processing them for meals. When looking at skeletons from this area, Patricia Bridges and colleagues found that female upper and lower limb strengths increased from Middle to Late Woodland times. This change is consistent with an ever-greater reliance on native cultigens where women were involved in more drudgery than ever before.

Sometime between AD 800 and 1100, maize began to be grown by people throughout much of the Eastern Woodlands, as is indicated by much greater amounts of charred maize in the fill of houses and pits.[20] Perhaps the heavy use of maize after centuries of neglect resulted from the introduction of a new variety better adapted to a temperate environment. But no morphological evidence has been found to support the possible spread of such a plant. Some might argue that the sudden appearance of carbonized maize relates to a shift in how food was prepared. If true, then kernels and cobs might be more likely to be burned, hence preserved, later in time. For-tunately we have an independent measure of maize consumption to test that idea: the stable carbon isotope signatures of human bones, a direct indication of what people ate. As it turns out, the skeletal evidence is entirely consistent with the botanical information. Both indicate a shift in dietary composition at the same time. Furthermore, the plant remains and human bones show that within any particular region the change in diets took place over a period spanning no more than a few centuries, perhaps only a few generations. Viewed from an archaeological perspective, this shift was indeed rapid.

Maize in the midcontinent was grafted onto well-established plant cultivation practices. Stone hoes, most notably large ones of tabular chert from the Mill Creek quarries in southwestern Illinois, began to be widely traded in the Midwest at this time.[21] The use of heavy hoes signals a greater need to prepare larger gardens and to weed them on a regular basis. Elsewhere maize was adopted without being preceded by a long tradition of growing native cultigens, mostly after AD 1000 and sometimes well after that date.

Regardless of what people might have grown, all of them collected nuts and berries and hunted large and small animals. In the midcontinent, many of these plants and animals thrived near human settlements where there were plenty of active and abandoned fields interspersed by intact wood-lands. Long occupations of particular areas had changed dense forests to vegetation mosaics consisting of shrubby growth to mature stands of trees. For example, bits of burned wood from archaeological sites in Ohio show that second-growth trees increased at the expense of those typical of deep forests.[22] People benefited from this transformation in vegetation cover: many edible plants and animals thrived in overgrown clearings, and saplings filled a need for straight, narrow poles for houses.

79 Bone fishhooks and splinters that possibly served as gorges are occasionally found on Late Woodland sites, such as these specimens from southwestern Illinois. The hook is 0.7 in (1.8 cm) long.

Hunting practices changed across much of the Eastern Woodlands somewhere between AD 600 and 800 when numerous small arrowheads first appear.[23] Opinion is divided over whether bows and arrows were new to the Eastern Woodlands or had been present for a long time, but they only became common during a period that spanned a few centuries. Light bows and arrows – as opposed to heavy spears held by hand or thrown with an atlatl – would have been particularly desirable if locally depleted game forced hunters to travel over longer distances in search of prey. Such hunting practices took place in at least some places, such as in the middle Ohio Valley where hunting camps have been found in remote rockshelters. Bows and arrows would also have been useful in the opportunistic hunting of small mammals and birds that frequent fields and clearings. People in the midcontinent were spending more of their time in these places, as indicated by the quantities of cultivated plants that were consumed. It would have been simple for people who were tending their crops to carry a bow and quiver of arrows in the event that they happened upon anything to shoot.

The use of fish was also increasing at this time along the major midwestern and southeastern rivers.[24] Such a development is consistent with a more sedentary existence by greater numbers of people who necessarily placed heavier demands on what local areas could produce. People occupying wide floodplains naturally turned to fish, which were not only abundant but easily caught in shallow ponds. Fish and other aquatic animals made up a correspondingly smaller part of the diets of people who lived along narrow upland streams lacking extensive backwater lakes. But the major river valleys were not the only places where people focused much of their attention on food from wetlands. Other such areas included the Saginaw drainage basin where a large bay from Lake Huron takes a big bite out of east-central Michigan. The inhabitants of the Atlantic and Gulf coasts also continued to collect what marshes, bays, and estuaries could provide.

79

## Life within groups

For the most part there is little to indicate any great differences in social standing within Late Woodland communities.[25] Grave goods, when present, tend to be a rather unimpressive lot, typically utilitarian objects and small personal ornaments. Nevertheless, people were often buried in different ways in roughly contemporaneous nearby sites, and even within a single burial ground. Bodies ended up in mounds, but also in flat cemeteries, on cremation platforms, and in village sites. Often intact bodies were buried, although many were either cremated or defleshed in some manner.

Perhaps the burial grounds are telling us that many Late Woodland societies were divided into roughly equivalent descent groups that used funerals as one means of signaling their separation from other members of their communities. The artifacts, however, indicate that nobody enjoyed much greater access to special goods than any of the other people who shared a particular burial ground. Residential structures confirm this lack of social differentiation. One house within a village looked very much like the rest, as long as due allowances are made for inevitable differences in household size, composition, competence, industriousness, and good fortune.

This rather egalitarian situation began to change after AD 700, particularly in and around the Mississippi Valley south of present-day St. Louis. Here there developed marked differences in the size, longevity, and internal characteristics of permanently occupied settlements. The largest of these sites were planned communities with one or more mounds next to public plazas. Their appearance signals the emergence of chiefdoms. There is some evidence that a few people of high rank were being singled out for special treatment when they died. The individuals buried in small clusters of graves in Mound C at Lake George made up only a tiny fraction of the site's inhabitants.[26] About half of them had died as juveniles, which is typical of preindustrial societies, and their presence along with adults is consistent with the mound being reserved for a particular descent group. Admittance did not depend on what one achieved during a long and active life. Thus kin-group affiliation was of great importance in determining who enjoyed privileges that included burial in a mound within the biggest site in the area.

## Deteriorating relations

Contacts were maintained between the members of different societies as indicated by items such as copper and marine shell that crossed long distances.[27] But the exchange of such items had dropped off from what it had been just a few centuries earlier, although in some places it picked up once again at the end of this period. These objects would have been passed from one person to the next, probably as gifts that accompanied quite ordinary social transactions such as arranging marriages, settling disputes, and acknowledging friendships.

The leaders of the nascent chiefdoms in the south undoubtedly did what they could to get these prized items from their counterparts in neighboring societies. Yet existing evidence, such as it is, indicates that even the most important residents of the mound centers possessed only a few such items.

At Lake George, for example, the people in Mound C did not have many special goods, or at least they chose not to dispose of them in funerary contexts. No matter how influential these people might have been, it seems that they did not exercise any direct or effective control over the long-distance movement of items fashioned from non-local materials. They certainly held no monopoly over the use of them.

Relations among many groups had deteriorated badly by the end of the first millennium AD. Victims of violence, including people shot with arrows, have been identified in many skeletal collections.[28] While extremely useful for hunters, bows and arrows doubled as ideal weapons for warriors who skulked around the villages of their enemies waiting for some hapless person to wander by.

Despite the bloodshed, fighting usually had not yet reached the point where it justified the effort needed to build palisades around villages. The chance that some losses might occur must have been weighed against the greater certainty that a diversion from tasks such as food production posed a significant threat to survival. Occasionally, however, people found it necessary to erect substantial defensive works, such as at Toltec – perhaps these defenses were a reflection of the kind of society that was beginning to arise in the southern Eastern Woodlands. Chiefs at this time probably maintained only a tenuous hold over societies riven by internal disputes among rivals backed by their own supporters. Their historic-period counterparts were forever plagued by the threat of usurpers who were always ready to pounce on any sign of weakness. In the coming centuries the widespread development of chiefdoms was accompanied by the common appearance of walls around settlements, especially the largest ones.

## A period of transition

Much more work has to be done before we understand the origin of chiefdoms in the southern Eastern Woodlands, but a bare outline of what happened is beginning to emerge. The following version of events relies heavily on what took place in the midcontinent, an area particularly well studied.

There can be no doubt that the Middle Woodland shift to a much greater reliance on several native cultigens enhanced the productivity and reliability of locally available resources. People were able to expand into places with fewer and more scattered wild foods, a capability that is most noticeable as a principally Late Woodland movement into settings far from major river valleys. Yet whatever gains were realized by a heavier use of indigenous crops, they were eventually offset by continued population growth.

By the late first millennium AD, people were facing a landscape that would have appeared full. Attractive areas were already occupied, claimed as hunting territories, or lay between hostile groups. Venturing into no-man's lands, let alone trying to live in them, was an extremely hazardous business, judging from the situation in early historic times. Thus it had become increasingly difficult for communities that budded off existing ones to carve out suitable areas for themselves. More people than ever before meant that there was a greater chance hunters would impinge on their neighbors' territories, especially during bad years when they had to travel widely in a desperate search for food. People began to be attacked on a regular basis at this time, as seen by skeletons with injuries from clubs and arrows.

Eventually the balance between maintaining an existing way of life and protecting oneself tilted toward a greater concern with defense. Vulnerable groups of people could no longer remain strung out along both major rivers and much smaller tributaries. So to alleviate their plight they sought safety in numbers – in many places, villages became larger and river valleys more crowded.[29] Thus people had formed themselves into groups that were more formidable politically and militarily. Not to do so was to invite disaster.

Population density obviously increased wherever people gravitated toward one another. Pressures on local environments were correspondingly greater, causing people to seek ways of boosting the amount of locally available food. Fortunately an obvious solution was at hand: they could shift to maize.

For the people of the midcontinent, maize was likely to have been marginally more productive than a mix of indigenous seed crops, although any difference in yield was more than offset by higher field maintenance requirements for maize and the greater reliability of a mix of hardy native plants.[30] Yet the yield-to-cost ratio shifted decisively toward maize as population densities increased, because growing maize enhanced harvest efficiency and flexibility. A wider range of people, from young children to the elderly and disabled, can be of real help when harvesting maize. Cobs are easily picked off stalks, and less effort is needed to prepare maize for long-term storage: it can be dried and stored as is, or shelled. In contrast, seeds from the native

80  The remnants of houses, storage pits, and hearths, as well as fragments of stone tools and pottery, tell us much about how people lived. This drawing shows part of a Late Woodland village in southern Illinois.

cultigens had to be stripped off the plants and then dried or parched before storage. Mature corn can also be left on the stalks until people are ready to pick it, as long as one does not mind some loss from animals. This flexibility was critical for individual households because competing demands on the limited labor they had available were always a problem, especially during harvest season. Late summer to early fall was the busiest time for collecting the food needed to make it through a cold and barren winter.

By maximizing efficiency and flexibility at harvest time – precisely when scheduling concerns were the greatest – people were making a rational choice that benefited them directly. That does not necessarily mean that people were any healthier than before, only that they had to shift their emphasis to a new food source. Thus the impetus to grow maize bubbled up from below; that is, from decisions made by individual households. It was not dictated from above, despite whatever advantages the leaders of nascent chiefdoms might have realized from surpluses produced in good years. After all, the shift to maize-based diets took place equally rapidly in the northern Eastern Woodlands where chiefdoms never developed. But there too people were living in clusters of villages separated by long stretches of infrequently used and often bitterly contested land.

People gravitated toward places with the greatest productive potential, but they could not avoid the threat of hard times. When primary sources of food failed – and in the fullness of time they were certain to do so – it was no easy matter to get enough alternative food to eat. Populations by this time had risen well beyond the level where people could slip back into an exclusively hunting-and-gathering way of life. Moreover, the existence of watchful enemies made it dangerous to disperse into infrequently used land where wild resources were more abundant. Unevenness in local productivity gave the leaders of strong lineages in especially favorable locations an opportunity to expand their influence. These lineage heads were the ones who possessed the means to help people eke out a living during the most difficult times. Inevitably people became indebted to situationally advantaged leaders who, over the long run, were able to attract and retain the most supporters, thus giving birth to the first chiefdoms.

While maize was of critical importance in many places – and it is emphasized in the archaeological literature – it should be recognized that agriculture was not a necessary prerequisite for the emergence of chiefdoms in some parts of the Southeast. Coles Creek people in the lower Mississippi Valley continued to rely heavily on wild plants, including acorns, for several centuries after chiefdoms had appeared.[31] Even in the central Mississippi Valley where great amounts of maize were grown, the principal settlements were located right next to large backwater lakes and swamps. Aquatic resources were absolutely essential if large numbers of people were to be supported over long periods of time. The central role of wetlands in the development of chiefdoms in the southern Eastern Woodlands deserves more attention than it has received.

# 6 · Chiefs Come to Power: Mississippian

Societies with higher population densities and greater political centralization that included inherited leadership positions legitimized by widely shared beliefs and customs – societies often called chiefdoms – had become increasingly common by the eleventh century AD. They were scattered across the Southeast and southern Midwest, and extended up the tributaries of the Mississippi River as far as southern Wisconsin. In the sixteenth century, Spanish adventurers such as Hernando de Soto encountered a number of them as they cut bloody paths through the Southeast, but within a century or so most of these chiefdoms had vanished. They had fallen victim to the population loss, sociopolitical disorganization, and unrest that followed sustained contact between the peoples of the Old and New Worlds. In contrast, the midwestern chiefdoms that had expanded northward around 1,000 years ago during the Medieval Warm Period mostly disappeared a century or more before the Spaniards plunged into the Southeast. They fell apart during a time of population movement and conflict accompanying deteriorating climatic conditions that took a turn for the worse in the fourteenth century.

While archaeologists refer to most of these chiefdoms as Mississippian, the two terms are not freely interchangeable. Not all Mississippian groups – that is, those with certain kinds of pottery and houses – were chiefdoms. In some of them a ranking of people appears to have been weak or absent, and there is little or no evidence to suggest fixed leadership positions. Moreover, not all late prehistoric chiefdoms are labeled Mississippian, even when that category is stretched to its furthest limits. Here the emphasis is on chiefdoms, the dominant sociopolitical form in the southern Eastern Woodlands, not how societies are categorized in terms of artifacts and buildings.

## Mounds for chiefs

Mounds are once again a good place to begin. They were used for different purposes and were often essential elements of community layouts. Most of them were rather small, and many have been plowed down to the point where they are hardly discernible. But some were massive piles of earth, including the largest mound ever built in the United States – Monks Mound at Cahokia in southwestern Illinois.

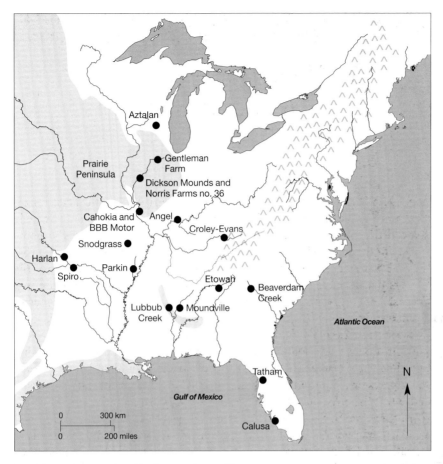

81 Selected sites mentioned in Chapters 6, 7, and 8.

Often these flat-topped mounds supported wooden structures that took 82, 83 different forms depending on when and where they were built, and how they were used. It has long been recognized that some mounds were the "dwelling-sites for chiefs," as described by Clarence B. Moore who, a century ago, burrowed into many of them while traveling through the Southeast in a steamboat aptly named the *Gopher*.[1] These platforms literally raised the houses for the highest-ranked people above the dwellings of lesser folk. Thus the buildings on earthen platforms were effective reminders of the high social standing of the people who occupied them. But not all mounds supported the houses of chiefs and their immediate kinsfolk. Important structures such as sweat lodges and council houses were also put on them, as were charnel structures for the bones of prominent ancestors.

Many mounds were raised in stages made up of distinctive layers of fill. Occasionally it appears that special soils were chosen, presumably because they held some symbolic significance. For example, excavations in the Snod-grass mound in northeastern Alabama exposed several stages that were each separated by layers of either red or blue-gray soil.[2] Any buildings that happened to be standing on the mounds were leveled when they were expanded in this way. Adding more earth to an existing mound was an effective means of getting an impressive platform with the least effort. But size was not the only consideration: building onto an earlier platform also established a connection with the past that legitimized the positions of the living.

Debris-filled deposits have been identified in some mounds.[3] Much of what these dumps contained must have come from the meals eaten by the people who lived on the mounds. Some of the trash probably also came from well-attended feasts sponsored by these prominent people. One such deposit was discovered in a platform mound at Beaverdam Creek in northeastern Georgia. While broken pottery and a wide array of food remains were consistent with everyday refuse, the bones from meaty parts of deer were more common than they were in ordinary village waste. It would not be surprising if special cuts of meat were served in feasts calculated to impress guests, much like in historic times.

Continuity in the use of socially or ritually significant ground can sometimes be traced back to a time before mound construction began. The remains of structures, including oversized ones, have been identified below

82 Soil stains where wall posts once stood show that buildings were often built on the flat surfaces of Mississippian mounds. Postmolds for large circular and rectangular structures were exposed in this 1939 excavation of a mound at the Rudder site in Alabama. The layer where the buildings stood was buried by later deposits of soil, as shown by the cross-section of mound fill to the right of the excavated postmolds.

83 Some flat-topped mounds had ramps up their sides, providing access to the summits. This one was found in 1940 during the excavation of one of the Bessemer site mounds in Alabama.

the lowest levels of a number of mounds. Their relationship to later earthen platforms is especially clear when the alignments of the initial buildings and the earliest mound stages are the same. An excavation at Lubbub Creek in west-central Alabama revealed that the shape of the initial rectangular mound conformed to the positions of a series of earlier rectangular structures and an enclosing fence that once stood on the original ground surface.[4]     84

84 Structures built on the original ground surface had the same orientation as this platform mound at Lubbub Creek in Alabama. Much of the mound was destroyed before excavations (shaded) exposed postmolds and wall trenches that belonged to several buildings.

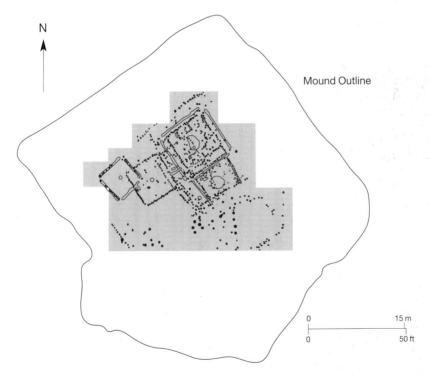

N

Mound Outline

0       15 m

0       50 ft

Even later enlargements of the Lubbub Creek mound retained the same orientation, but little is known about what was on these surfaces because the mound was partly flattened before being excavated.

Excavations in platform mounds have also uncovered signs of charnel houses, bone deposits, and other burials that were typically accompanied by many fine objects made from precious materials such as marine shell and copper. One of these bone deposits was discovered about 50 years ago in the Wilson, or Junkyard, mound near Cahokia when it was hurriedly excavated to make way for the Indian Mound motel.[5] As so often happens, the new building was named after something it destroyed! While doing what they could to see what was in the mound, the excavators uncovered a 14 by 18-ft (4.3 by 5.5-m) area with the remains of over 180 people. Most of the bones were stacked in neat piles, each containing parts of more than one individual. Many of the bones were scratched where stone tools were used to cut away soft tissue. Not all of the bones were cut, so it is likely that only pieces of desiccated tissue had to be removed from some of the skeletons.

85   Piles of bones were placed alongside one another in the Wilson mound in Illinois. Shell beads were scattered amongst the bones, as were whelk shells (shaded).

N

0        0.9 m

0        3 ft

Scattered around the stacks of bones were thousands of marine shell beads, as well as many entire whelk shells. Few other artifacts were found, although the remainder did include personal ornaments such as earspools. Thus it appears as if the members of this group were for the most part treated similarly.

A periodic cleaning out and replacement of mortuary houses is well documented at the Harlan site in northeastern Oklahoma.[6] Here, a burial mound consisting of three overlapping cones of earth held the remains of over 190 people. Many of them were represented by disarticulated bones, and grave goods were scattered indiscriminately among them. The preservation of bones was not always the same, so it is likely that the skeletons had accumulated over a lengthy period as important people happened to die. The remnants of several burned buildings beneath and within two other mounds were also discovered – they are thought to have been charnel houses that originally held bones later buried elsewhere. A post in the tunnel-like entrance to at least one of the buildings prevented easy access to its interior. Such barriers helped keep children and animals out of the charnel houses. Similar structures in the lower Mississippi Valley dating to the historic period were equipped with doors for that very purpose.

These buildings and other mortuary areas held only a small fraction of the total population – the people who enjoyed high rank, largely because of their birth into select kin groups. Prominent burial places served as readily understood reminders of the legitimacy of the prestigious positions held by people who could claim a relationship to illustrious ancestors. These genealogical histories need not have been accurate, only widely accepted as being true. Like all oral traditions, they would have been freely edited and embellished to suit the purposes of the living.

The clearest evidence of the importance of links to ancestors, real or not, comes from the Great Mortuary in the Craig Mound at the Spiro site (see box p. 130).[7] Old bones and grave goods were dug up, moved to the Great Mortuary, and buried with several people who had recently died. The body parts must have come from artifact-rich contexts, presumably also mounds, judging from the number of objects as well as their different styles and preservation. While the people who built the Great Mortuary knew that skeletons and impressive artifacts could be found in mounds, they had no real idea about which bones belonged to specific individuals. Forensic experts today have a hard time doing just that using the best tools of modern science. Bones from large animals were even picked up, presumably mistakenly, along with those from humans. A special effort was made to collect skulls, or at least parts of them; they were among the easiest to recognize as belonging to humans, quite apart from whatever symbolic significance they might have had. After the mortuary was closed, cedar poles were erected to mark its location. Continuity with the Great Mortuary and its link to revered ancestors was thereby maintained long after all traces of it, other than the upright poles, had disappeared from view.

86

pl. XVIII

## An amazing discovery at the Craig Mound

One of the finest examples of a mortuary deposit for important people was largely destroyed by looters who dug into the Craig Mound in the 1930s.[8] It was the largest mound at the Spiro site along the Arkansas River in east-central Oklahoma. The pot hunters encountered a hollow chamber that they subsequently enlarged; fortunately, they were stopped before destroying everything in this remarkable mortuary deposit. More careful excavations subsequently clarified what was originally in the mound, and our present understanding stems largely from James Brown's compilation of field notes, photographs, and collections.

The Craig Mound was one of 11 mounds at Spiro, a site occupied for about 500 years. The principal feature in the Craig Mound – the Great Mortuary that dated to about AD 1400 – has understandably received the most attention since it contained one of the most impressive collections of grave goods ever found in the Eastern Woodlands. The Great Mortuary was

86 Excavations were undertaken in the Craig Mound to clean up after the looting of the Great Mortuary in the 1930s.

87 One of the best-known red cedar masks from the Craig Mound at Spiro, Oklahoma, had deer antlers and shell inserts that accentuated the eyes and mouth. Height 11.4 in (28.9 cm).

made all the more interesting and mysterious by the discovery of a cavity that had never completely filled with soil. Among the bones and artifacts were many wooden objects and baskets that normally do not survive long burial. Several additional layers of soil were laid down on top, along with still more burials. As the mound was raised upward, the position of the Great Mortuary was marked by cedar poles planted over it. Continuity with the mortuary was thereby maintained for about two generations until moundbuilding ceased. Eventually the Craig Mound was covered with a mantle of soil, presumably to signify the closing of the cemetery.

The Great Mortuary, a rectangular floor surrounded by low earthen ridges, was located on an earthen platform covering earlier burials. The floor, badly damaged by the pot hunters, was covered by split cane and appears to have been rectangular, measuring 37 by 55 ft (11.3 by 16.8 m). Broken artifacts and disarticulated bones were laid on it, as were baskets and cedar litters arranged in several rows. The litters and baskets held more disarticulated bones and fine artifacts, sometimes great quantities of them, that had been removed from other locations and then buried in the Great Mortuary. A number of intact bodies were also laid out on the floor, probably belonging to people initially buried there. The artifacts found alongside the bones included, among other things, engraved marine shell cups and tens of thousands of shell beads. Posts arranged in a circle were erected on the floor and were in turn covered with earth. Rotting and settling eventually resulted in the cavity that attracted so much attention when it was first discovered.

88  Several large pits in Cahokia's Mound 72 contained the skeletons of sacrifical victims who were packed closely together.

Another well-known example of a mound with a lengthy history is Mound 72 at Cahokia.[9] Once again, several small piles of earth along with their burials were enlarged and joined together by the later addition of still more soil and graves. A final capping layer signaled the closing of the cemetery, which by this time had developed into a low linear mound. Many people were buried there, including some who must have held key positions, such as two people, probably males, found with many thousands of marine shell beads. Placed alongside them were three intact bodies and a bundle of bones. A short distance away lay the remains of seven more people and additional fine objects.

Mound 72 is noteworthy because it contained the remains of what seem to have been sacrificial victims. Most of them were crowded into five rectangular pits that held from 19 to 53 people. For the most part they were adults, with females being more common in three pits and males in one (poor preservation limited what could be said about the skeletons in the last pit). In one of the pits, bodies were tossed in haphazardly, and one individual had a stone arrowhead lodged in a lower vertebra. Elsewhere in the mound four men were laid out neatly alongside one another. They were missing their heads and hands – both figured prominently in the iconography of that time – so they too probably lost their lives during some ceremony.

Cahokia was not the only place where humans were sacrificed.[10] The heads of four people buried together at Dickson Mounds in west-central Illinois were also removed, but here they were replaced by pots. Such practices continued up to about 300 years ago in the lower Mississippi Valley when Frenchmen described the killing of adults and children upon the deaths of chiefs and their immediate kin. Thus human sacrifices to honor the most important members of these societies had a long history.

Archaeologists rarely find clues about what precipitated the renewal of mound surfaces, the replacement of structures, or the opening and closing of mortuary features.[11] But we can say something about what happened in a mound at Beaverdam Creek. A platform mound was built over two large sequential structures, both of which were surrounded by low earthen embankments. When the first building was torn down, a man's body decorated with many ornaments, including those made from copper and marine shell, was carefully laid out on the embankment. The earthen ridge for the next structure was put directly over the corpse, so only a short time elapsed between the funeral and work on the new building. Perhaps the destruction of the first structure was related to this man's death – just such a custom was described during the historic period in the lower Mississippi Valley. If that was the case, then the dead man's successor found a way to confirm his own descent, legitimize his succession, bury his predecessor, and build a more impressive structure all in one go.

While mounds occupied prominent positions in major sites, easy access to them was occasionally denied.[12] Rows of posts have been found around the bases or summits of mounds; even if not parts of solid fences, the posts

## The biggest of them all: Cahokia

Far more earth was moved to make the mounds at Cahokia than anywhere else.[13] The site is located on the Mississippi River floodplain where long fingers of well-drained fertile soil once stretched their way through shallow lakes, vegetation-choked swamps, and frequently inundated boggy ground. There were over 100 mounds at Cahokia, far more than at any other Mississippian site. The biggest of them – Monks Mound – dwarfs even the largest mounds built anywhere else in the Eastern Woodlands.

Time has not treated Cahokia well. Many of its mounds have been plowed down or leveled by urban sprawl, and much of this destruction has taken place alongside Highway 40, a particularly seedy strip that runs straight through the heart of the site. For a while, the best (safest) place for excavators to enjoy hard-earned drinks at the end of the day was in a house of ill-repute, which has since been torn down. Fortunately much of Cahokia, including Monks Mound, is now preserved by the state of Illinois as a park, which has gradually expanded over the years.

About half of the earth moved to build the mounds was used to make Monks Mound, which is about 100 ft (30 m) high and covers 13.8 acres (5.6 ha). It contains about 814,000 cu. yards (622,000 cu. m) of soil, has four terraces, and large wooden buildings once stood on its flat surfaces. The site's inhabitants also leveled the area to the south of Monks Mound to make an immense plaza.

Large wooden structures used for special purposes were erected in some parts of the site, including big circles of posts called "woodhenges." Posts near their centers marked spots where observers could use the positions of the posts in the outer ring to track the sun's progress throughout the year. While the woodhenges could be used to mark the passing of the seasons, they would no doubt have had more ritual than practical significance since people knew perfectly well when to plant and harvest their crops.

The most heavily occupied part of Cahokia was a natural levee along the southern side of an old river channel. Evidence of occupation tends to drop off toward lower-lying ground. The size of the site is difficult to measure because at least some habitation materials are scattered across most of the high spots in this part of the

89 Cahokia's main plaza was surrounded by mounds, as shown in this computer-generated image based on topographic data collected in 1966. Monks Mound is at the northern edge of the plaza.

90 The twin mounds that define the southern edge of the main plaza are two of the large mounds at Cahokia, yet are still dwarfed by Monks Mound opposite them.

floodplain. The mounds usually said to be part of the site are distributed across an area of about 3.9 sq. miles (10 sq. km). But the limits of this area, and all other estimates of site size, are to a large extent arbitrary.

The core of the site consisted of mounds that were arranged around a large rectangular plaza. Monks Mound was located at the northern end of this open area, the most prestigious position closest to the old river channel, again underscoring the critical importance of wet places. The mounds and plaza were surrounded for a century or so by a stout palisade reinforced by bastions, which was replaced on several occasions. Many more mounds, several plazas, and residential areas were distributed around the walled precinct.

We do not know exactly when the first mounds were built, but it is thought that work had started on Monks Mound by the tenth century AD.

Moundbuilding certainly picked up during the eleventh century. At its most heavily occupied point early in the Mississippian period, the site was occupied by 3,000 or more people, a large population by the standards of its time. But by the start of the fourteenth century the site had fallen into noticeable decline. The number of its inhabitants had dropped, and places where public architecture once stood had reverted to residential use. Even old mounds were used for common burials by that time, these mounds had lost much or all of their earlier significance. Moundbuilding continued into the fourteenth century, although it had tapered off from earlier times. The site and the surrounding floodplain were largely deserted by about AD 1400. Its abandonment was part of a broader pattern of population redistribution and reduction in southern Illinois and adjoining areas.

could still mark off sacred places. A charnel house used by the historic Taënsa of the lower Mississippi Valley, for example, was surrounded by poles with skulls impaled on them. A line of heads rotting in the hot sun was a clear warning that this sacred place should only be approached with caution on appropriate occasions.

Dirt for mounds was dug from large pits or scraped up from nearby areas, including village deposits and swamps. These soils show that many mounds were built in one or several bursts of effort. The people who performed this work probably did so on special occasions, such as during annual ceremonies or at critical points in the lives of their leaders. Some mounds, however, required much greater investments of labor and long construction histories, as indicated by their size and many separate mantles of earth.[14] It might have taken several generations, even a few centuries, before the largest mounds reached their final dimensions. That was certainly true of the biggest of them all, Monks Mound, that – at 100 ft (30 m) – towered over all other mounds at Cahokia.

pl. x

It is commonly assumed that building big mounds – especially those at Cahokia – required large populations and strong coercive measures to motivate reluctant laborers. It is easy to come to such a conclusion after trudging up Monks Mound on a hot and sticky midsummer's day. But first impressions can be deceptive. A recent estimate of the labor needed to build the mounds shows that it was well within the capabilities of the local population at Cahokia, assuming that the work was spread out over several centuries.[15] A population of no more than a few thousand people could have constructed Cahokia's mounds if each household contributed one laborer for less than two weeks each year. Far less earth was moved at other sites. Many of the Mississippian mounds, perhaps even the majority of them, would have required the effort of only a few dozen people working for no more than a few weeks. Separate layers of fill show that often the work was not all done at one time. So nowhere did the commitment to moving earth have to interfere with essential household activities. In mounds, chiefs got an impressive monument that was not only permanent but also cheap.

## Artifacts and symbols

The finest objects to have survived are often found in mounds that contain the bones of people who held prominent positions in their societies. Conspicuous displays of unusual items – there was nothing subtle about where important people were buried – made it plain who possessed the power to obtain great numbers of objects, such as marine shell beads, that were probably used as gifts to smooth relations among people and to acknowledge key social interactions. But in addition to being a form of wealth, some artifacts served as insignia of office, underscored the roles of chiefs and other prominent people, reinforced the naturalness of inequities in the social order, and depicted supernatural beings.

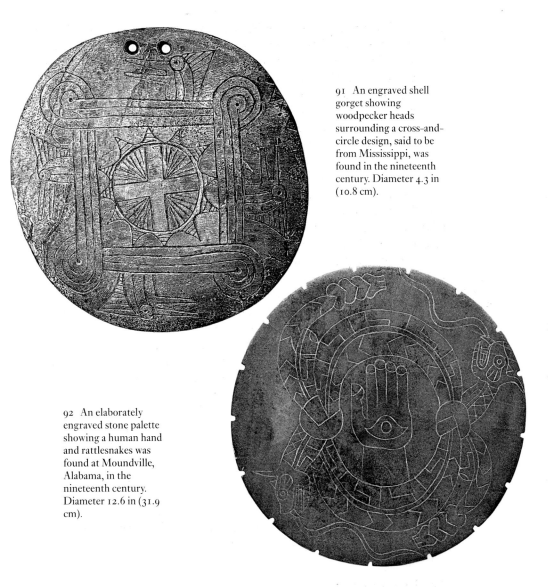

91 An engraved shell gorget showing woodpecker heads surrounding a cross-and-circle design, said to be from Mississippi, was found in the nineteenth century. Diameter 4.3 in (10.8 cm).

92 An elaborately engraved stone palette showing a human hand and rattlesnakes was found at Moundville, Alabama, in the nineteenth century. Diameter 12.6 in (31.9 cm).

Many of these artifacts and the designs on them are commonly referred to as being part of a Southern Cult or Southeastern Ceremonial Complex.[16] Despite what the words "cult" or "complex" might imply, these items are unlikely to be a sign of a tightly integrated, uniformly understood, and universally held vision of the natural and supernatural worlds. Instead, they are best viewed as indicative of beliefs that were widely, but variably, shared by culturally diverse groups of people. The artifacts and images were not distributed evenly across the southern Eastern Woodlands, and there was stylistic variation among them.

91, 92

The most elaborate items associated with key people tend to emphasize a few themes, the importance of ancestors and war being prominent among

93 Short-nosed god masks fashioned from pieces of shell, such as this one found in Alabama in the nineteenth century, were occasionally worn as ear ornaments. Height 1.4 in (3.6 cm).

them. A collection of bones and precious artifacts in charnel structures is consistent with the respect given to strong and wise ancestors. With the passage of time, some of these ancestors could have been promoted to legendary status in orally transmitted origin myths whose content and emphasis drifted over time to accommodate new realities. Mortuary facilities associated with mounds in major settlements were important means of providing a readily understood connection to the past. A long ancestral pedigree – or the conscious construction of it, much like what happened at Spiro – provided an aura of legitimacy to the positions of chiefs and their immediate kin groups. Some artifacts were probably direct references to pl. XX ancestors, such as carved wooden figures in the Great Mortuary at Spiro.[17] Similar effigies were noted in early historic descriptions of charnel houses, 94, pl. XIX and stone figures have been found in midwestern and southeastern sites, including several in mounds.

94 Stone figures, such as this one from Ware in Illinois, have been discovered in the most important parts of some sites, especially mounds. Height 11.2 in (28.5 cm).

95  A man holding a mace and head was carved on this shell gorget from Castalian Springs in Tennessee. Two suspension holes are located to the right. Diameter 3.8 in (9.7 cm).

Some artifacts provide clues as to what occupied the attention of chiefs and other key people.[18] Large marine shells and copper plates have been found that were decorated with warriors in bird-of-prey costumes or bird-man composites. Some of these figures brandished maces and clutched severed heads. Opinion is divided over whether actual men or mythical heroes were depicted, but the reference to bold, decisive, and swift action – essential in war – is obvious. Resolute and inspiring leadership was critical for chiefs who had to be ever watchful of rivals at home and enemies from neighboring chiefdoms. Items from mounds also point to an active involvement of key people in a rich ceremonial life. Rattles and scarifiers, for example, must have been used in various rituals and on special occasions, much like they were in later times. The rattles included small ones from a large burial mound at Mitchell, a major site near Cahokia, where realistic turtle carapaces and plastrons were fashioned from thin copper sheets. A copper-covered wooden turtle rattle was also found in the Craig Mound at Spiro. Among the other Spiro rattles were several where human heads were carved out of cedar and then covered by copper.

Occasionally ordinary people were buried with ritually significant artifacts, including bits of crystals.[19] During the historic period, crystals were used in the Southeast for divination purposes when setting out to hunt, going to war, and healing the sick. Here we see evidence of personal rituals

pl. XIV

95

practiced by common people that had a long history and existed alongside whatever beliefs might have propped up the positions of chiefs.

Interestingly, a number of objects of ritual or symbolic significance – among them crystals, but also bird-wing fans, rattles, and scarifiers – were buried with people of both high and low rank. So too were arrows and "discoidals" (pill-shaped polished stones that were rolled across a specially prepared field and pelted with poles in the widespread "chunkey" game). Their presence acknowledged the significance attached to hunting game, heading off to war, and participating in competitive games. While artifacts used by the most important people were often more elaborate in the sense that they were frequently made from materials such as copper, these objects and whatever they signified were nonetheless part of the ritual lives of all segments of these societies. Certain rituals might have been appropriated and elaborated by chiefs for their own benefit, but they remained firmly rooted in long-standing and widely shared beliefs and customs. In this regard, distinctions between members of chiefly lineages and common people were more a matter of degree than of kind.

The centrality of the quest for food is revealed by many of the artifacts used for special purposes, especially by ordinary people. A figurine carved of reddish Missouri fire clay from a site near Cahokia is indicative of a deep concern with growing crops and, more generally, fertility.[20] This squatting woman grasps a hoe that rests on a chimeric serpent with carnivore's teeth. The snake's tail divides and metamorphoses into squash or gourd vines that wind their way up the woman's back. These plants, as we have seen, were important contributions to diets for many thousands of years. A number of Mississippian groups occasionally made pottery vessels that depicted animals, and these pots were typically buried with ordinary people. While their precise meaning has long been forgotten, wetland species, including fish, ducks, beavers, frogs, and snapping turtles, figure prominently among the animals on these pots. So the importance of water for many Mississippian people was underscored by the pottery used on ceremonial occasions such as funerals.

96

97

96 This figurine was found during the 1979–1980 excavation of the BBB Motor site, a small site near Cahokia. It shows a woman holding a hoe that rests on the back of a serpent. Note the way the stone blade is lashed to the handle of the hoe. Height 7.9 in (20 cm).

97 Fancy pottery vessels occasionally depicted animals, often those that inhabit wetlands, such as this frog pot from Arkansas. Length 11.5 in (29.2 cm).

## Where they lived

House sizes, shapes, and construction details varied from one place and time to the next. Despite such differences, these structures were all supported by frameworks of upright poles firmly embedded in individually dug holes or in narrow trenches. The wall trench was an innovation that followed the    98, 104

98 The walls of this roughly square house are indicated by trenches, some of which contain partially excavated postmolds. Many of these buildings were uncovered during the 1940–1942 CCC excavation of Jonathan Creek, a large settlement in western Kentucky. Another building is located in the foreground, while palisades (one with a bastion) can be seen in the background.

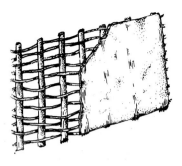

99 Wattle and daub construction, commonly used by Mississippian people to build their houses, consisted of mud plastered on a framework of posts and horizontal sticks.

PL. XII
99

100

widespread availability of large stone hoes – it would have been far easier to excavate a narrow trench with one of these tools than to dig many separate postholes with mussel shell scoops and the like. The walls of buildings sometimes consisted of bundles of thatch lashed to branches bent around the posts. Elsewhere wattle-and-daub – mud thickly plastered against frameworks of horizontal branches and vertical posts – was common. House floors were often dug into the ground, and the resulting loose dirt was mounded up against the outer sides of the walls. This construction technique produced the "hut rings" noticed in the nineteenth century, which for the most part have been plowed away.[21] Extra wall trenches or rows of post-molds show that building walls were occasionally replaced, and the houses were usually enlarged when that was done.

Food was stored in pits and in above-ground granaries.[22] In some places, people dug numerous storage pits near their houses. The pit walls were presumably lined, but there is little left to tell us exactly how that was done. In the Cahokia area, for example, archaeologists have occasionally found limestone slabs on the pit floors, and one pit had a thin layer of charred grass still in place. But storage pits were not common at all Mississippian sites, such as those in eastern Tennessee – here food must have been stored in above-ground granaries. Many hearths and scattered postmolds for light

100 Limestone slabs covered the floor of this storage pit, found in 1979 at the Julien site in southwestern Illinois.

101 Mound B is one of the largest mounds at Moundville; this is how it appeared in 1935.

frameworks such as drying racks and canopies have also been discovered by excavators. "Smudge pits" – small pits packed with carbonized corn cobs and twigs – were used to make thick smoke, sometimes within buildings. Thatch-covered roofs and walls soon crawl with insects, and the smoke would have helped to get rid of these pests.

The principal sites were distinguished from all others by their size and internal layout. Most of them had no more than a few mounds, often only one of them, with central plazas ringed by wooden buildings and mounds that supported residential, charnel, and council houses. The main plazas at the largest mound centers, such as Cahokia, were sometimes accompanied by smaller ones located elsewhere within the settlements. Various ceremonies must have been held in the plazas, much like what happened in historic-period Creek towns. These "square grounds" were used when entertaining visiting dignitaries and conducting community-wide ceremonies, as noted by William Bartram, whose feast in a late eighteenth-century town was described previously (pp. 111–12). The plazas in prehistoric towns were open and seemingly free of debris, but not necessarily empty.[23] Mounds were located in the plazas at Moundville and Cahokia, the one at Moundville being almost the largest at the site. The butt end of an enormous bald cypress post was found in the plaza at the Mitchell site. This post must once have been an impressive sight: it was over

109

pl. XI

pl. VIII

102 The bottom end of a large bald cypress post was found in a pit when the Mitchell site, Illinois, was excavated in the early 1960s. The post had snapped off at ground level when it was being taken down many hundreds of years ago.

102   3 ft (0.9 m) in diameter at its base, and had broken near the ground when an attempt was made to remove it. The plazas, mounds, and important buildings were surrounded by dwellings for ordinary folk, whose houses were typically smaller than those of the chiefs and other important people, but had an otherwise similar layout.

The mounds at Moundville (see box p. 146), one of the largest Mississippian towns, are especially interesting because of their distribution according 103   to size.[24] The biggest mound lay at the northern, or river, side of the plaza, and the amount of earth used in mound construction tended to diminish to the south. Vernon Knight has suggested that the sizes of the mounds were consistent with a ranking of principal kin groups where the paramount chief occupied the place of honor overlooking everybody else. By this arrangement the leading members of this society were trying to impose a sense of order, stability, and legitimacy on the social standing of different groups of people.

The inhabitants of some mound centers spread themselves out across fairly large areas.[25] Cahokia is a fine example of one of these settlements, yet even here the central core of the site is easily identified because mounds, including Monks Mound, ringed an enormous plaza. The most heavily used parts of Cahokia, those along the banks of an abandoned river channel, grade into the sparser occupation of the surrounding floodplain.

Other mound centers were more compact.[26] Thick middens with nicely delineated edges are especially noticeable where a settlement's growth was constrained by palisades. Good examples of such sites can be found near the St. Francis River, a tributary of the Mississippi in northeastern Arkansas. Archaeologists who mapped many of these sites 50 years ago described rectangular areas that rose up above the surrounding floodplain. Slight depressions where plazas were located could be seen in the middle of the higher deposits of debris and soil thrown up from defensive ditches. These settlements with their stinking piles of refuse would certainly have been public health nightmares.

Topographic features, as well as the locations and orientations of earlier public and domestic architecture, influenced the overall layouts of mound centers.[27] The general orientation of many towns was determined largely by the lakes and streams that ran alongside them, but the use of space could change over time. The development of sites such as Cahokia and Moundville was accompanied by the imposition of a fixed site plan, including a large plaza and mounds, on areas that were already in use.[28] Thus at least occasionally there was a purposeful, perhaps even forced, restructuring of settlement layouts to make room for the needs of chiefs and other important people.

The large sites were inhabited by anything from a few hundred to several thousand people, although sites approaching the upper end of this range were rare.[29] Even the largest one, Cahokia, was perhaps inhabited by as few as 3,000 people during its peak of occupation; it was unlikely to have been much more than about twice that size. This estimate, derived from structures in various parts of the site, differs from frequently cited figures of up to 40,000 people, which are based more on enthusiasm than solid evidence. Similar societies elsewhere in the world, after all, had nothing like the higher estimates for Cahokia. In fact, the upper end of the commonly cited population range for Cahokia exceeds that of the largest cities in the first United States census in 1790. Here again is an example of the mischievous effect of big mounds on the fertile imaginations of writers over the past two centuries.

Archaeologists usually find innumerable settlements of one kind or another scattered around the mound centers.[30] The locations and internal configurations of these small settlements represented a balance among labor demands, resource distributions, and defensive needs. In some places

## A suitably named site: Moundville

Moundville, which lies on a high terrace overlooking the Black Warrior River in west-central Alabama, is one of the largest Mississippian sites.[31] Simply viewing the mounds ringing a huge plaza conveys an impression of its former greatness. The site is also important because it has been the subject of considerable archaeological attention, including excavations that took place during the Great Depression when a road was put through the site.

The mounds and plaza were accompanied by extensive habitation areas indicated by abundant debris and building remnants that covered about 185 acres (75 ha). About 29 large and small mounds have been identified, although one is said to have been a natural rise. Most of the mounds fronted the plaza, but several of them were located either beyond or within it. The largest mound, which is 57 ft (17.3 m) high, was located along the northern, or river, side of the plaza.

At least some of the mounds contained human remains, including the most important members of this society. The plaza is largely devoid of cultural materials, and low spots were filled to make a level surface, showing that this open area was specially

103 Large and small mounds surrounded the large plaza at Moundville, Alabama. One can drive around the site on the road alongside the mounds.

104 Several wall-trench structures are shown in this 1939 excavation, undertaken before a road was built through Moundville.

prepared and used as public, not residential, space.

A palisade surrounded the mounds, plaza, and residential areas. This wall, complete with bastions, was replaced at least six times, indicating that the site's inhabitants were concerned about defense for a long time. The palisade protected the three exposed sides of the site; the steep and heavily eroded fourth side overlooks the river.

The mounds were built over several centuries. In fact, Moundville and the chiefdom it dominated were quite long-lived relative to most others. Moundbuilding began as early as the late eleventh century or shortly thereafter, and picked up in the thirteenth century, by which time the overall site layout was established.

During the peak period of occupation the site had perhaps as many as 1,000 inhabitants. By the late fourteenth century, some mounds had been abandoned while others were being enlarged. Mound use continued through the sixteenth century, although the site and what it represented were slowly flickering out. If the route of de Soto's expedition has been reconstructed correctly, the Spaniards encountered only a weak chiefdom that included Moundville as well as other settlements. Within another century, the site was completely deserted and the surrounding area depopulated. Except for the mounds and whatever else could survive the passage of time, all remnants of the once-powerful chiefdom had disappeared.

105 A compact village known as Snodgrass in the Missouri Bootheel was excavated in the late 1960s and early 1970s. An outer defensive ditch surrounded houses (both shaded), pits, and an inner wall (black).

houses were clustered together in an orderly fashion, sometimes around small plazas, producing compact settlements occupied by several dozen to a few hundred people. They include the Snodgrass site in southeastern
105  Missouri where a ditch, which was part of a defensive work, surrounded closely spaced houses. At the King site in northwestern Georgia, houses surrounded an open area where a central post and a large public structure were located. It was one of many sites where the general layout of large towns, complete with an open central area, was replicated in a smaller settlement.

Elsewhere, scattered single-family houses were the norm. This does not necessarily point to the absence of secular and sacred institutions forming local communities – merely to the problems faced by archaeologists in recognizing the existence of such communities. Fortunately, near Cahokia, areas ranging up to several tens of acres have been dug, and this work has uncovered signs of dozens of widely spaced farmsteads on floodplain ridges. These families were probably part of dispersed settlements centered on small clusters of buildings, including "sweat lodges," that have also been excavated. Sweat lodges were cramped structures heated by hot rocks or hearths and were widely used during both the prehistoric and historic periods. Several centuries ago in Virginia, for example, Native Americans took "great delight in Sweating," and would "use this to refresh themselves, after they have been fatigu'd with Hunting, Travel, or the like, or else when they are troubl'd with Agues, Aches, or Pains in their Limbs."[32] Upon leaving, people often finished their experience with a cold dip in a nearby stream. Whatever transpired in and around the special-function buildings in the Cahokia area, including the sweat lodges, it probably promoted close relations among households with shared political and economic interests.

Far to the south of Cahokia – in what is today western Arkansas, northern Louisiana, and contiguous parts of eastern Oklahoma and Texas – the early historic-period Caddo people lived in scattered houses amongst their gardens, groves of trees, and patches of shrubby growth and grass.[33] Villages were up to several miles long, and encompassed structures used for community purposes. In its general form, the dispersed arrangement of houses resembled earlier settlements found around Cahokia and in other parts of the southern Eastern Woodlands.

Permanently occupied settlements were surrounded by widely scattered camps used when hunting, fishing, or collecting wild plants. Isolated arrowheads, most of which were simple triangles, show that hunters often sought out game such as deer that were in short supply in the immediate vicinity of large sites. But it seems that most people spent the majority of their lives near their villages.

The picture of a rather sedentary life is reinforced by the kinds of chipped stone tools and debris from sites such as those around Cahokia.[34] Here most tools were made by simply grabbing a convenient chert core and knocking off just enough flakes to get one suitable for the task at hand. Little or no effort was spent shaping these flakes or preparing cutting edges. Carefully fashioning tools, keeping them for a long time, and sharpening them when dull was not important, probably because people spent so much of their time close to home where cores were readily available.

Stone hoes, including the widely traded Mill Creek chert hoes in the Midwest, represent a notable exception to the general pattern. When broken, these tools were reworked to make still serviceable, albeit smaller, hoes. When not being used, these valuable tools were hidden in pits or along the walls of houses. The effort involved in obtaining the chipped stone hoes and

106

106 Several Mill Creek hoes were found in 1979 when a pit at the Julien site in southwestern Illinois was cleaned out.

taking care of them is consistent with a more intensive use of land at this time. They would have been a much-appreciated addition to the digging stick or mussel-shell hoe when preparing and weeding fields used for several consecutive years.

## Scattered chiefdoms

The chiefdoms of this time were mostly scattered along major stream valleys where edible plants and animals were plentiful, but there were, of course, exceptions to this pattern. Among them were the Calusa of southwestern Florida who were contacted by Spaniards in the opening years of the sixteenth century.[35] These people were fortunate enough to live in an exceedingly rich coastal environment, a reliable source of food every bit as good as the river valleys in the continental interior.

Contemporaneous sites tended to be clustered where resources were most abundant. Our best estimates for these pockets of population indicate that they extended along rivers from as little as six miles to something in excess of ten times that distance (10 to 100 km).[36] Most of the site concentrations are in the bottom end of that range. The largest ones were located in unusually resource-rich locations, such as the mosaic of well-drained ridges and wetlands within the central to lower Mississippi Valley.

Population estimates for these concentrations of sites are largely guesswork.[37] For the most part they were probably inhabited by no more than several thousand people, occasionally a few tens of thousands. The largest of the prehistoric populations did not exceed the biggest of the historically known tribes, which also tended to number in the low tens of thousands.

The population aggregates were separated by sparsely occupied land that encompassed both prime valley segments and less productive uplands. These areas harbored abundant game, yet hunters would have avoided many of them; in the historic period, long-standing animosities between neighboring societies could make them extremely dangerous places.[38] Such conditions also prevailed during late prehistoric times, to judge from discoveries of palisaded villages and the skeletons of grievously wounded and horrifyingly mutilated people.

As might be expected, the social boundaries defining separate groups of people, which often had uneasy relations with one another, acted as barriers to gene flow.[39] Dawnie Steadman's measurements of skulls from west-central Illinois show that the Mississippians were more divided up into regional populations than their immediate predecessors. The osteological data are fully compatible with archaeological evidence for a patchy distribution of groups that had only irregular contact with one another.

The locations of these settlement clusters and the most powerful sites did not remain fixed over time.[40] For example, the occupation of much of the Ohio and Mississippi river confluence region had dropped to the level of archaeological invisibility by the early fifteenth century. Some of this decline is more apparent than real because people moved from river bottomlands to the surrounding uplands. Sites are difficult to detect in large expanses of hilly terrain creased by small streams. Yet it is hard to believe that a redistribution of people was the entire story. It seems that the original population actually declined, although by how much is not known. The Savannah River valley was another such place. It was abandoned about a century before de Soto's mid-sixteenth-century expedition cut through the deep forests of the Southeast. By the time the Spaniards arrived, the valley was a thoroughly overgrown, rarely frequented, and dangerous place between warring chiefdoms.

It is clear that over the half-millennium of the Mississippian period, the places where people were concentrated and the most powerful societies were located blinked on and off like the twinkling of Christmas tree lights. While the general nature of these societies remained largely the same over several centuries, their geographical distribution did not.

## What they ate

It was once widely believed that maize, squash, and beans came to the Eastern Woodlands as an integrated complex from Mesoamerica, and reigned supreme in late prehistoric times because together they provided a balanced diet. It was also thought that chiefdoms could not have arisen without the stable source of food that only these plants could provide. But like so many ideas, they have not withstood the assault of hard data. Squash was grown several thousand years before the other two plants appeared. Beans were introduced well after the shift to maize, and they were rarely if ever eaten by some Mississippian people, including those at Cahokia.[41]

The move to maize described in the previous chapter was accompanied by changes in workload and the frequency and severity of tooth decay.[42] In northwestern Alabama, the bones of Mississippian women show they were stronger than earlier hunter-gatherers, particularly in their arms. In addition to working in fields, these women probably pounded maize in large wooden mortars for hours on end, much like their historic-period descendants. Similar increases in workload, however, did not occur everywhere, because once again we see considerable diversity within broadly defined ways of life. The addition of significant amounts of maize to the diet – that is, the introduction of sticky food rich in carbohydrates – also promoted tooth decay. Cavities both on crowns and at the gum line led to abscesses that drained into the oral cavity. Molars were especially prone to decay, and often fell out at an early age. Calculus, or tartar, also built up on everyone's teeth.

Even after maize became a dietary staple, several native plants continued to be grown, especially in the midcontinent (as in earlier times, they made up much smaller parts of the diet in the Deep South). Even in the early eighteenth century people were seen scattering the seeds of an unidentified native plant over sand bars scoured by the river in the lower Mississippi Valley.[43] These sprouted and grew without further attention in the fertile alluvial soil.

Despite the importance of various crops, wild plants and animals continued to form part of meals everywhere in the southern Eastern Woodlands. Wetlands remained an important and reliable source of food in the major valleys. The mix of resources gave subsistence practices a certain resiliency that enabled people, within limits, to substitute one food for another. But even large stretches of fertile soils and productive wetlands were subject to

107  In many parts of the Southeast, women who lived in Mississippian communities probably pounded maize each day in large wooden mortars much like those used in the historic period. This drawing is based on a photograph of a Hitchiti woman in Oklahoma.

devastating droughts and floods. Severe shortages are precisely what the inhabitants of Cahokia would have faced had the 1993 flood occurred many hundreds of years earlier. This flood took place during late summer instead of in the spring when they usually occur. An equivalent event in prehistoric times would have destroyed crops and stored food on all but the highest ground. Late floods also interfered with fishing – the best places to fish were shallow pools that normally dry up during the steamy summer months, not vast sheets of floodwater.

Greater numbers of people in the most densely settled places depleted the animal populations near their settlements, most importantly deer. One of the better-known examples of problems from intensive hunting comes from the Lewis and Clark expedition in the opening years of the nineteenth century.[44] These men had trouble getting enough meat along the Missouri River where hunters from large villages were active. Easy hunting only resumed when they entered infrequently used land claimed by competing tribes. Around Cahokia, as well as in other heavily populated spots, deer would certainly have been in short supply, unlike in sparsely occupied places such as the narrow valleys of southeastern Kentucky.[45] Excavations at Croley-Evans, for example, a site with one mound along the Cumberland River, yielded an abundance of bones from deer, but few fish. Fishing along the Cumberland was not nearly as good as in the Mississippi Valley, whereas hunting pressure on game was much less, so the people of these two valleys had correspondingly different diets.

While maize was of central importance in many diets, it was not eaten in all of the late prehistoric chiefdoms.[46] In the lower Mississippi Valley it did not become a dietary staple until as late as the thirteenth century, several hundred years after mound centers had first appeared. A late switch to maize must have been related to the presence of exceedingly rich natural settings that provided a sufficiently stable and plentiful supply of food. Maize was also consumed only in limited quantities, if at all, in much of peninsular Florida, as shown by the stable carbon isotope signatures of human bones. The Calusa were one of the groups that did not rely on maize agriculture, but took advantage of shallow-water resources that were abundant, dependable, and concentrated near settlements. Thus their wild foods mimicked the critical characteristics of crops in fields.

## Chiefs and followers

Social relations in Mississippian times were based on kinship. That was as true of the highest-ranking members of these chiefdoms as it was for common people. The widespread occurrence of charnel houses and deposits of bones in mounds indicates that important people were often treated as members of groups that were presumably defined by birth or marriage. Yet group affiliation was not the entire story. Mostly adult bones were found in the Harlan, Spiro, and Wilson mound deposits. So access to the most impor-

108 Clusters of well-made arrowheads sorted by shape and material were found with important burials in Mound 72 at Cahokia.

tant mortuary areas was partly a function of an individual's age, even though membership in a select social group was of paramount importance.

While the people who filled the highest social positions needed acceptable pedigrees, they also had to be vigorous and decisive leaders. Artifacts emphasizing warlike themes indicate that chiefs had to be effective in war.[47] Clusters of similarly aligned arrowheads, which were sorted by shape and raw material, were uncovered when excavating Cahokia's Mound 72. These points must have been attached to arrows held in quivers that decayed long ago. Fine stone points also have been found in mortuary contexts at other sites. Ceremonial stone axes and maces fashioned after actual weapons were also buried, and menacing warriors or bird–man figures decorated marine shell cups and copper plates.

But chiefs were more than war leaders – they had to be persuasive and respected. Judging from what happened during the historic period, chiefs were constrained by a need to consult with leading members of their societies and to reach consensus on weighty matters. They could not push too far or they would risk alienating powerful factions within their own societies. They probably played a part in settling disputes that were likely to develop when greater numbers of people began living in closer proximity to one

108

109 This mound at Town Creek in North Carolina provides an impression of what a building on a platform would have looked like to the residents of major settlements. These buildings were used for various purposes, such as residences for the most important people and as charnel houses for their ancestors' bones.

another. A more formalized means of dealing with intractable problems that could not be resolved locally would have become important as individual households and larger descent groups found it increasingly difficult to move away from sources of trouble. After all, it was in a chief's self interest to dampen tensions before they spun out of control.

Like their historic-period counterparts, chiefs probably did whatever they could to maintain full granaries with food donated from ordinary people.[48] This food was probably used to help maintain their own households, to entertain visitors, such as emissaries from neighboring groups, and to distribute to their supporters on special occasions. Because yields were inherently unpredictable, prudent households – that is, those that survived over the long run – had to adopt strategies that normally yielded modest surpluses. Each household held onto much of the surplus it produced, as indicated by large storage pits in many sites, but possessed only limited means of keeping food for much more than a single year. So in good times, gifts to chiefs were essentially painless because ordinary people could not otherwise use the surplus they produced. All that chiefs had to do was to figure out how to lay their hands on the extra food that already existed. They presumably did so through appeals to fulfill time-honored obligations accompanied by threats of ritual sanctions and the more palpable menace of many warriors.

The sharp edge of occasional shortages could have been blunted by the judicious deployment of food that chiefs already had on hand. While it would be difficult to demonstrate that food was actually given to needy families, the historic-period Creek did distribute it in this manner.[49] Local crises presented ambitious chiefs with the chance to augment their reputations through highly visible acts of generosity; it would be surprising if they overlooked such golden opportunities.

Chiefs and their close kinsfolk possessed a disproportionate share of the finest objects available, many of which were made from non-local materials. Having great numbers of these items is consistent with chiefs being points of contact with the leading members of neighboring societies. Symbolically significant gifts were probably exchanged when sealing alliances, making peace, and fulfilling tribute obligations, much like what took place in historic times.

Highly valued goods trickled downward through social hierarchies, often ending up in the hands of ordinary people. While people of low rank did possess items such as marine shell beads, they tended to be fewer, smaller, and of poorer quality than those belonging to chiefs and their kinsfolk. By selectively doling out gifts, chiefs could have shored up their positions by making people indebted to them. Chiefly largesse was probably coupled with carefully staged events that included feasts, for which there is direct evidence in mound deposits.

Most chiefs exerted limited control over the occupants of a few communities around the principal settlements. In these situations there was one level of decision-making above the largely consensual agreements made within local villages. These simple chiefdoms are recognized archaeologically by the presence of a single center – the seat of the local chief – surrounded by sites that were generally smaller and occupied for shorter periods of time. While the principal sites in these societies had public architecture that typically included mounds, these communities were usually not all that much grander than ordinary villages.

There were also chiefdoms with two levels of decision-making above the local community. Archaeologically speaking, they can be distinguished from simple chiefdoms by having two or more contemporaneous major centers, each surrounded by its own group of closely affiliated, but smaller, settlements. Occasionally a principal site, such as Cahokia and Moundville, dwarfed its outlying mound centers. These complex chiefdoms must have been knit together through relationships among leading people, the strength and permanence of which depended on the efficacy of the principal chief. Even the largest of them resembled an aggregation of simple chiefdoms with one being ascendant over the others.[50] Thus these societies consisted of two or more similarly constituted, economically self-sufficient, and politically quasi-autonomous districts led by locally important chiefs who resided in their own mound centers.

If this picture of complex chiefdoms is correct, then their rise and fall involved little more than the addition or subtraction of structurally similar groups, each headed by its own chief. The formation of such complex chiefdoms through the coalescence of formerly discrete parts could be rapid, as seems to have been the case at Cahokia.[51] Lesser chiefs, however, would have been always watchful for opportunities to advance their positions relative to their peers, sometimes to the detriment of the paramount chief. The de Soto expedition had direct experience of this tendency on their march through the Southeast in the mid-sixteenth century. Even the largest and most powerful chiefdoms suffered from this inherent instability. At Cahokia, there was a long period when a stout palisade studded with bastions surrounded the central group of mounds, including Monks Mound. No nearby society at that time represented a credible threat to Cahokia given the great disparities that existed in warrior mobilization potential. Danger more likely sprang from within.

While a few high-ranking individuals were very much in evidence, most people never held positions of any significance.[52] The majority of the houses within a particular society, as well as the artifacts they contained, resembled one another. But there are some indications of differences in status, even within small settlements. In the dispersed communities around Cahokia, a few houses were built next to ritually significant buildings, most notably sweat lodges. These houses were perhaps occupied by people whose roles in these communities were tied to the ritual and social activities, such as sweat baths, that took place in the special-function buildings. In southeastern Missouri, somewhat larger houses were built in the innermost part of the compact Snodgrass village. The most influential families might have lived in the centrally located houses, but there is no evidence from domestic architecture and artifacts that they enjoyed much – if anything – in the way of genuine material advantages.

Common folk were usually buried in simple graves near their houses or within separate cemeteries, although there was regional variation in precisely how bodies were handled and graves constructed.[53] For example, shallow graves lined with stone slabs are commonly found in Tennessee, Kentucky, and nearby parts of adjoining states. Groups of graves, in clusters or rows, suggest that family or lineage affiliation was important when deciding precisely where a grave should be dug. In her worldwide survey of mortuary practices, Lynne Goldstein has pointed out that formally arranged cemeteries are commonly used by sedentary villagers to mark rights of access to essential resources, principally land. So the prehistoric burial grounds are consistent with a situation where survival depended on a local kin group's investments in fields and stores of food.

Bodies were usually buried with rather plain ornaments, pottery that included vessels depicting animals, and everyday tools.[54] The distribution of these objects sometimes varied according to age and sex – tool kits used for flint knapping, for example, were usually buried with men.

110

110  This bowl in the shape of an owl came from the East St. Louis Stone Quarry cemetery in southwestern Illinois. The site was excavated in 1980 just before it was to be destroyed by a highway. The depiction of wild animals on pottery used for special purposes, such as funerary offerings, is consistent with the importance these people would have placed on a detailed knowledge about the natural environment.

A few people were buried with more precious items such as marine shell beads, some graves yielding as many as a thousand or more of these beads. These individuals might have been village headmen or elders who earned their positions through special kin connections, unusual abilities, or simply long life. Whoever they were, they were not otherwise distinguishable from everyone else buried in these cemeteries.

So it seems that ordinary people did pretty much what everyone else of their age and sex were also doing. Despite occasional claims to the contrary, there is no evidence indicating that some people supported themselves by producing goods that they, in turn, exchanged for the food and other goods they needed to live.[55] Members of common households, not full-time specialists, seem to have been involved in the production of salt in Illinois and Arkansas, as well as utilitarian Mill Creek hoes in Illinois. Nor does it appear that such specialists made the fancy objects used for displays of wealth, as insignia of high rank, and in various ceremonies.

If evidence of craft specialists who supported themselves by what they produced can be found anywhere, it ought to be at Cahokia. Much attention has focused on fine goods, especially marine shell beads, but the beads from Cahokia and nearby sites are so irregular it is clear that no special skills or equipment were involved in making them. Moreover, the chert microdrills

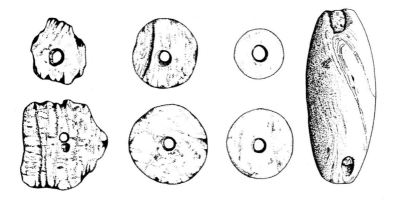

111 Six whelk shell disk beads from the Wilson mound are arranged, from left to right, by quality of workmanship. The two middle beads are typical of the majority found in the Cahokia area. Holes drilled off center in the seventh bead *(far right)*, a large whelk columella bead from Cahokia's Mound 72, have been repaired with carefully fitted shell plugs. The columella bead is 1.8 in (4.5 cm) long.

used for drilling holes in beads were easy to produce, and they were made by 111 the residents of both mound centers and outlying communities. Many of these microdrills have been picked up from fields near Monks Mound, consistent with the possibility that high-status families who had access to the most shell also made the most beads. These people had ample opportunities to work on beads during the long cold winter months when there were few competing demands on their time; that is, no time had to be taken away from basic subsistence-related tasks when making these ornaments. Perhaps the finest beads – some of them are symmetrical, highly polished, and found in matched sets – were made by a few particularly talented people who gained a local reputation for their abilities and by their occasional work earned a place to live in a prestigious part of the site. Chiefs and other influential people might have had a hand in sponsoring the production of beads, especially the best ones, when they were needed for ritually and socially important events. But even the most able bead-makers would have spent the bulk of their time doing what everyone else had to do to survive.

Did any of the advantages enjoyed by the most important members of these societies have a noticeable effect on their health?[56] Here we must turn to skeletal samples, such as they are. So far, osteologists have failed to find evidence showing that highly ranked people, as a rule, ate markedly better food or had fewer illnesses than anyone else. The stable carbon isotope signatures of skeletons from Moundville indicate that people throughout the social hierarchy had about the same proportion of maize in their diets. The prevalence and severity of the diseases they suffered from were also about the same. These illnesses included two communicable infections that produced skeletal lesions similar to those of modern tuberculosis and the 112

112 An effigy bottle from Arkansas depicts a hunchback that some researchers believe might be a deformity from tuberculosis. Height 7.7 in (19.5 cm).

treponematoses. The treponematoses include venereal syphilis and yaws, among others, although the precise form of the pre-Columbian infection is unknown and unlikely to have been identical to one of the present-day diseases.

The inhabitants of Mississippian chiefdoms were not the only people in the Eastern Woodlands to suffer from these diseases. In fact, one early eighteenth-century explorer described a "Burning of the Limbs, which tortures them grievously, at which time their Legs are so hot, that they employ the young People continually to pour Water down them."[57] They must have been suffering from the treponemal infection, which we know from skeletons often affected the legs, typically the distal femora and tibiae.

It is possible that chiefs and their close kinsfolk benefited during hard times from the stores of food they had amassed during the previous year or so, but clear-cut and consistent signs of such advantages are not found in their skeletons. They were perfectly capable of distinguishing themselves from everyone else by how they dressed, where they lived, and the way they were buried. Yet they were little different from the lowliest members of their societies in terms of their physical well-being. Here we see the very real limits of chiefly power – it was more show than substance.

## Friends and foes

The long-distance exchange of goods, which had dropped off in Late Woodland times, picked up during the Mississippian period. These objects appear to have moved across long distances by passing through innumerable hands, presumably as gifts accompanying social transactions among both chiefs and ordinary households.[58] Jon Muller has shown that there is a decline in the amounts of non-local artifacts as distances from sources increase, a pattern true of nicely carved marine shell gorgets and utilitarian Mill Creek chert hoes alike. The fit between distance and artifact abundance is not perfect, but then neither are the incomplete and –worse – biased data. Even the appearance of some items from distant places shows that they were in circulation for a long time. The surfaces of whelk shell pendants from the Dickson Mounds and De Frenne cemeteries, both in Illinois, were smoothed from prolonged use. Many years, perhaps even several generations, had elapsed before these particular seashells ended up being buried in the continental interior.

113

Another clue to the long journeys of precious objects comes from the marine shell beads from Cahokia and nearby sites.[59] It is not uncommon to find whelk shell beads with the small holes and narrow interconnected tracks characteristic of shells that wash up onto beaches. The presence of these beads is consistent with an exchange network where the poorest material had the greatest chance of moving the farthest. The unfortunate people at the end of a long sequence of transactions had to be pleased with whatever they could lay their hands on, even if it was not the best material in circulation at that time.

113 Whelk shell pendants from the Midwest sometimes show the effects of long use. These heavily worn pendants are from Dickson Mounds in west-central Illinois.

## Mesoamerican contacts?

There has been much ill-informed and strangely persistent speculation by enthusiasts who are tireless in their attempts to find ties between the civilizations of Mesoamerica (Mexico and nearby Central American countries) and the Southeast. Distinctive foreign artifacts are one of the clearest ways to demonstrate the existence of such contacts and, until recently, there was absolutely no evidence of such a connection. But now a scraper made from Mesoamerican obsidian has turned up in a collection of objects from the Great Mortuary at Spiro.[60] So it is natural to ask what this find might mean in terms of contact with Mesoamerica.

One small tool falls far short of proving there was direct contact with Mesoamerica. In fact, what is more extraordinary than the discovery of this scraper is the absence of anything else like it in the Eastern Woodlands. In other parts of North America, and

elsewhere in the world, a very few odd artifacts are known to have crossed vast distances through innumerable hands. Spiro is exactly where we might expect to find such an object. It was positioned on the western fringe of the Eastern Woodlands, and its inhabitants maintained contacts with people in the

Many of the items that crossed long distances must have been passed from one chief to the next. These were the people who were able to hoard dispro-portionately large numbers of the finest and most highly prized objects, which often served as symbols of high rank. But however much archaeologists focus on the significance of non-local raw materials and the artifacts made from them, exchanges of these items were probably incidental to the real purpose of the dealings chiefs had with one another. Some form of contact had to be maintained if chiefs were to secure allies in times of need and, if at war, to arrange the resumption of peaceful relations. Such interactions were probably accompanied by gifts, including symbolically meaningful objects that were highly valued in part because they had long histories attached to them. In fact, it is possible that the overall amount of non-local materials in circulation increased because of the demand by chiefs for prestige goods used to solidify their local positions and to seal negotiations with their counterparts elsewhere.

While chiefs and their close kinsfolk dominated the trade in valued goods, they were never able to secure a monopoly over it. A movement from one small village to the next is the simplest explanation for the lack of a

Southern Plains who, in turn, communicated with groups in the arid Southwest. The southwestern groups clearly had access to some Mesoamerican objects. Moreover, a scraper ending up in Spiro's Great Mortuary is perfectly consistent with the workings of southeastern chiefdoms. Precious and unusual objects – in this instance, a scraper prized for its novelty, not for its functional value –

tended to gravitate toward chiefs. Much the same thing happened during the sixteenth century when Spanish artifacts often ended up in the biggest sites with the most important people.[61]

114 The Great Mortuary was located within the Craig Mound, one of several mounds to be seen at the Spiro site in Oklahoma.

noticeable decline in non-local goods from outlying sites near Cahokia when the main mound center's position of regional dominance had deteriorated.[62] But the kinds of materials did change – a possible indication of altered alliance networks across the region. The continued access to non-local goods, despite a marked erosion of the chief's position, is not at all surprising. After all, valued objects moved over long distances for thousands of years before there were any chiefs around to tell people what to do, and they continued to be traded in the historic period well after chiefdoms had vanished.

Exchange had its counterpoint in conflict, which broke out regularly. By the eleventh century AD, the numbers of palisaded settlements had plainly increased and they remained common from that point onward.[63] Palisades were made of upright posts, now detectable as long lines of large postmolds 115 or trenches, around which pliable branches must have been woven. Some of the walls were thickly plastered with mud, such as at Aztalan, a northern Mississippian outlier in south-central Wisconsin. Nineteenth-century visitors to Aztalan described great quantities of burned daub, mistakenly called brick, that littered low ridges where walls once stood. Mississippian palisades were often studded with bastions at roughly 98-ft (30-m) intervals,

115 In 1940–1942, young men in the CCC excavated Jonathan Creek in Kentucky, and plow-disturbed soil from a large area was removed by hand. In this part of the site, postmolds belonging to a palisade and houses are partially dug. Work at the site was halted soon after the United States entered World War II.

well within overlapping bow fire, and were further strengthened by embankments and ditches. The defensive works at Angel in southwestern Indiana show the lengths to which people had to go to protect themselves. Here a strong palisade, reinforced with square bastions, was erected on a low embankment, with another wall a short distance in front. Attackers who had climbed over the first wall were forced to charge across an open area to reach the main palisade, a feat that could only be accomplished with great loss of life.

Walls were not only thrown up in times of immediate peril, but were permanent fixtures around many sites. Wooden palisades were repaired or replaced as necessary, and new ones erected as settlements expanded or contracted over time. Their maintenance indicates that the threat of attack by a strong and determined foe could last for decades, if not generations.

Fighting mostly consisted of small-scale raids and ambushes where only a few people at a time were killed; at least that is the impression one gets from cemeteries where the skeletons of victims are mostly arranged singly or in small groups. But people must also have been worried about large groups of determined warriors, as shown by the strong defenses at many sites. Once warriors managed to gain entry into an enemy's principal town, they did whatever they could to despoil the chief's charnel structure. That is what took place in the sixteenth century when de Soto's men saw their victorious allies break off the engagement in order to toss human bones around and take war trophies.[64] Defiling a charnel house struck at the core of a chief's aura of legitimacy and power; an inability to protect the bones of one's illustrious ancestors was a sure sign of feeble leadership.

## The rise and fall of chiefdoms

One of the most important outcomes of work since the 1980s is the realization that the Mississippian world was highly volatile: chiefdoms rose and fell, and the distributions of people changed accordingly. Some chiefdoms remained in place for several hundred years, although their longevity was usually measured on the order of a few generations.

Opinion differs over what lay behind the emergence of chiefdoms, but several clues point us in the right direction. They include a change in population distribution and density; the character of natural landscapes,

116 At some sites, natural features accentuated the impressive nature of mounds used principally by chiefs and their close kinfolk. They include these two mounds at Ocmulgee in Georgia.

especially the risk of catastrophic shortfalls in essential foods; a shift in technology, including the move to maize agriculture; and a descent to unprecedented levels of violence.

By the end of the first millennium AD, warfare had become firmly embedded in the fabric of everyday life, and things took a turn for the worse in the eleventh century. People seeking safety gravitated toward one another, presenting capable and charismatic war leaders with new opportunities to recruit followers, thereby augmenting and solidifying their positions. At the very least, a reputation for ferocity was central to chiefly power, and success in combat was a means of social advancement for other people, as shown by warlike themes depicted on Mississippian artifacts and the sketchy comments of early European explorers. Such a reputation also helped chiefs deal with disaffected members of their own societies.

Deteriorating intergroup relations coupled with higher local population densities meant that people enjoyed fewer options for switching to alternative foods during times of hunger. Even the richest parts of the Eastern Woodlands were susceptible to periodic shortages of food, some of which must have led to outright famine as in historic times. So it is not surprising that favorable locations were critical for chiefs to achieve long-term success. Nowhere is this clearer than in the Mississippi Valley near Cahokia where the major mound centers were located in places with a good mix of fertile soil, permanent wetlands, and regularly inundated ground, all of which were essential to support many people through good and bad years.[65] When mounds were present in less desirable places, they were rather low heaps of soil that a few people could build in a short time. The debris near these small mounds tends to be sparse, consistent with light or short occupations.

Chiefdoms spread rapidly across the southern Eastern Woodlands once they had emerged late in the first millennium AD. Their broad distribution within only a few centuries of their initial appearance makes sense if conflicts were really as pervasive as indicated by victims and palisades. The losers of disputes that broke out in the weakly knit chiefdoms might have been tempted to move away, provided they were strong enough to carve out a place for themselves elsewhere. If prehistoric chiefs were anything like their historic-period counterparts, they could enlist the aid of friendly neighboring groups in times of need and exert some influence over weakly affiliated groups that could be intimidated by the threat of raids.[66]

While the organizational advantages of chiefdoms over more egalitarian societies may not have provided much of a competitive edge, it was apparently sufficient. New chiefdoms soon developed through the coalescence of formerly discrete and loosely integrated constellations of villages. Not to join was to risk being displaced by numerically superior foes or incorporated into the orbits of aggressively expanding chiefdoms.

Once begun, the growth of complex chiefdoms was made possible by an ever-increasing disparity in the capacity to wage war. Outward growth was eventually halted by limits on the paramount chief's capacity to project his

117

117 Mississippian settlements often looked much like this palisaded village in Georgia (a painting based on excavations at Rucker's Bottom). People in many places had to be careful to defend themselves against their enemies.

or her authority over long distances and to maintain control over a society that retained much of its original segmented structure. A principal chief's influence over lesser chiefs, all of whom could draw upon the support of their own people, could be expected to diminish as distance from the major center increased. Thus it is likely these societies were prone to disintegration at their edges where the chief's authority was the weakest. Cahokia's collapse, for example, seems to have been accompanied by the rise of one or more rivals at the periphery of its earlier sphere of influence.

The self-sufficient nature of each district made it possible for ambitious subchiefs to break away or to usurp the highest position should favorable circumstances present themselves. Signs of discontent and enfeebled leadership would be apparent long before the final vestiges of chiefly authority faded away. Cahokia's final collapse, for example, was presaged by an extended period when the population of the mound center and neighboring sites declined.

Even in the best of circumstances, chiefs inevitably experienced reversals of one kind or another that they were powerless to stop. Their positions were surely tested during times of repeated shortages, especially if coupled with losses at the hands of their enemies. In such situations the demands on common people that had become codified through long practice could become increasingly onerous, prompting a lack of cooperation or even outright resistance. Precisely this problem – in this instance, repeated droughts indicated by tree-ring sequences – contributed to the fifteenth-century collapse of chiefdoms along the Savannah River.[67] A century later, de Soto's men only found a tangled and uninhabited wilderness.

The midwestern Mississippian chiefdoms that expanded northward during the Medieval Warm Period eventually fell apart during a time of unrest that was probably related, directly or indirectly, to a deterioration of climatic conditions.[68] Many formerly strong chiefdoms were showing signs of weakness by the thirteenth century, and the once-impressive river valley societies had all but disappeared by the beginning of the fifteenth century. Anything that increased the risk of back-to-back shortfalls surely eroded the authority of chiefs – no matter whether their problems stemmed from poor harvests or losses at the hands of their enemies. Conflicts accompanying movements of people pressed onward by hard times certainly added to any difficulties midwestern chiefs faced when struggling with a greater uncertainty in harvests. And we know that populations fought and replaced one another in at least some parts of the Midwest. This movement is seen most clearly by the appearance around AD 1300 of loosely affiliated villages classified as Oneota in the central Illinois Valley. This was an area where chiefdoms had been present for over two centuries. While the causes of a widespread disappearance of the major midwestern chiefdoms have yet to be fully explained, their collapse surely came about through the interaction of both natural and social forces.

**XIII** (*opposite*)  Mica found in Mound 25 at Hopewell in Ohio was cut into various shapes, including this hand with curiously elongated fingers. Length 11.4 in (29 cm).

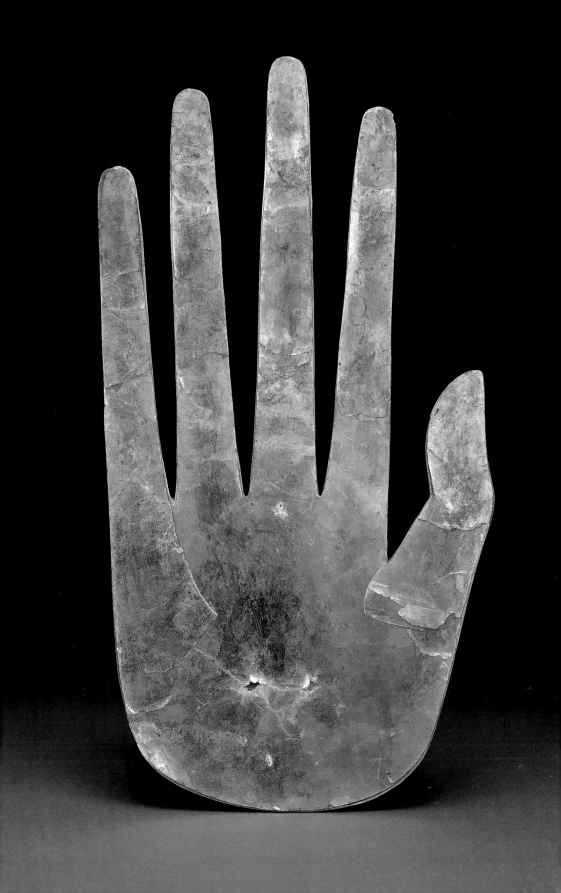

**XIV**  This elaborate shell gorget from eastern Tennessee shows two bird-men with bird wings, feet, and tails. They have deer antlers, wear earspools and necklaces with shell pendants, and clutch long, sharp objects. Diameter 4.5 in (11.5 cm).

**XV**  A Mississippian-period head pot from western Kentucky with elaborate incised facial decorations. Diameter 7.3 in (18.5 cm).

**XVI**  Head pots similar to this one from eastern Arkansas have been found at a number of Mississippi Valley sites. Diameter 7.1 in (18.1 cm).

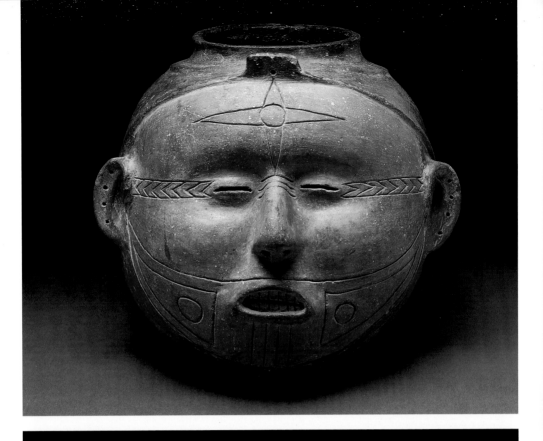

**XVII** Birds of prey, such as this copper plate from Mound City in Ohio, were depicted on some ritually significant Middle Woodland objects. Length 12 in (30.6 cm).

**XVIII** (*opposite*) A "forked eye" design, thought to be derived from markings on the peregrine falcon (a bird known for its swift and powerful flight), is shown on this copper plate from the Craig Mound at Mississippian-period Spiro in eastern Oklahoma. Its head appears to have been cut out of a larger plate, several of which were found nearby, the feather then riveted on. Length 9.4 in (24 cm).

**XIX** (*overleaf*) Two stone human figures were found in a grave alongside Mound C at the Mississippian-period Etowah site in Georgia. They were broken, apparently from being dropped into the pit. Height 24 in (61 cm).

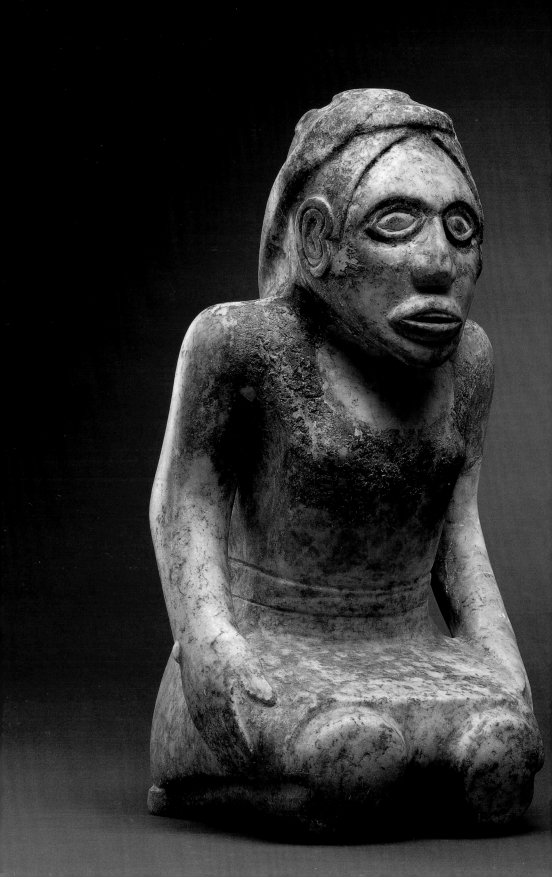

**XX** This red cedar human figure was one of several found in the Craig Mound at Spiro in eastern Oklahoma. Height 12.8 in (32.5 cm).

# 7 · Northern Villagers: Late Prehistory

By the second millennium AD, agricultural villagers were scattered from the prairie and forest transition eastward through the Midwest and into the northeastern and mid-Atlantic states. These culturally distinctive groups are known by various names that include, among others, Oneota in Minnesota, Iowa, Wisconsin, and Illinois; Fort Ancient in Ohio, Kentucky, and West Virginia; Monongahela in Pennsylvania, Maryland, and West Virginia; and Owasco and Iroquoian in Ontario, New York, and Pennsylvania. Much time has been spent on refining cultural classifications based on artifacts, architecture, and community layouts. Yet these distinctions, real though they may be, should not obscure the fact that life was not all that much different for sedentary villagers across the northern Eastern Woodlands. They relied heavily on maize, lived in permanent villages, and their settlements were clumped together. People were often fearful of their enemies, and the situation generally worsened in the fifteenth century as climatic conditions deteriorated, culminating in the Little Ice Age.

Archaeologists believe that the societies at this time were tribes, rather than chiefdoms. In these societies constellations of villages were loosely held together by shared interests and social institutions that fostered cooperation among the members of separate settlements. Permanent hereditary leadership positions were lacking, and decisions affecting the community were made through consensus. While some people had a disproportionate say in community affairs, including senior members of lineages or especially capable or charismatic individuals, their influence tended to be limited to specific contexts where they had earned the respect of their fellow villagers.

There were, however, exceptions to this pattern. A few chiefdoms with hereditary leaders developed no later than the early sixteenth century in the mid-Atlantic states, and they lasted to the early seventeenth century.[1] They include the Powhatan of southeastern Virginia that came to ruin soon after Jamestown's founding in AD 1607. In terms of artifacts and architecture, these chiefdoms had roots extending deep into the earlier societies of the mid-Atlantic region, not to the Mississippian chiefdoms to the south. Much like elsewhere, the origin of these chiefdoms was accompanied by greater tensions among groups of people. In this instance, hostilities at least partly

118 In 1938, a hunter traipsing over Tussey Mountain in central Pennsylvania found this pottery jar tucked in a small cavity formed by a rock slide. It was put there hundreds of years earlier, the opening then sealed with several additional rocks. Height 10.4 in (26.4 cm).

resulted from competition that ultimately stemmed from population movement as climatic conditions worsened.

While a distinction is drawn here between the northern constellations of tribal villages and the southern chiefdoms, there was considerable overlap between them in terms of the size of communities and the demands of everyday life on self-sufficient households. Cultural connections are particularly apparent between the midwestern societies, especially the Oneota and Fort Ancient groups and their Mississippian neighbors to the south. Objects were occasionally exchanged, ending up in contexts far removed from their points of origin. More importantly, there was a communication of ideas and, at some level, shared beliefs. For example, pots and mussel shell spoons indicative of food offerings were buried with people in northern Illinois, a practice shared with their Mississippian contemporaries in the southern part of the state.[2]

### Burial in mounds

Compared to what took place among the southern chiefdoms, the northern villagers put little effort into building mounds. They include the effigy mounds in the upper Midwest, some of which might date as late as AD 1200. These mounds, which are generally poorly dated, were discussed in Chapter 5 (p.106 ff.) so they require no further attention. Mounds were present in other places, mostly in the Midwest, although they tended to be widely scattered and were usually rather small piles of earth.[3] They included several low mounds of the Grand River group in central Wisconsin where excavators found only a few burials and even fewer grave offerings, most notably pottery. There was likewise only a modest array of burial artifacts, mostly pottery, personal ornaments, and tools, at the Gentleman Farm mound in northeastern Illinois. This site is notable because it is the best-known mound in northern Illinois with extensive ash deposits that came from graveside ceremonies. Here is evidence for continuity in beliefs between prehistoric and more recent times because some historic-period groups in the upper Midwest also lit fires near graves. Overall, there is a lack of any clear ranking of people in these mounds, as well as in the other burial grounds scattered across the northern Eastern Woodlands.

One Oneota mound dating to this period, Norris Farms no. 36 in west-central Illinois (see box p. 180), deserves special attention because it is particularly well documented – it was excavated by Alan Harn in the mid-1980s to make way for a road.[4] A little over 2 ft (0.7 m) of dirt was piled up on a steep bluff that commanded an excellent view of the Illinois River flood-plain; the mound was so low and spread out that the natural contours of the narrow and steeply sloping ridge crest were barely changed. For a few decades around AD 1300, graves were dug in and around the mound. The oval cemetery grew as new graves were added to its edge, mostly on the side that overlooked the valley.

The burials at Norris Farms were accompanied by a rather modest group of artifacts, mostly personal ornaments, everyday tools, and pottery. The kinds and numbers of artifacts varied from one grave to the next, and some of them occurred more often with certain age and sex groups. Yet nobody really stood out from the rest of the group. Personal characteristics or family circumstances must have had a strong influence on what was placed in a grave. But so too did ritual concerns, as shown by a child buried with an adult's severed hands. As mentioned previously, hands were also depicted on Mississippian artifacts used for ceremonial purposes, once again indicating similarities in the beliefs of widely distributed people. Infant mortality was high, and just over half these people died before reaching maturity. As the Iroquois saying goes, "an infant's life is as the thinness of a maple leaf."[5] About two-fifths of the men and women at Norris Farms who made it to adulthood lived beyond the age of 45 years, so the skeletons are consistent with the deaths expected to occur in a preindustrial society. The overall picture is one of a cemetery for all group members with little or no differentiation among them except by age and sex.

Other mounds built at this time include a few in Virginia, one of which was explored by Thomas Jefferson.[6] His mound was about 40 ft wide and 7.5 ft high (12.2 by 2.3 m), and contained many jumbled bones. They had been moved from their initial place of burial, as indicated by the disordered arrangement of bones and the use of skulls as handy containers for small bones. Deposits of bones were encountered at different levels, so the mound was not built all at once. But without modern dating methods, Jefferson had no way of knowing when or for how long the mound was used. The bones

## Death at Norris Farms no. 36

The Norris Farms no. 36 cemetery provides us with a good picture of warfare in late prehistoric times.[7] Many of the 260-plus people buried in this completely excavated mound were killed by their enemies. They included one-third of all men and women (people over the age of 15 years), as well as a few children. People were shot with arrows and smacked with clubs, including stone celts usually used for chopping wood, and many of the bodies were scalped or decapitated, some also dismembered. Scavenging animals then fed on the exposed corpses. Eventually whatever survived – intact bodies, partially decayed pieces of them, or disarticulated and scattered bones – were discovered and returned to the cemetery for proper burial.

No more than a few victims were put in a single grave, and these burial pits were scattered across the cemetery. When several individuals were placed in one grave their skeletons were often in

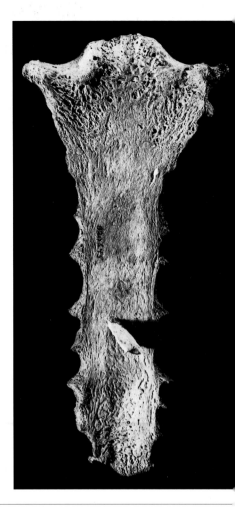

119 Arrows that had passed through this man's body were embedded in the back of his sternum. Only the tip of the upper arrowhead remains (right side, one-third of the way down); the lower one sticks out of the bone. Such wounds were certainly lethal.

belonged to both adults and children, although Jefferson felt there were too few of the latter, presumably in light of the high childhood mortality of his day. He quite reasonably concluded that the deficiency in children was at least partly a result of poor preservation.

More mounds have been discovered in the Piedmont and mountainous parts of Virginia since Jefferson's time, but there were never very many of them.[8] As far as we know, all were used for mortuary purposes. More bone deposits containing people of all ages and both sexes have also been found, as have single burials. Unlike Jefferson, we now know that the piles of bones were part of a broader pattern of ossuary burial in late prehistoric and early historic societies distributed from the mid–Atlantic states into New England and across the Great Lakes area.[9] Relatively few ossuaries, however, were

120 Many of the people who were killed and buried in the Norris Farms cemetery were scalped. Incisions are usually most numerous on the frontal bone, apparently the first part of the scalp that was cut and lifted up.

the same state of disarticulation, indicating that similar amounts of time had passed between death and burial. Thus it appears that small groups of people were sometimes attacked and died together. These victims tended not to be the healthiest members of the community, diminishing their chances of fleeing or protecting themselves. They suffered from debilitating conditions, including diseases that affected bone, unhealed fractures, or permanently dislocated joints.

Considering the extent of carnivore damage and disarticulation in some skeletons, it is likely that many people were killed in rarely frequented spots, probably while foraging for food. Others were attacked closer to home,

judging from the presence of complete skeletons without signs of carnivore damage. A few survivors – they were scalped, beaten, or shot with arrows – show that villagers occasionally managed to struggle home before succumbing to blood loss and exposure. Several of these maimed people lived for many months, or even years, after their ordeals.

The number of victims was certainly higher than the skeletal evidence would indicate because fatal injuries do not always result in recognizable damage to bone. The loss of life was truly appalling, and nobody was spared the disruptions in family life that sudden death inevitably brought.

enclosed in mounds, so Jefferson had the good fortune to find a rather unusual site.

Low embankments, sometimes accompanied by ditches, were occasionally built throughout the Great Lakes region.[10] Inevitably archaeologists disagree over whether these earthworks were used for defensive or ceremonial purposes. There is no reason, of course, why all enclosures had to serve the same purpose. After all, they were built over several centuries by culturally different groups of people. Many of the embankments were probably intended for ceremonial events, if we follow the same reasoning used on the much more numerous Middle Woodland enclosures. Normal habitation debris is often mostly absent, such as at the Mikado site in northeastern Michigan. Here the builders of the earthen embankment incorporated a number of openings that greatly reduced its effectiveness as a defensive barrier. Several openings were also present in other earthen rings. They included those at Rifle River, also in northeastern Michigan, where everyday debris is sparse. Yet other embankments and ditches were certainly defensive structures, especially if they surrounded compact residential areas loaded with refuse. Settlements protected by palisades, as indicated by rows of postmolds, were common in these troubled times.

## The shift to crops

About a millennium ago in the northern Eastern Woodlands maize was added to diets that were otherwise based largely on wild plants and animals.[11] This transition occurred, on average, several centuries later than it did across much of the southern Midwest and Southeast. Once again, a change in diets can be picked up from charred plant remains carefully sifted from village refuse and the stable carbon isotope composition of human bones. Beans were only later added to diets, becoming common somewhere around AD 1300. Not long thereafter these two plants along with squash, which had a long history in the Northeast, became the mainstays of the diets of many people – they were the "three sisters" of the Iroquois. These plants were grown together, and a number of low corn hills or ridged fields have been found, especially in Michigan and Wisconsin. A seventeenth-century description of farming practices in New England gives us a general impression of their appearance: "The Indians ... at every Corn-hill, plant with the Corn, a kind of French or Turkey-Beans: The Stalks of the Corn serving instead of Poles for the Beans to climb up with. And in the vacant places between the Hills they will Plant Squashes and Pompions; loading the Ground with as much as it will bear."[12]

121    The cultivation of crops was accompanied by fishing, hunting large and small mammals and birds, and gathering wild plants, especially nuts. People in coastal areas were especially fortunate because they could easily catch fish, including those that swam up rivers in great numbers to spawn. One example of how these resources influenced settlement choice is the distribution of early seventeenth-century sites in Virginia's Tidewater, such as those belonging to the Powhatan. The sites tended to be situated near the best

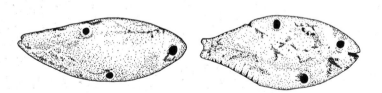

121  Fish lures, such as these two from Norris Farms, were used in the upper Midwest. The lures are from 2.9 to 3.1 in long (7.4 to 7.9 cm).

places for aquatic foods.[13] Once again, river or wetland resources had as much, if not more, influence on choices about where to live as the requirements for growing crops.

Like all other people in the Eastern Woodlands, these sedentary villagers hunted various kinds of game. Patchworks of active and abandoned fields along with swaths of secondary growth around permanent villages were ideal habitats for deer. But even their numbers would have been greatly reduced by relentless predation, forcing men to take part in long hunting trips.

## Village life

As soon as archaeologists started digging large parts of sites they recognized signs of "a fairly settled life," as occupations of Pennsylvania's Monongahela villages were described back in the 1930s.[14] Excavations of settlements commonly uncover the remains of houses, pits, hearths, and postmolds. Storage pits would have resembled those of seventeenth-century New England: "The Natives commonly Thresh it [maize] as they gather it, dry it well on Mats in the Sun, and then bestow it in holes in the Ground (which are their Barns) well lined with withered Grass and Matts, and then covered with the like, and over all with earth."[15] The walls of the houses, regardless of their size or shape, typically consisted of rows of poles covered by thatch or bark. Often the circular to rectangular houses were so small that only single families, which consisted of parents, children, and perhaps a few relatives, could have packed into them. There were also examples of an unprecedented and distinctive kind of residential structure: the multi-family longhouse. 122

122 Longhouses looked like this reconstruction at the Lawson site in Ontario, except here the walls are a bit too high and the roof not sufficiently curved.

Longhouses roughly similar to the ones used by the seventeenth-century Iroquois and Huron had a several-hundred-year history in Ontario and New York.[16] Related families, each with its own space, belongings, and hearth, occupied the historic-period longhouses. Many prehistoric buildings likewise have hearths running right down their middle, so several families must have lived in them as well. The poles supporting walls could not have lasted more than several years before they rotted, so it is not surprising that archaeologists often find superimposed rows of postmolds where walls were repaired or replaced. Houses were often lengthened or shortened when such work was undertaken to accommodate changes in the number of families that occupied them.

When much of a settlement is excavated, it is not unusual to find at least one longhouse that was much bigger than the others. Such buildings were presumably for village leaders.[17] In the historic period, these structures were both residences and places where important social functions took place. But they were otherwise similar to the rest of the buildings. The amount of storage space relative to the number of occupants shows that important families were no better off than their neighbors. Thus a disproportionate say in village affairs – to the extent it actually occurred – did not translate into greater access to essential goods, at least not nearly enough to improve the well-being of even the most influential households.

Longhouses were also built in some of the Oneota villages in Iowa, Illinois, and Wisconsin, although the artifacts, especially the pottery, at these sites were stylistically quite different from the items found in Iroquoian villages.[18] The presence of longhouses, therefore, does not mean that there were particularly close connections among all of the people who used them. In fact, their probable descendants spoke completely different languages. But it does seem that roughly similar social and economic demands favored living arrangements that underscored close ties among village members.

Many villages had houses and other features arranged in a circle or oval around open spaces.[19] Compact residential areas coupled with centrally located public spaces promoted a sense of community, facilitated cooperation among households in the essential chores of everyday life, and provided an additional margin of safety from marauding enemies. In the Ohio Valley, small mounds were even associated with a few Fort Ancient villages. Little is known about them, although they contained burials and other features. Elsewhere the houses were jumbled together, particularly in the Iroquoian area where longhouses were often crowded into areas encircled by palisades. Contemporaneous villages were about the same size within any particular region. So the great disparity in site size, composition, and configuration that was so typical of the southern chiefdoms was lacking.

Compact villages have naturally received the most archaeological attention – they are the easiest to identify – but these settlements were not the only ones that existed. Some of them were made up of no more than a few houses. Of course, there were also scattered short-term camps

123  Villages occupied by the immediate predecessors of the historic-period Iroquois and Huron in New York and Ontario were often surrounded by palisades, such as this reconstruction of a wall at the Lawson site in Ontario.

used by small groups of people for special purposes, such as hunting and fishing.

As social relations in many places worsened in the several centuries following AD 1000, people found it increasingly necessary to live behind walls.[20] Palisades give the appearance of having been thrown up as needed without much planning – they were no bigger than necessary to surround most, and typically all, houses. The wooden palisades were sometimes accompanied by low embankments and shallow depressions. For the most part the ridges seem to have been no more than attempts to pile up just enough soil to help keep the wall posts upright. These embankments did not greatly strengthen the defensive barrier in the way they did at many of the large mound centers in the southern Midwest and Southeast, and the adjacent low spots were soon filled with village refuse.

Most of the palisades can be best visualized as screens that kept enemies from slipping into villages unobserved – they were not stout enough to withstand the attack of a large party of determined warriors. Walls were stronger

123

124 This pipe depicting a human head is from the Otstungo site in New York. The face is 2.8 in (7 cm) high.

in Ontario and New York where serious fighting apparently broke out fairly frequently, especially as time wore on. Here substantial walls are indicated by multiple rows or thick bands of postmolds. But even these palisades lacked the strength and regularity of most Mississippian walls. The height of one of these palisades – it was at the Kelso site in central New York – could be estimated from angled soil stains for poles that had once crossed one another.[21] The poles would have intersected each other at 12 ft (3.7 m), and their free ends must have stuck up a bit higher, making the wall hard to climb over. The protection that palisades provided was often enhanced by putting villages on easily defended hilltops and running walls along steep slopes, particularly in the hilly Northeast.

It is commonly thought that Iroquois villages were occupied for no more than a single generation, often much less, and this also appears to be true of settlements elsewhere.[22] No matter how good a particular spot was, the large game near villages was soon depleted, treks to gather firewood lengthened, and piles of smelly garbage accumulated. At some point the effort of every-day life outweighed resistance to moving elsewhere, building new houses, and clearing more land for fields. People were forever repairing and replacing houses, as well as preparing additional fields, so this work could just as easily be done at a new location.

The inhabitants of permanent villages typically numbered no more than a few hundred people, and often much less.[23] In a study of ossuary skeletons, Douglas Ubelaker found that his estimate of average community size, just over 200 people, was consistent with John Smith's early seventeenth-century eyewitness counts of warriors in villages around the lower Potomac River. Villages from the Great Lakes and middle Ohio Valley into the

Northeast and mid-Atlantic states began to get bigger between the late thirteenth and fifteenth centuries. Some of the late settlements were occupied by up to a thousand or more people – as big as all but the very largest Mississippian mound centers to the south. Increases in village size took place at about the same time as relations among people deteriorated, as shown by more palisades. People were unlikely to come together to form large settlements unless there was a compelling reason to do so. More villagers meant a greater use of local game and firewood, as well as fewer alternative foods when harvests failed. Still, the inconveniences of life in a big village were no match for worries over safety, and villages grew accordingly.

## Clusters of settlements

People were concentrated in rich natural settings, and long expanses of unoccupied land separated clusters of closely affiliated villages.[24] Population concentrations throughout the northern Eastern Woodlands and out onto the Plains to the west did not remain fixed over time. Local movement would have been prompted by problems stemming from a prolonged use of areas near settlements. But people also migrated over long distances, often pushed onward by the attacks of determined enemies.

Communities that found themselves on the leading edges of population expansions sometimes suffered terribly. This is what happened to villagers at Norris Farms who were part of a southward Oneota push into Illinois around AD 1300. At least one-third of the adults were killed by their enemies. In situations where the loss of life was this great, the capacity to produce sufficient food was surely compromised, jeopardizing the lives of surviving household members. As the search for widely scattered resources became increasingly hazardous, people would have been tempted to risk curtailing their foraging trips on the thin hope that whatever was missed would not be needed later in the year. If the fear of enemy warriors also prompted the formation of work parties that were larger than absolutely necessary, the efficiency of food production surely dropped, as did the yield. 119, 120

Any reduction in the return of food was a serious matter. Theirs was a precarious existence and concerted attacks, especially when combined with a bad year, could push people over the edge into outright starvation. That happened to the mid-seventeenth-century Huron when they were forced from their homes by their enemies, the Iroquois. Many of the refugees – "dying skeletons eking out a miserable life, feeding even on the excrements and refuse of nature" – died from hunger and attendant disease over a long, hard winter.[25]

The jostling of populations, which had always taken place, took on a new urgency as early as the fourteenth century when climatic conditions deteriorated.[26] The worst effects were felt where the cultivation of maize was already pushed to its northern limits. Any movement spurred on by hard times had a domino-like effect as groups successively bumped into one

125 In the late sixteenth century, Englishmen visited the village of Pomeiooc in coastal North Carolina. This drawing shows a palisade, ring of buildings, and inner common ground. The general layout of the village is similar to those erected over a several-hundred-year period in the mid-Atlantic region.

125    another. Conflicts spread accordingly, as shown by palisaded villages whose numbers increased while their distribution broadened.

It took until the fifteenth century before walls around settlements became common in the mid-Atlantic Piedmont and Coastal Plain. New forms of pottery along the Potomac River have been interpreted as a downstream movement of people. By the time Englishmen arrived at Jamestown in AD

1607, the Powhatan and their allies of Tidewater Virginia were not only fighting their enemies beyond the Fall Line to the west, but were also busy holding off more northerly people, possibly Iroquoian speakers.

In these troubled times, distinct groups of people must have found it advantageous to forge alliances to defend themselves. Such political arrangements leave little tangible evidence of their existence, so are difficult to detect from archaeological materials alone. Of the historic-period alliances, the best known was the long-lasting but loosely knit League of the Iroquois.[27] It seems to have reached its Five Nations form by AD 1600 – before Europeans settled permanently in the Northeast – although close ties among some of its member groups date a century or more earlier. Its formation was a lengthy process, not a single event. One principal reason for the League's formation was to quell fighting among related groups distributed across upstate New York. It also put them in a good position, numerically speaking, for the turbulent times that accompanied the establishment of European colonies early in the seventeenth century.

# 8 · A Trail of Tears: Native American and European Contact

Demonstrating continuity across the prehistoric to historic divide is not easily done in most places. Shocking population losses in the historic period were coupled with movement and dramatic cultural change. Some groups disappeared without a trace. Others sought out new places to live, sometimes far from their original homes, or joined formerly distinct groups of people. Only where contact between Native Americans and Europeans was early and continuous is it a simple matter to move from long prehistoric sequences to historically known tribes. For the most part these areas are located along the Atlantic and Gulf coasts that were inhabited by people such as the Powhatan in Virginia and the Calusa in Florida. There are fewer examples of seamless connections in the continental interior, although they include the well-known Iroquois and their bitter enemies the Huron.

## The last mounds

As we have seen, only after the original inhabitants were all but gone – that is, by the early nineteenth century – did there develop a widespread interest in the antiquities of the Eastern Woodlands. Mounds, being hard to miss, naturally attracted the most attention. But it was all too easy to believe that the ancestors of decimated groups had nothing to do with them. The few examples of mound use in accounts left by early European travelers made little impression on popular opinion.

Members of the de Soto expedition had actually seen mounds used as platforms for structures. They even put up a large cross on a mound – it was probably the large one at Parkin in northeastern Arkansas – at the request of the chief to break a drought.[1] Good fortune intervened, and it rained. The reputation of the Spaniards was thereby boosted at a point when they sorely needed help.

Up to the early eighteenth century, the Natchez of southwestern Mississippi continued to bury chiefs and other important people in mounds. That was when Antoine Simon le Page du Pratz saw what took place upon the death of the chief's brother, who also happened to be his friend.[2] The body was carried on a litter to a charnel house on a mound, and several people – among them wives, close advisors, and a child – were strangled.

126

127

126 The large mound at Parkin in Arkansas is quite likely to have been where de Soto erected a wooden cross during his stay in the Mississippi Valley.

*Mort et Convoi du Serpent piqué*

*Temple*.

127 An early eighteenth-century burial of an important man among the Natchez is shown in this drawing. People were killed as the funeral procession made its way to the charnel structure, which sat on a mound.

This building's wattle-and-daub walls were said to have been about 10 ft (3 m) high, and the posts were cut from cypress trees, a wood resistant to rot. Perched on its roof were three large wooden birds, all facing east. The entire episode – burial in a charnel structure on a mound and human sacrifices – has an unmistakably Mississippian flavor. But the days of this society were numbered, like so many others across the Eastern Woodlands.

There is also evidence for the late use of mounds in the form of European artifacts.[3] In the Southeast, most of these objects date to the sixteenth century, and they include items that were given away or lost by the de Soto and other Spanish expeditions. At the early sixteenth-century Tatham mound in central Florida, there are even two skeletons from people whose arms had been chopped off by swords or axes wielded by the practiced hands of Spanish soldiers. European objects, including silver ornaments and copper kettles – they were a century or more younger and often of French origin – have also been found in mounds in the upper Midwest. These discoveries were made long ago, so it is unclear whether the individuals with these foreign items were among the people who built the mounds. But there can be no doubt that graves were dug into existing mounds. They include an early nineteenth-century grave house consisting of crossed sticks – in the upper Midwest, small structures over individual graves had a long history – built on the back of a turtle mound in Waukesha, Wisconsin. By choosing such a location, a connection was made to a symbolically significant spot, in this instance an effigy mound that was already several centuries old.

## Depopulation and removal

Catastrophic population decline is the root cause of the many problems Native Americans experienced during the contact period. Losses were so great that European settlers could reasonably view the Eastern Woodlands as a hardly used, even pristine, wilderness. The great reduction in native numbers was taken as a sure sign that a bountiful land was being providentially opened to the burgeoning European populations at home and in the new colonies.

The major culprits for the horrific losses were several newly introduced diseases, among them smallpox and measles. Wars and mistreatment certainly claimed their share of lives, but diseases and their aftermath caused the greatest declines in Native American numbers. Late sixteenth-century Englishmen at Roanoke, the now-famous Lost Colony on a North Carolina barrier island, found it remarkable that "within a few dayes after our departure from euerie such towne, the people began to die very fast, and many in short space; in some townes about twentie, in some fourtie, in some sixtie, & in one six score."[4] For the Native Americans, the disease was "so strange, that they neither knew what it was, nor how to cure it; the like by report of the oldest men in the countrey neuer happened before." Nobody knew what caused infectious diseases, although the outcome was obvious to all.

The Roanoke experience was to be repeated on innumerable occasions in later years with the same devastating effect.

We have a fairly good idea of what happened when the epidemics hit from descriptions of disease outbreaks in the Americas and the Pacific Islands, including those that occurred relatively recently in isolated populations. When many members of a community fall ill in short succession, only a few of them are able to provide even rudimentary care for the sick, such as keeping them adequately supplied with fluids. Yet these diseases – while terrible enough – were just the beginning of the problems faced by the people of eastern North America. In addition to coping with the emotional distress of losing family members and friends, people had to reconstruct viable households and other social institutions to carry on with the tasks necessary for survival. And it had to be done quickly. Failure to complete essential chores such as planting or harvesting during the height of an epidemic would come back to haunt the survivors during lean times of the year.

While all people were proficient in the basics of everyday life, enabling them to reconstruct functional households and communities, that was not true of their grasp of oral traditions. Origin myths, rituals, and the like can have long and resilient histories, but they are vulnerable to the sudden and unexpected deaths of the relatively few individuals who possess intimate knowledge of them. So much cultural knowledge was also lost.

Diseases transmitted from one person to the next, such as the great killers measles and smallpox, spread erratically from their points of introduction, with the overall history of any particular disease outbreak dictated by innumerable chance events. For the pathogens to hop from one group to another, people had to come into contact with one another at precisely the right time. Thus during any single epidemic some groups suffered horribly whereas others were spared. Hard-hit communities had to merge to survive – at least that is what happened later on when we have adequate written accounts of the desperate plight of refugees.

Weakened and dispirited groups were irresistible targets for their traditional enemies – and there was no shortage of them judging from the conflicts that dated back many centuries. Temporary imbalances in the capacity to mobilize warriors must have been a common occurrence. The situation was made that much worse by groups becoming engulfed in wars promoted by European powers intent on expanding their political and economic spheres of influence.

Frightful loss of life from the new diseases reduced all groups but, while some societies hung on, others disappeared altogether.[5] The strong chiefdoms distributed across the Southeast proved to be particularly vulnerable. They were hit early and hard, especially those along the Mississippi River. In the 1500s these southeastern groups bested several Spanish attempts at conquest, de Soto's ill-fated expedition among them. But most of the large and powerful chiefdoms did not last more than a few generations after de Soto's journey. Only remnants of these societies were in evidence during the

128 Spanish bells, called Clarksdale bells, have been found at contact-period sites, including this one from Little Egypt in Georgia. It could very well have been carried by the de Soto expedition. Diameter 1.1 in (2.8 cm).

late 1600s when explorers once again made their way through the Mississippi Valley. The Coosa chiefdom, which consisted of pockets of people distributed over as much as several hundred kilometers in northwestern Georgia and eastern Tennessee, likewise impressed de Soto's men. But later Spanish expeditions make it clear that this chiefdom was in decline only a few decades after de Soto's men remarked upon its size and strength.

Densely settled chiefdoms, and those like Coosa where formal connections were maintained among geographically separate concentrations of people, facilitated the spread of highly contagious diseases. Sudden, unexplained, and uncontrollable loss of life surely eroded the authority of chiefs, even if they managed to escape death from the disease itself. Moreover, with so many people dying, the normal succession to chiefly office was frequently disrupted. Feeble leaders and ambiguous claims on newly vacated chiefly positions set the stage for disruptive fighting among rival factions.

The Chickasaw in northeastern Mississippi are particularly interesting because by the eighteenth century they had turned into a major force in the region.[6] Their ascendancy was in marked contrast to the situation only two centuries earlier when heavily populated and powerful chiefdoms were located in the nearby Mississippi Valley. Jay Johnson has shown that, prior to de Soto's time, people in the Chickasaw area generally lived in small, widely spaced communities. This dispersed pattern of settlement – and a more atomized society than the tightly knit river-valley chiefdoms – put these upland folk at an advantage when epidemics struck by reducing the likelihood of intercommunity contact and, hence, the transmission of pathogens. They too suffered horrific losses, but fared relatively better than the inhabitants of the Mississippi Valley to the west.

There are additional signs that the spread of epidemic diseases such as smallpox was likely to be interrupted in societies comprising constellations of loosely allied villages.[7] The Mohawk of central New York, one of the Iroquois Nations, and the Powhatan of Virginia's Tidewater survived intact until the early 1600s when the English, French, and Dutch established lasting toeholds on the continent. That is also true of groups in the hills of North Carolina, only they made it to the end of the seventeenth century before suffering crippling losses. These groups lacked the regular communication of chiefdoms such as Coosa where far-flung people were

129  Native Americans were active participants in the great cultural changes that took place following contact with Europeans. They avidly sought out new goods, but drove hard bargains to get the most useful ornaments, tools, and guns. Their settlements contained a mix of traditional and newly introduced objects, as shown in this depiction of an early nineteenth-century Kickapoo house in central Illinois.

united, however tenuously and temporarily, under one political umbrella. Thus the clusters of villages that were only weakly tied together tended to remain relatively unscathed longer than the strong Mississippian chiefdoms.

Culture change was accelerated by the incorporation of native groups into European economies. The fur trade was especially important: in the north, Native Americans sought beaver pelts; in the south, they went after deer hides. Existing rivalries were accentuated as groups competed for positions near sources of guns and other increasingly necessary goods. The disruptive effect of trade – in which Native Americans were active, not    129
passive, participants – produced a more volatile cultural setting than had ever existed before.

Despite grievous losses, Native Americans long remained formidable obstacles to the westward expansion of Euroamerican settlers.[8] They often maintained themselves as viable social and economic units by incorporating new members from weaker groups. The League of the Iroquois, for example, succeeded by dampening internal tensions and facilitating the incorporation of additional people, including defeated enemies. It appears that the largest of the southeastern societies also maintained their numbers over long periods, although their sizes fluctuated over time from disasters offset by influxes of more people. It is noteworthy that the reduction of the overall southeastern population was not accompanied by a corresponding great decline in village sizes, merely fewer of them. Safety in numbers at both the community and group levels was mandatory in these troubled times.

While we can be sure that populations plummeted after AD 1500, the magnitude and timing of this loss are hotly debated. Current population estimates for the United States and Canada at the time of Columbus range from 2 to 18 million, a large number of whom lived in the fertile and well-watered Eastern Woodlands.[9] The low estimate is derived from crude census information taken from various documents, many of which certainly postdate great losses from epidemics. The high figure was obtained by extrapolating from rather speculative population density and resource productivity estimates. It was supported by a figure for the precontact Timucua of Florida that was obtained by ratcheting the population upward in a series of steps corresponding to supposed sixteenth-century pandemics. Thus the devastating epidemics are said to have appeared early, happened frequently, and spread uniformly across vast areas. Other researchers, including the present author, think it is unlikely that such events occurred repeatedly in the Eastern Woodlands during the sixteenth century. The debate is not over whether horrifyingly large numbers of people died when the epidemics hit – they certainly did – but over the likelihood that diseases would have spread widely and frequently from one group to the next. Recent archaeological work shows that groups of people were much more unevenly distributed across even the best land than was recognized when the high estimates were proposed. Communication among many of these geographically discrete populations appears to have been irregular enough that highly contagious diseases such as smallpox and measles must have often burned themselves out before being passed on to neighboring groups. Such epidemics no doubt spread beyond face-to-face contact with sick Europeans, but there is no reason to believe that the Timucua example is an accurate depiction of what happened to sixteenth-century Native Americans.

Fortunately we do not have to rely on any one argument about what should, or should not, have taken place before the widespread and sustained presence of Europeans on the continent. Dean Snow's analysis of the numbers and sizes of Mohawk settlements shows that the population did not decline until the early seventeenth century.[10] The site data are consistent with the appearance of destructive epidemics described by observers in various places. Snow's drop in the overall numbers of people is a century later than when the sharp decline should have taken place if the biggest population estimates based on supposedly huge sixteenth-century losses are anywhere near correct. While the United States and Canada were almost certainly occupied by more than 2 million people in AD 1500, it is difficult to believe there were more than two or three times that number.

In the early nineteenth century, what remained of Native American groups were for the most part pushed out of the eastern states. Some groups hung on tenaciously – they included, among others, the Iroquois in New York, the Cherokee in North Carolina, and the Chippewa and Menominee in Wisconsin – but most of them had either disappeared or moved beyond the Mississippi River, leaving only scattered remnants behind. For Euroamericans, the land occupied by Native Americans was simply too valuable to be left in their hands if any way could be found to force them off it. Various uprisings provided a ready excuse for moving people westward, although such justification was not always needed. With the growing disparity between the numbers of natives and newcomers, the former did not possess the means to protect their homes, nor could they effectively protest the injustice of broken treaties and the resulting loss of land.

Of the forced removals from the eastern states, one of the saddest became known as the Trail of Tears.[11] During the 1830s, the Cherokee were driven from their homes and put in stockades. Some managed to escape to the

130

130 Many people perished during their forced removal from the Southeast to Indian Territory, now the state of Oklahoma. This move has become known as the Trail of Tears.

rugged mountains and their descendants live there to this day. Most of the Cherokee, however, had no such luck. They were forced to march about 750 miles (1,200 km) all the way to Indian Territory – present-day Oklahoma, which only became a state in 1907 – with whatever possessions they could carry. Thousands died along the way from exhaustion and disease.

Only late in the nineteenth century did the plight of Native Americans begin to become a matter of widespread concern. By that time the struggle for a rich land was over. The last remnants of the groups that formerly occupied eastern North America had been shunted to the poorest land where they often suffered terribly from disease and privation. Their prospects for the future appeared bleak. Yet despite horrific population losses and enforced changes in their ways of life, the downward spiral in numbers was finally reversed. Today, Native Americans survive as rightfully proud descendants of long cultural traditions stretching far back to a time when they were the sole inhabitants of the Eastern Woodlands.

# Guide to Eastern Woodlands Sites

The many mounds and village sites incorporated into national, state, county, and city parks are well worth visiting. They bring life to what can otherwise be rather dry academic discussions of ancient times. Often interpretive centers put the sites in their proper cultural context.

This is not a comprehensive list of sites that are open to the public, although the well-known ones are identified. Other mounds are also preserved in odd corners of cities and the surrounding countryside. Many of them are also open to the public, particularly in Ohio, Wisconsin, and Florida. And local historical museums staffed by dedicated volunteers should not be forgotten – their often charming exhibits hold many treasures. Fuller descriptions of these sites along with local directions and hours of operation can usually be found on the internet.

It only takes a little extra planning to tack visits to sites onto cross-country road trips. In fact, there is no better way of seeing the country than exiting the interstates, finding back roads, and winding one's way to some remote spot. The sites and museums listed below are widely scattered, but there are enough in southern Ohio and along the lower part of the Mississippi Valley to plan a trip specifically to see them. And there is much else of historical interest in these areas besides prehistoric mounds.

## Midwest

There is no place better than southern Ohio to look for well-preserved mounds. While driving along monotonous Interstate 70 one should not overlook the opportunity to stop in Columbus and visit the **Ohio Historical Center**, which has outstanding exhibits, especially those on Middle Woodland (or Hopewell) societies. It is a fine place to start your mound tour. Other places to stop along this interstate include the Middle Woodland **Newark Earthworks State Memorial** and the **Flint Ridge State Memorial**, a quarry. They are located an easy drive from one another. Also a short distance off Interstate 70 is the **Sunwatch Indian Village**, a reconstructed Fort Ancient site near Dayton, Ohio, showing what life was like in a late prehistoric village. Just to the east, again not far south of the same interstate, is the **Indian Mound Reserve Park**. Many mounds and earthworks were once located near Chillicothe in Ross County where one can find the **Hopewell Culture National Historical Park** (Mound City) and **Seip Mound**. Rural roads take you through scenic countryside to the **Fort Ancient State Memorial** in Warren County, **Serpent Mound** in Adams County, **Miamisburg Mound** in Montgomery County, **Fort Hill State Memorial** in Highland County, and **Leo Petroglyph** in Jackson County. When in **Marietta**, you must see the Conus in the Mound Cemetery, an interesting graveyard filled with old tombstones. The city's Public Library sits on a mound called the Capitolium, and there is another – the Quadranaou – in a nearby park.

You should not miss seeing **Cahokia Mounds State Historic Site** near East St. Louis, Illinois. This UNESCO World Heritage site is a short drive east of downtown St. Louis, Missouri, just off Interstates 55-70 (the two are joined at that point). A climb to the top of Monks Mound, the biggest mound in the eastern United States, is rewarded with an excellent view of other mounds and the bank along an abandoned river channel where many people once lived. The relatively new interpretive center is one of the best of its kind. Mounds can also be found in **Albany Mounds State Park** in Albany, **Gramercy Park** in East Dubuque, **Beattie Mound Group** in Rockford, and **Indian Mounds Park** in Quincy. House basins and petroglyphs can be seen at **Millstone Bluff**, a Mississippian site in the beautiful Shawnee Hills. It is in the Shawnee National Forest in Pope County off State Route 147, east of Vienna. Petroglyphs can also be found in the **Piney Creek Ravine Nature Preserve** in Randolph County, a short drive from Chester. Exhibits on prehistoric and historic period life can be found at the **Field Museum of Natural History** in Chicago, the **Illinois State Museum** in Springfield, and the **Dickson Mounds Museum** in Lewistown.

In Indiana, one can see the **Angel Mounds State Historic Site**, a major Mississippian site in Evansville. The feature attraction of the **Mounds State Park** in Anderson is the Great Mound, one of the Adena small circular earthworks.

In southeastern Iowa, Middle Woodland mounds can be seen in **Tootlesboro State Park**. Later mounds are located within the **Effigy Mounds National Monument** in the northeastern part of the state.

The **Sanilac Petroglyphs** can be visited near Cass City in the east-central part of the Lower Peninsula of Michigan.

In Minnesota, the **Grand Mound State Historic Site** is located near the Canadian border. At the opposite end of the state is the **Jeffers Petroglyphs State Historic Site**. Several mounds overlooking the Mississippi River are in St. Paul's **Indian Mounds Park**.

Within an easy drive of St. Louis in Missouri you can visit the Archaic-period **Graham Cave Historic Site**, the **Mastodon State Historic Site** (the Paleoindian Kimmswick site), and late prehistoric petroglyphs at the **Washington State Park**. Cahokia is located just across the Mississippi River in Illinois. Farther south in Missouri's Bootheel, the **Towosahgy**

131

131 Mounds often became sources of civic pride, such as the ones shown in this picture from a century-old postcard from St. Paul, Minnesota.

**State Historic Site** gives visitors a good feel for the mound and plaza layout of major Mississippian settlements. It has been recently opened to the public, and this quiet spot is accessible by gravel road. Also in that part of the Bootheel is the largest mound of a Mississippian site known as **Lilbourn**. It is only a short distance from Interstate 55 in a cemetery near a town of the same name. Signs of nineteenth-century digging are clearly visible in this mound.

In southeastern Wisconsin there is **Aztalan State Park**, a Mississippian site with mounds that sits on the bank of the Crawfish River. Mounds can also be seen in many other places, such as on the grounds of **Beloit College** and the **University of Wisconsin**, as well as in the **Wyalusing State Park** near Prairie du Chien, **Perrot State Park** near Trempealeau, the **Lizard Mounds County Park** near West Bend, the **Indian Mounds and Trail Park** near Fort Atkinson, the **Man Mound County Park** near Baraboo, and the **Indian Mound Park** in Sheboygan. There are petroglyphs at the **Roche-A-Cri State Park**, a short drive south of Wisconsin Rapids.

## Southeast

The **Moundville Archaeological Park** near Tuscaloosa, Alabama, encompasses one of the largest Mississippian sites. Here mounds surround a huge plaza, and it is one of the best sites for getting an impression of the layout of a late prehistoric town. There is also a mound in **Florence**. An impressive rockshelter can be seen at the **Russell Cave National Monument**. **Shell Mound Park** is located on Dauphine Island at the mouth of Mobile Bay.

Just west of the Mississippi River in Arkansas one can see the **Parkin Archeological State Park**, an area probably visited by the battered remnants of de Soto's expedition in the mid-sixteenth century. The **Toltec Mounds Archeological State Park** – a site occupied in the late first millennium AD – is only a short drive from Little Rock, and is a delightful spot with trails that lead you past many mounds.

When in Tallahassee, Florida, you can see the **Lake Jackson Mounds State Archaeological Site**, a major Mississippian site. The **Mission San Luis de Apalachee**, also in the city, provides a good feel for life in seventeenth-century Spanish Florida. Mounds can also be seen at **Indian Temple Mound Museum and Park** in Fort Walton, **Fort George Island Cultural State Park** near Jacksonville, **Crystal River State Archaeological Park** near Tampa, **Philippe Park** in Safety Harbor, **Mound Key State Archaeological Site** near Fort Myers, **Randall Research Center** in Pineland, **Hontoon Island State Park** near Deland, and **Canaveral National Seashore** near New Smyrna. In Gainesville, there are excellent exhibits in the **Florida Museum of Natural History** at the University of Florida.

Several major sites are open to the public in Georgia. The **Etowah Indian Mounds State Historic Site** is a short drive from Atlanta. William Tecumseh Sherman's visit to the mounds as a young man gave him a feel for the lay of the land that he put to good use during his march on Atlanta in the Civil War. In addition, the **Ocmulgee National Monument** is in Macon, and the **Kolomoki Mounds State Historic Park** is near Blakely. Ocmulgee in particular is quite large, and provides visitors with lengthy hikes among the mounds. A rock mound in the shape of a bird, the **Rock Eagle Mound**, is located in the Rock Eagle 4-H Center near Eatonton; a rock wall stands in the **Fort Mountain State Park**; and there are petroglyphs at **Track Rock Gap** in the Chattahoochee National Forest.

Mississippian mounds can be seen at the **Wickliffe Mounds Research Center Archaeological Site** in western Kentucky. Recent first-rate work has greatly improved our understanding of this site – it has a colorful history as a tourist trap known as the "Ancient Buried City." Low stone walls are visible at **Indian Fort Mountain** near Berea, as are mounds in Ashland's **Central Park**.

In northeastern Louisiana it is possible to visit the Late Archaic **Poverty Point State Historic Site**. A Middle Woodland earthwork and mounds are preserved in the **Marksville State Historic Site** in a town of the same name.

In Natchez, Mississippi, one can see the **Grand Village of the Natchez Indians**. This settlement was described by Frenchmen who visited it 300 years ago. Several groups of mounds, including the Middle Woodland **Bynum Mounds** and Mississippian **Emerald Mound**, are located along the **Natchez Trace Parkway**, a pleasant road that takes you diagonally across the state. Just outside Greenville there is a Mississippian site, the **Winterville Mounds State Park**. In the east-central part of the state there is a large mound at the **Nanih Waiya State Historical Site**.

A reconstructed palisade and a few buildings at the **Town Creek Indian Mound** near Mt. Gilead in North Carolina give visitors an idea of life in this late prehistoric settlement.

The **Spiro Mounds Archaeological Park** – complete with reconstructed Craig Mound – is located on the eastern edge of Oklahoma. The site is not far off Interstate 40. In Okmulgee there is the **Creek Council House**, an attractive sandstone building dating to 1878, with small but fine exhibits.

A mound can be seen in the **Santee National Wildlife Refuge** near Santee, South Carolina, and a trail in the **Edisto Beach State Park** will take you to shell mounds.

In Tennessee, you can visit the **Pinson Mounds State Archaeological Park**, a Middle Woodland site only a short drive south of Jackson; hiking trails wind past mounds, an embankment, and through a wetland. Stone walls are on view at the **Old Stone Fort Archaeological Site** outside Manchester, and Mississippian mounds are located within the **Shiloh National Military Park** (the scene of a particularly bloody Civil War battle). You can see a partially reconstructed Mississippian settlement at the **Chucalissa Archaeological Museum** in Memphis. The **Frank H. McClung Museum** is located in Knoxville at the University of Tennessee.

## Northeast and mid-Atlantic

Museum-goers will get much out of visits to the outstanding **American Museum of Natural History** in New York and the **National Museum of Natural History** (Smithsonian Institution) on the mall in Washington, DC. In addition, the **State Museum of Pennsylvania** in Harrisburg has fine displays of life in prehistoric times, as does the **New York State Museum** in Albany. A reconstruction of an Iroquois longhouse can be seen at the **Ganondagan State Historic Site** near Rochester, New York.

The **Grave Creek Mound Historic Site** in Moundsville, West Virginia, is impressive and there is a fine view of the city, including the old state penitentiary, from the top. It is one of the tallest mounds in the Eastern Woodlands, and has long been a local attraction. In South Charleston, the **Criel** mound is located in a small park in the middle of town.

## Canada

The excellent **Canadian Museum of Civilization** is located in Hull, Quebec. In Ontario there is the **Serpent Mounds Park** and **Petroglyphs Provincial Park** near Peterborough, **Southwold Earthworks National Historic Site** near St. Thomas, and **Manitou Mounds National Historic Site** near Stratton. You can also see what life was like in an Iroquoian village by visiting the **Lawson Prehistoric Indian Village** at the London Museum of Archaeology, **Ska-Nah-Doht** near London, and the **Crawford Lake Conservation Area**, a short drive southwest of Toronto.

# Notes to the Text

Abbreviations

| | |
|---|---|
| GLO | General Land Office |
| ISA | Illinois State Archives |
| ISM | Illinois State Museum |
| NAA | National Anthropological Archives, Smithsonian Institution |
| NMNH | National Museum of Natural History, Smithsonian Institution |
| UMMA | University of Michigan Museum of Anthropology |
| WPA | Works Progress Administration |
| WSWMA | William S. Webb Museum of Anthropology, University of Kentucky |

**Preface** (pp. 7–10)
1 Foster 1873: 311, 349.
2 Fowke 1902: 3.
3 GLO, vol. 12, p. 76, ISA.
4 Brackenridge 1811: 3.
5 Moulton 1986: 77.

**Chapter 1** (pp. 11–21)
1 Krech 1999: 101–22.
2 Tanner 1987: 20–21.
3 Styles 1994: 48; white-tailed deer (*Odocoileus virginianus*).
4 Limp and Reidhead 1979: 72.
5 Goosefoot (*Chenopodium berlandieri* and other species).
6 Jefferson 1954 [1787]: 97–102; Bartram in Waselkov and Holland 1995: 211.
7 Brackenridge 1818: 154, 158.
8 Fowke 1898: 380.
9 Thomas 1894; Bureau of Ethnology was later changed to Bureau of American Ethnology.
10 Greber and Ruhl 1989: 2–5.
11 Phillips *et al.* 1951.
12 Thomas 1894: 20.
13 Hoffman 1835: 67–68.
14 Anonymous 1869b: 4.
15 Anonymous 1869a: 4.
16 Squier and Davis 1848: 75–76.
17 Putnam 1887: 188; Willoughby 1919: 163.
18 Jefferson 1954 [1787]: 98.
19 Brown 1996: 41–52; Phillips and Brown 1978: 3–5.
20 Committee on Basic Needs in American Archaeology, 22 Jan. 1945: 1–2, Johnson Papers, NAA.
21 WPA Quarterly Report, July–September 1940: 22, WSWMA.

**Chapter 2** (pp. 22–33)
1 Meltzer 1993: 30.
2 Guthrie 2001: 550–60, 566–68.
3 Dillehay 1997; Dillehay and Pino 1997: 48; Meltzer 1997: 754; Meltzer *et al.* 1997: 662.
4 Mandryk *et al.* 2001: 302–08; Mann and Hamilton 1995: 457–65.
5 Anderson 1990: 164, 1996: 30; Anderson *et al.* 1996: 9; Meltzer 1997: 754.
6 Adovasio *et al.* 1990; Clausen *et al.* 1979: 609, 611; Meltzer 1993: 72–75.
7 Severinghaus and Brook 1999: 931; Taylor *et al.* 1997: 826; Yu 2000: 1737–41.
8 Graham 1986: 139–41; Graham and Lundelius 1984: 224–46, 231, 234; Graham *et al.* 1996: 1601–02; Jackson *et al.* 2000: 503; Jacobson *et al.* 1987: 280, 286.
9 Anderson 1990: 170–71, 1996: 31, 34–36, 50; Anderson and Gillam 2000: 59; Morse and Morse 1983: 80.

10 Fairbridge 1992: 15, 17; Goodyear 1999: 468–69; Meltzer 1993: 29; Stright 1990: 439–46.
11 O'Steen 1996; Wiant 1993.
12 Birmingham and Eisenberg 2000: 72; Broster and Norton 1996: 296; Dincauze 1993: 45–47; Freeman *et al.* 1996: 402; Futato 1996: 308–10; Goodyear 1999: 434; Meltzer 1988: 8–10; Tankersley and Morrow 1993: 122–26.
13 Alroy 2001: 1895; Martin 1973; Mosimann and Martin 1975.
14 Griffin 1967: 176; Meltzer 1988: 3–4; Webster 1981.
15 Graham *et al.* 1981: 1115–16.
16 Bentley *et al.* 1993: 273–74; Campbell and Wood 1988: 56.
17 Dunbar and Webb 1996: 333–50; Goodyear 1999: 444–45; Meltzer 1988: 24; Webb *et al.* 1984: 388; Pleistocene bison (*Bison antiquus*).
18 Clausen *et al.* 1979: 609; Graham 1986: 135–37; Meltzer 1988: 6–8, 25, 1993: 122; Meltzer and Smith 1986: 12–13; Storck and Spiess 1994: 134–37.
19 Curran 1999: 8; Meltzer 1988: 26–33, 1989: 11, 33; Shott 1989: 224; Tankersley 1990: 283–84.
20 Meltzer 1988: 26–33; Meltzer and Smith 1986: 13; Morse and Morse 1983: 72–75; Tankersley 1990: 275, 294.
21 McGahey 1996: 378; O'Steen 1996: 104–05; Tankersley 1990: 294.
22 Ahler 1991: 5; Chapman and Adovasio 1977: 620, 624; Daniel 1998: 29–37; Driskell 1996: 322–26; Fowler 1959: 24; Jefferies 1996a: 42–46; Kimball 1996: 177–83; Mitchie 1996: 266; Morey and Wiant 1992: 225; O'Steen 1996: 101; Sassaman 1996: 73–75; Smith 1986: 16–17.
23 Ahler 1991: 6.
24 Meltzer and Smith 1986: 16–17; Smith 1986: 11–13.

**Chapter 3** (pp. 34–53)
1 Webb 1939: 14.
2 Baker *et al.* 1992: 380, 384–6; Dahl-Jensen *et al.* 1998: 270; Delcourt *et al.* 1999: 25–27; Wright 1992: 129.
3 Delcourt *et al.* 1999: 19; Guccione *et al.* 1988: 77–78; Schuldenrein 1996: 8–9, 26; Smith 1986: 22, 25.
4 Blanton 1996: 201; DePratter and Howard 1981: 1292–94; Dunford 1999: 43–46; Fairbridge 1992: 17; Schuldenrein 1996: 7.
5 Bense 1994: 75–76, 86; Cook 1976: 44, 76–77, 79–81; Jefferies 1983: 202–03, 1996a: 55; Jefferies and Lynch 1983: 307–11.
6 Newsom 2002: 203–04; Smith 1986: 28–30, 1989: 1567–68; Watson 1989: 559; squash (*Cucurbita pepo*) and bottle gourd (*Lagenaria siceraria*).
7 Sassaman 1996: 68–69, 71, 1999: 76–77; Webb and DeJarnette 1948: 50–55.
8 Smith 1986: 30; Sassaman 1993: 16–22.
9 Bense 1994: 82, 91; Brown 1985a: 215–16; Brown and Vierra 1983: 185; Dye 1996: 145, 154, 158; Griffin 1967: 178–79; Jefferies 1996a: 57–58, 77; Jefferies and Lynch 1983: 311–14; Marquardt 1985: 72–83; Marquardt and Watson 1983: 330–31; Milner and Jefferies 1998: 120–23; Sassaman and Ledbetter 1996: 76–79; Smith 1986: 24–27; Webb 1950: 357–59; Webb and DeJarnette 1942: 306–19; Webb and Haag 1940.
10 Brown and Vierra 1983: 185–89; Jefferies 1983: 199–200, 202; Jefferies and Lynch 1983: 301–02, 315; Styles and Klippel 1996: 118; Webb and Haag 1940: 68–70.
11 Emerson and McElrath 1983: 228–38; Fortier 1983: 248–51; Higgins 1990: 102–06.
12 Buikstra 1981: 126, 129, 131; Jefferies and Lynch 1983: 319; Mensforth 1990: 89; Milner and Jefferies 1998: 123, 126–29; Powell 1996: 120–24.

13  Moulton 1990: 169; Moulton's word clarification.
14  Ruff 1999: 315–17.
15  Dye 1996: 141; Emerson and McElrath 1983: 230–32; Jefferies 1983: 202–03.
16  Jackson and Scott 2001: 189–90, 193–95.
17  Russo 1996b: 178, 181–96; Smith 1986: 28.
18  Décima and Dincauze 1998: 157–59, 165.
19  Jefferies 1983: 203–04, 1996a: 54, 70.
20  Fritz 1995: 6–8; Smith 1989: 1566, 1995: 12–13; Watson 1989: 562.
21  Smith 1989: 1567–68, 1995: 196; Watson 1989: 563; erect knotweed (*Polygonum erectum*), marsh elder (*Iva annua*), maygrass (*Phalaris caroliniana*), little barley (*Hordeum pusillum*), and sunflower (*Helianthus annuus*).
22  Crites 1993: 147; Fritz 2000: 230–31; Hart and Sidell 1997: 528, 532; Petersen and Sidell 1996: 688, 693; Smith 1989: 1567–69, 1995: 184–201.
23  Bense 1994: 76, 88; Brown 1985a: 218, 223; Jefferies 1995b: 133, 1996a: 61–62, 1996c: 232; Marquardt 1985: 78, 80–81.
24  Gibson 1996: 289–91, 2000: 80–91, 96–105; Kidder 2002: 95–99; Saunders *et al.* 2001: 76; Webb 1977: 16–19, 28–53.
25  Jefferies 1996b: 468, 472–75, 1996c: 225–30; Johnson and Brookes 1989: 142–43.
26  Jefferies 1996c: 233.
27  Jefferies 1996a: 46; Milner 1999: 120–22; Smith 1997: 250–56.
28  Jackson and Scott 2001: 189–90; Russo 1996a: 261–71, 276–81; Saunders *et al.* 1997: 1796–98.
29  Gibson 1996: 289–91, 2000: 80–91; Kidder 2002: 90–99; Smith 1986: 32–34; Webb 1977: 16–19, 28–31, 40–43, 48–52.
30  Gibson 1996: 293; Kidder 2002: 90–91; Russo 1996a: 262; Smith 1986: 29, 32.
31  Erasmus 1965: 285; Fowke 1902: 85.
32  Gibson 2000: 96, 109
33  Gibson 1996: 301–02, 2000: 172–6; Smith 1986: 30, 32–33.
34  Gibson 1996: 294–96; Russo 1996a: 266–81, 1996b: 194.
35  Albertson and Charles 1988: 29–33; Charles 1996: 86–87; Charles and Buikstra 1983: 127–28, 130; Klepinger and Henning 1976: 105–09, 128–33.
36  Albertson and Charles 1988: 33–38; Charles 1996: 86; Charles and Buikstra 1983: 132; Klepinger and Henning 1976: 105–09.

**Chapter 4** (pp. 54–96)
1  Ashley 1998: 208–13; Bense 1998: 259; Esarey 1986: 240; Smith 1986: 42.
2  Webb 1940: 51, 1941b: 228–36, Fig. 2, 1942a: 309, 332, 1942b: 427, Figs. 22, 23, 1943a: Fig. 7, 1943b: Fig. 2.
3  Milner and Jefferies 1987; Webb 1942b.
4  Milner and Jefferies 1987: 40.
5  Copper breastplates are roughly rectangular plates with rounded corners and generally two suspension holes.
6  Clay 1983: 113–16.
7  Brown 1979: 213–15; Greber 1979: 30–36, 1983: 13–38; Greber and Ruhl 1989: 52; Konigsberg 1985: 131.
8  Greber and Ruhl 1989: 172–78; Morgan 1952: 90, Fig. 94; Song *et al.* 1996: 252–62.
9  Brown 1979: 213–15; Mills 1922: 269–79.
10  Abrams 1992: 85–90.
11  J. Brown 1979: 215–18, 1981: 34–36; Bullington 1988: 227–33; Griffin *et al.* 1970: 13–123; Leigh *et al.* 1988; Van Nest *et al.* 2001: 635, 636–42.
12  Braun *et al.* 1982: 9–27; Buikstra 1976: 35, 42; Griffin *et al.* 1970: 13–123; Leigh 1988: 198–209; Leigh *et al.* 1988: 71–72, 77.
13  McKern 1931: 206–11, 242–47, 252–56, 263–67, 272–327.
14  Ford 1963: 9–45.
15  McKern 1931: 210–13.
16  Walthall 1979: 200–02.
17  Jefferies 1976: 3–5, 6–18.
18  Leigh *et al.* 1988: 51, 56.
19  Jefferies 1976: 20; McGimsey and Wiant 1986: 534–41
20  Fowke 1928: 414, 422; Jefferies 1994: 73–82; Knight 1990: 34–49, 168–69; Mainfort 1986: 15–17, 82; Milanich 1994: 174–79; Pickard 1996; Toth 1974: 11.

21  Ford and Willey 1940: 14–16, 22–30, 35–45, 122–26.
22  Milanich 1994: 173–79.
23  Jefferies 1994: 76–82; Knight 1990: 34–49, 168–69; Mainfort 1986: 15–17, 82; Pickard 1996.
24  Fowke 1928: Plt. 64; Garland and Beld 1999: 140–42; Jackson 1998: 215; Jones and Kuttruff 1998; Kellar 1979: 100–02; Mainfort 1986: 7; Mainfort and Carstens 1987: 58–59; Toth 1974: 9–13.
25  Clay 1987: 46; Fenton and Jefferies 1991: 43; Fowke 1902: 220–21, 332; Griffin 1947: 190–91; Squier and Davis 1848: 8–103; Thomas 1894: 451; Vickery 1979: 60–61; Webb 1941a: 141–42; field notes, WSWMA.
26  Webb 1941a: 142–58.
27  F.L. Cowan, personal communication, 2001.
28  Squier and Davis 1848: 8–75.
29  Fowke 1928: 492; Griffin 1947: 190–91; Shetrone 1925: 48–50; Vickery 1978: 59–60; Bohannan field notes, WSWMA.
30  Clay 1985:12–17, 1987: 49; Squier and Davis 1848: 8–103.
31  Connolly 1998; Essenpreis and Moseley 1984; Faulkner 1996: 7–8, 10; Jefferies 1976: 43–44; Prufer 1997; Riordan 1996; 1998.
32  Lepper 1996: 233; Riordan 1996: 248, 251–52, 1998: 81.
33  Connolly 1998: 93–95; Squier and Davis 1848: 47–103.
34  Fowke 1902: 159–62; Greber 1997: 218; Jackson 1998: 207; Jones and Kuttruff 1998: 52; Lepper 1996: 233, 1998: 126; Prufer 1997: 316–19, 324; Riordan 1996: 248, 252–53, 1998: 81–82.
35  Fowke 1902: 159–60; Greber 1997: 213–14; Jones and Kuttruff 1998: 50, 52; Lepper 1996: 232, 1998: 123.
36  Drooker 1997: 273; Fletcher *et al.* 1996: 116–23, 133; Willoughby 1919: 153–60; Squier and Davis 1848: 96–97.
37  Connolly 1998: 90.
38  Baby and Langlois 1979; Smith 1992: 210–12.
39  Greber and Ruhl 1989: 11–13, 23, 27, 77–78, 80, 90, 191–92, 257; Shetrone 1926: 27–29, 43, 74–76, 109, 140; Squier and Davis 1848: 26–29; Mound 17 is also referred to as Mound 29.
40  F. L. Cowan, personal communication, 2001.
41  Griffin 1967: 184.
42  Brown 1979: 214–15; Essenpreis and Moseley 1984: 26; Greber and Ruhl 1989: 23, 77–78, 80, 90, 191–92, 257; Mills 1907: 64–65; Shetrone 1926: 27–29, 43, 74–76, 109, 140.
43  Jefferies 1976: 21–27; Snyder 1962 [1895]: 195; Walthall 1979: 203.
44  Griffin 1967: 184.
45  Milner 1999: 122.
46  Butler 1979: 151–53; Fortier 1989: 58–94; Leeper and Yerkes 1997: 180–83; Pacheco 1996: 25–28; Smith 1986: 39–41, 44, 1992: 213; Stafford 1985: 449–50; Stoltman 1979: 129–32.
47  Butler 1979: 151–52; Smith 1986: 39, 44, 1992: 214–16, 240–43; Stafford 1985: 447, 454–55; Stoltman 1979: 131.
48  Coughlin and Seeman 1997: 240; Genheimer 1997: 295; Leeper 1996: 234; Pacheco 1996: 19.
49  Bense 1998: 257–62.
50  Smith 1989: 1567, 1995: 184.
51  Riley *et al.* 1994: 493–94; Smith 1989: 1570; Watson 1989: 560.
52  Styles *et al.* 1985: 434–35.
53  Bense 1998: 253–55.
54  Konigsberg 1985: 126, 129; Milner and Jefferies 1987: 40; Webb and Snow 1945: 247.
55  Buikstra 1976: 33–40; Bullington 1988: 237.
56  Braun *et al.* 1982: 9–10; Dragoo and Wray 1964: 196–98; Fenton 1998: 33, 102, 122, 200–01; Greber and Ruhl 1989: 29–30; Griffin *et al.* 1970: 28; Leeper 1996: 232; Mills 1907: 58–59; Neumann and Fowler 1952: 201–02, 209–10; Shetrone 1926: 163–66; Webb and Baby 1957: 61–71.
57  Jefferies 1976: 49–50.
58  Schnitger 1989: 112–14, Plt. 24; von Furer-Haimendorf in Schnitger 1989: 164–66.
59  Dillehay 1990: 230–34.
60  Mills 1907: 76; Seeman 1995: 130–32.
61  Shetrone 1951: 25.

**Chapter 5** (pp. 105–123)

1 Phillips 1970: 20.
2 Birmingham and Eisenberg 2000: 110, 138; Goldstein 1995: 102–05. Mallam 1976: 2, 104–09; Salkin 2000: 533; Stoltman and Christiansen 2000: 501, 507.
3 Birmingham and Eisenberg 2000: 110, 125–28; Goldstein 1995: 105–07; Salkin 2000: 533; Stoltman and Christiansen 2000: 501–04.
4 Birmingham and Eisenberg 2000: 117; Goldstein 1995: 102, 109–10, 119–20.
5 Goldstein 1995: 102, 105, 113; Mallam 1976: 38–40; Salkin 2000: 536; Stoltman and Christiansen 2000: 512.
6 Birmingham and Eisenberg 2000: 171; Buikstra and Goldstein 1973: 3–4; Butler and Wagner 2000: 701–02; Chapman 1980: 78–137; Charles *et al.* 1988: 85–102; Conner 1991: 240–43; Esarey 2000: 394; Halsey 1999: 234; Nassaney 2000: 721; Pollock and Henderson 2000b: 628; Reeder 2000: 194, 205–06; Schroedl *et al.* 1990: 183; Seeman and Dancey 2000: 599–600; Smith 1986: 52.
7 Atwell 1991: 237; Charles *et al.* 1988: 85–102; Conner 1991: 240–43.
8 Kidder 1998: 130; Williams and Brain 1983: 333–36, 352.
9 Rolingson 1990: 11–17; 1998: 2, 95.
10 Bartram in Waselkov and Braund 1995: 62, 246–47.
11 Rolingson 1990: 3, 5, 11–17, 1998: 2–3, 22–23, 95–100; Thomas 1894: 243.
12 Belovich and Brose 1992: 8, 14, 17–20.
13 Butler and Wagner 2000: 698; Muller 1986: 150–53; Pollack and Henderson 2000b: 621.
14 Butler and Wagner 2000: 697; Pollack and Henderson 2000b: 628, 630; Railey 1984: 29, 84–90.
15 Kelly 1990a: 87–105, 1990b: 126–35.
16 Kidder 1992: 95; 1998: 129–30; Nassaney 2000: 718–19; Rolingson 1998: 101–04.
17 Birmingham and Eisenberg 2000: 103; Butler and Wagner 2000: 696, 702; Green 1993: 206–08; McElrath and Fortier 2000: 97, 100; Muller 1986: 128–29; Nassaney 2000: 719; Pollack and Henderson 2000b: 632; Seeman and Dancey 2000: 602; Smith 1986: 52.
18 Fritz 1990: 416–24; Johannessen 1984: 202, 1993: 59–66; Simon 2000: 42, 46, 48, 52; Smith 1989: 1570.
19 Bridges *et al.* 2000: 227–30.
20 Buikstra 1992: 95; Fritz 1990: 398, 408–09; Johannessen 1984: 203, 1993: 63, 66; Katzenberg *et al.* 1995: 344–46; Smith 1986: 51, 1989: 1570.
21 Brown *et al.* 1990: 265–70; Cobb 2000: 65.
22 Seeman and Dancey 2000: 589; Wymer 1997: 156–57, 159.
23 Blitz 1988: 130–31, 135; Butler and Wagner 2000: 695; Nassaney 2000: 715–17; Seeman 1992: 41; Seeman and Dancey 2000: 594; Shott 1996: 288.
24 Brashler *et al.* 2000: 555–56; House 1990: 19; Styles 1994: 43, 2000: 85–90.
25 Atwell 1991: 237; Butler and Wagner 2000: 701–02; Charles *et al.* 1988: 85–102; Esarey 2000: 394; Schroedl *et al.* 1990: 183; Seeman and Dancey 2000: 600; Smith 1986: 52.
26 Williams and Brain 1983: 42–56, 334–35.
27 Kelly 1990b: 130; Muller 1986: 140; Nassaney 2000: 715–16, 721; Smith 1986: 52.
28 Milner 1999: 122.
29 Kelly 1990b: 130–36; Knight and Steponaitis 1998: 11; Milner 1998: 174–75.
30 Rindos and Johannessen 1991: 43; B. Smith 1987: 47–51.
31 Fritz 1990: 411, 1995: 9, 2000: 238–39; Kidder 1998: 129–30.

**Chapter 6** (pp. 124–168)

1 Moore in Morse and Morse 1998: 29.
2 Krause 1990: 75–86.
3 Anderson 1994: 210–11; Blitz 1993: 82; Rudolph 1984: 38, 41; Wesler 2001: 38.
4 Blitz 1993: 74–85.
5 NMNH, ISM, and UMMA notes and collections.
6 Bell 1972: 18–19, 110, 142–45, 160–65, 179–81; J. Brown 1981: 32–34; 1996: 23, 170–71; Du Pratz 1972 [1774]: 334.
7 Brown 1996: 53–103, 188, 319, 421.
8 Brown 1996: 12–13, 53–103, 161, 166–67, 188–89, 195,

419–21.
9 Fowler *et al.* 1999: 3–13, 64–79.
10 Conrad 1991: 128–29; Du Pratz 1972 [1774]: 337–39; Le Petit in Thwaites 1896–1901 vol. 68: 131–33; Swanton 1911: 264–67.
11 Anderson 1994: 196–99; Du Pratz 1972 [1774]: 339; Le Petit in Thwaites 1896–1901 vol. 68: 129; Rudolph 1984: 35–39.
12 Anderson 1994: 178–79, 182, 209, 212; Black 1967: 266; DeJarnette and Wimberly 1941: 61; Larson 1971: 60; Price and Fox 1990: 24; Smith 1969: 66; Swanton 1911: 262–69.
13 Fowler 1997; Milner 1998: 106–14, 121–24, 144–46; Pauketat 1998: 122–28.
14 Fowler 1997: 87; Milner 1998: 144–46; Muller 1997a: 273.
15 Milner 1998: 146–50; Muller 1986: 200–04, 1997a: 273–75.
16 Knight *et al.* 2001: 129–31.
17 Brown 1996: 96, 189, 194, 531; Knight *et al.* 2001: 132.
18 Brown 1985b: 114–23; 1996: 532–34; Knight *et al.* 2001: 134–36; Phillips and Brown 1978: 119–20, 124–30, 153; Winters 1974: 38–42.
19 Brown 1996: 534–37; Goldstein 1980: 58, 65; Harn 1980: 16, 26; Hudson 1976: 166–69, 244, 343, 356–57; Milner 1998: 135–36; Perino 1971: 18, 22–24, 50, 54, 112–13, 126–30.
20 Emerson 1997: 198–205; Milner 1983: 52, 1984: 240.
21 Thomas 1894: 31.
22 Milner 1998: 97; Schroedl 1998: 88.
23 Fowler 1997: 24; Knight 1998: 48; Porter 1974: 294–97.
24 Knight 1998: 50–52, 60.
25 Fowler 1997: 193–200; Milner 1998: 109–14; Stout and Lewis 1998: 152.
26 Phillips *et al.* 1951: 329–35; Stout and Lewis 1998: 152.
27 Milner 1998: 110–13; Payne and Scarry 1998: 40; Stout and Lewis 1998: 154–55.
28 Knight and Steponaitis 1998: 15; Milner 1998: 113, 156–57.
29 Milner 1998: 121–24; Muller 1997a: 213–15; Schroedl 1998: 90; Steponaitis 1998: 42–43; Wesler 2001: 150.
30 Hally and Kelly 1998: 49–54; Kidder 1998: 147; Milner 1998: 100–02; Muller 1997a: 22; Price and Griffin 1979: 31–45; Smith 1978: 488–91; Stout and Lewis 1998: 154.
31 Knight and Steponaitis 1998: 2–6, 13–24; Steponaitis 1998: 39, 43.
32 Beverley 1947 [1705]: 218–19.
33 Early 2000: 129–30.
34 Milner 1998: 81–87.
35 Marquardt 2001: 158, 166–68; Widmer 1988: 260–76.
36 Brain 1988: 266–72; Hally 1993: 161; Hally and Kelly 1998: 49; Harn 1994: 29–30; Milner 1998: 64; D.F. Morse 1990: 78–83; P.A. Morse 1990: 123–24; Welch 1998: 134.
37 Fenton 1998: 21; Knight and Steponaitis 1998: 20; Milner 1998: 120–25; Muller 1997a: 206–21; Rountree and Turner 1998: 266.
38 Anderson 1994: 94–95; DePratter 1991: 29–34; Martin and Szuter 1999: 43–44.
39 Steadman 2001: 69–71.
40 Anderson 1994: 326–29; Butler 1991: 271–74; Cobb and Butler 2002: 628, 636–38; Hally and Rudolph 1986: 37–78; Mainfort 2001: 184–85; Milner 1998: 169–73; Smith 1986: 59; Smith 2001: 147; Williams 1980: 109.
41 Johannessen 1984: 207; Lopinot 1997: 170; Rindos and Johannessen 1991: 39; common bean (*Phaseolus vulgaris*).
42 Bridges *et al.* 2000: 234; Larsen *et al.* 1991: 182–86.
43 Du Pratz 1972 [1774]: 156–57.
44 Martin and Szuter 1999: 38–40.
45 Jefferies 1995a: 260.
46 Fritz 1990: 419–21, 1995: 8–10; Hutchinson *et al.* 2000: 110–15; Kidder 1998: 130; Marquardt 2001: 162; Widmer 1988: 260–76.
47 Brown 1975: 19–22; 1996: 436–37, 469–88; Fowler *et al.* 1999: 102–04; 168–70; Phillips and Brown 1978: 108, 119, 124–30.
48 Muller 1997a: 84–85, 92, 395.
49 Bartram in Waselkov and Holland 1995: 127, 159–60.
50 Milner 1998: 158–60.
51 Milner 1998: 168; Pauketat 1994: 171–72.
52 Milner 1998: 101, 138; O'Brien 2001: 158, 222–28, 295; Price and Griffin 1979: 47, 139.

53  I. Brown 1981: 2–14; Goldstein 1980: 97–106; Milner 1998: 135; Peebles 1971: 71–72; Sullivan 1987: 24; Webb and DeJarnette 1942: Fig. 70.

54  Cobb and Pope 1998: 4, 6, 13; Goldstein 1980: 65; Harn 1980: 14–33; Milner 1998: 135–36; Peebles 1971: 71–72, 1983: 192; Perino 1971: 14–57.

55  Cobb 2000: 149–53, 186; Early 1993: 230–34; Milner 1998: 138–43; Muller 1997a: 301–53.

56  Buikstra and Williams 1991: 162, 165, 168; Powell 1991: 176–79, 1998: 112; Schoeninger and Schurr 1998: 128–29.

57  Lawson 1709: 223.

58  Brown et al. 1990: 268–70; Muller 1997a: 368–79; ISM and NMNH collections.

59  Milner 1998: 164.

60  Barker et al. 2002: 104–07.

61  Gentleman of Elvas in Smith 1968: 64; M. Smith 1987: 91–92, 102–03, 2000: 90.

62  Milner 1998: 165.

63  Barrett 1933: 256–65; Black 1967: 120–228; Milner 1999: 120, 123–24.

64  Garcilaso de la Vega in Varner and Varner 1951: 292–93, 438, 493.

65  Milner 1998: 157–59; Schroeder 1997: 209–18.

66  Du Pratz 1972 [1774]: 350–54; Muller 1997a: 78, 101.

67  Anderson et al. 1995: 277.

68  Cobb and Butler 2002: 628, 636–38; Esarey and Santure 1990: 166; Milner 1999: 125–26; Milner et al. 1991: 593; Smith 1986: 59.

**Chapter 7** (pp. 177–189)

1  Potter 1993: 149–50; Rountree and Turner 1998: 273.

2  Milner and Schroeder 1992: 63.

3  Birmingham and Eisenberg 2000: 171–72; Brown 1967: 4, 9–14, 42; Drooker 1997: 87–88, 200, 279–80; Emerson 1999: 31–33; Griffin 1966: 102–04; Jeske 1927: 156–63; Kreisa 1993: 44–8; Krogman 1931: 415.

4  Milner et al. 1989: 56–57; Santure 1990: 66–71; Santure and Esarey 1990: 106–10.

5  Fenton 1998: 29.

6  Jefferson 1954 [1787]: 97–102.

7  Milner et al. 1991: 582–93; Santure 1990: 66–74.

8  Gold 2000: 195–206; Hantman 1990: 683–84, 2001: 108.

9  Dodd et al. 1990: 353–56; McManamon et al. 1986: 8–14; O'Shea 1988: 76–79; Ubelaker 1974: 8–40; Ward and Davis 1999: 218.

10  Brose 2001: 57–58; Brown and Sasso 2001: 221–22, 224; Hinsdale 1924: 4–7, 10; Kullen 1994: 4–14; Milner and O'Shea 1998: 185–88, 195–201; Neusius et al. 1998: 202–04, 229–30; Thomas 1894: 516–18; Zurell 1999: 244–48.

11  Brown and Sasso 2001: 217, 224; Buikstra 1992: 89–96; Emerson 1957: 12, 14; Fenton 1998: 22; Fritz 1990: 423–24; Gallagher and Sasso 1987: 141; Hart 1999: 63; Hart and Scarry 1999: 656; Katzenberg et al. 1995: 343–45; Little 2002: 114; Smith 1989: 1570; Thomas 1894: 550; Warrick 2000: 437.

12  Winthorp 1963 [1678]: 1067.

13  Rountree and Turner 1998: 275–77.

14  Butler 1939: 46.

15  Winthorp 1963 [1678]: 1066.

16  Dodd 1984: 204–14, 274; Fenton 1998: 23; Finlayson 1985: 125, 411, 414; Ramsden 1990: 378–79; Ritchie 1980: 305–10, 314–15; Snow 1994: 28–30, 40–46; Warrick 1984: 60, 2000: 434–54.

17  Dodd 1984: 207; Fenton 1998: 25; Finlayson 1985: 411; Ramsden 1990: 374; Warrick 1984: 20, 42, 44.

18  Alex 2000: 207–08; Birmingham and Eisenberg 2000: 167; Brown and Sasso 2001: 216; Hollinger 1995: 144–50; Markham 1991: 102, 110–11; McKusick 1973: 14–16; Overstreet 1997: 283, 286; Rodell 2000: 390–91.

19  Brose 1994: 176, 2000: 103–07, 2001: 56–58; Custer et al. 1995: 34; Drooker and Cowan 2001: 91–95; Finlayson 1985: 44; Griffin 1978: 554–57; Hart 1993: 97–101; Nass and Hart 2000: 134–40; Nass and Yerkes 1995: 66–68; Pollack and Henderson 2000a: 202–07; Sharp 1996: 167–69; Ward and Davis 1999: 106; Warrick 1984: 92.

20  Milner 1999: 119–20, 125.

21  Ritchie 1980: 307.

22  Fenton 1998: 23; Snow 1995: 1602.

23  Brose 1994: 176, 2001: 57; Custer et al. 1995: 28; Dodd et al. 1990: 357; Drooker and Cowan 2001: 90; Overstreet 1997: 283; Snow 1994: 38, 1995: 1603; Stewart 1995: 194; Ubelaker 1974: 66–69; Ward and Davis 1999: 106; Warrick 1984: 12, 2000: 447.

24  Alex 2000: 168–69; Esarey and Santure 1990: 166; Milner 1999: 125–26; Milner et al. 1991: 593; Rodell 2000: 388; Snow 1994: 48–50, 2001: 20, 22; Warrick 1984: 65, 2000: 434–54.

25  Ragueneau in Thwaites 1896–1901 vol. 35: 89–91.

26  Brose 2000: 108; Milner 1999: 126; Potter 1993: 126–38, 176–77; Rountree and Turner 1998: 279, 281; Stewart 1995: 195; Warrick 1984: 65.

27  Fenton 1998: 68–72, 130; Kuhn and Sempowski 2001: 303, 311–12; Ritchie 1980: 316–17; Snow 1994: 60, 231.

**Chapter 8** (pp. 190–198)

1  Gentleman of Elvas in Smith 1968: 110; Garcilaso de la Vega in Varner and Varner 1951: 432–33.

2  Du Pratz 1972 [1774]: 333–39.

3  Birmingham and Eisenberg 2000: 172–73; Hutchinson 1996: 55–56, 62; Hutchinson and Mitchem 1996: 48; Krogman 1931: 419; Langford 1930: 82–83; Latham 1855: 27, Plt. 19; Mitchem 1989: 103–09; P.A. Morse 1990: 130; M. Smith 1987: 91–92; Thomas 1894: 51–52, 376.

4  Harriot 1972 [1590]: 28.

5  Brain 1988: 272; Mainfort 2001: 188–89; Smith 2000: 34–49, 2001: 150; Williams and Brain 1983: 414–15.

6  Johnson 2000: 89–90; Johnson and Lehmann 1996: 48, 50–51.

7  Snow 1995: 1603, 1996: 164–65; Ward and Davis 1993: 413–18, 422–32; 2001: 140–41.

8  Fenton 1998: 247, 250; Muller 1997a: 194–96, 1997b: 355–59.

9  Dobyns 1983: 37–42, 291–95; Ubelaker 1988: 291.

10  Snow 1995: 1603, 1996: 164–65.

11  Thornton 1987: 114–18.

# Further Reading

The literature on the prehistory of eastern North America is vast, although fine introductions to various topics, regions, and time periods can be found in Anderson 1994; Bense 1994; J.A. Brown 1985b; Jefferies 1995b; Kelly 1990b; Meltzer 1993; Milanich 1994; Muller 1986, 1997a; B.D. Smith 1986, 1992, 1995; M.T. Smith 2000; Snow 1994; Ward & Davis 1999; and Warrick 2000. Lengthy works on several important sites include Gibson 2000 (Poverty Point); Rolingson 1998 (Toltec); Milner 1998 and Fowler 1997 (Cahokia); J.A. Brown 1996 (Spiro); and Knight & Steponaitis 1998, edited volume (Moundville).

ANONYMOUS 1869a 'An Indian Velocipede,' *Missouri Democrat*, April 19, p. 4.
— 1869b 'The Big Mound,' *St. Louis Daily Times*, April 16, p. 4.
ABRAMS, ELLIOT M. 1992 'Archaeological Investigation of the Armitage Mound (33-At-434), The Plains, Ohio,' *Midcontinental Journal of Archaeology* 17:79–111.
ADOVASIO, J.M., J. DONAHUE, AND R. STUCKENRATH 1990 'The Meadowcroft Rockshelter Radiocarbon Chronology 1975–1990,' *American Antiquity* 55:348–54.
AHLER, STEVEN 1991 'Modoc Matting and Beads: Cultural Complexity in the Early Archaic Period,' *The Living Museum* 53:3–6.
ALBERTSON, DONALD G., AND DOUGLAS K. CHARLES 1988 'Archaic Mortuary Component,' in *The Archaic and Woodland Cemeteries at the Elizabeth Site in the Lower Illinois Valley*, eds. D.K. Charles, S.R. Leigh, and J.E. Buikstra. Research Series 7. Kampsville, IL: Center for American Archeology.
ALEX, LYNN M. 2000 *Iowa's Archaeological Past*. Iowa City: University of Iowa Press.
ALROY, JOHN 2001 'A Multispecies Overkill Simulation of the End-Pleistocene Megafaunal Mass Extinction,' *Science* 292:1893–96.
ANDERSON, DAVID G. 1990 'The Paleoindian Colonization of Eastern North America: A View from the Southeastern United States,' in *Early Paleoindian Economies of Eastern North America*, eds. K.B. Tankersley and B.L. Isaac, Greenwich, CT: JAI Press.
— 1994 *The Savannah River Chiefdoms: Political Change in the Late Prehistoric Southeast*. Tuscaloosa: University of Alabama Press.
— 1996 'Models of Paleoindian and Early Archaic Settlement in the Lower Southeast,' in *The Paleoindian and Early Archaic Southeast*, eds. D.G. Anderson and K.E. Sassaman. Tuscaloosa: University of Alabama Press.
ANDERSON, DAVID G., AND J. CHRISTOPHER GILLAM 2000 'Paleoindian Colonization of the Americas: Implications from an Examination of Physiography, Demography, and Artifact Distribution,' *American Antiquity* 65:43–66.
ANDERSON, DAVID G., DAVID W. STAHLE, AND MALCOM K. CLEAVELAND 1995 'Paleoclimate and the Potential Food Reserves of Mississippian Societies: A Case Study from the Savannah River Valley,' *American Antiquity* 60:258–86.
ANDERSON, DAVID G., LISA D. O'STEEN, AND KENNETH E. SASSAMAN 1996 'Environmental and Chronological Considerations,' in *The Paleoindian and Early Archaic Southeast*, eds. D.G. Anderson and K.E. Sassaman. Tuscaloosa: University of Alabama Press.
ASHLEY, KEITH H. 1998 'Swift Creek Traits in Northeastern Florida,' in *A World Engraved: Archaeology of the Swift Creek Culture*, eds. M. Williams and D.T. Elliott. Tuscaloosa: University of Alabama Press.
ATWELL, KAREN 1991 'Analysis of Burial Program,' in *The Kuhlman Mound Group and Late Woodland Mortuary Behavior in the Mississippi River Valley of West-Central Illinois*, eds. K.A. Atwell and M.D. Conner. Research Series 9. Kampsville: Center for American Archaeology.
BABY, RAYMOND S., AND SUZANNE M. LANGLOIS 1979 'Seip Mound State Memorial: Nonmortuary Aspects of Hopewell,' in *Hopewell Archaeology*, eds. D.S. Brose and N.B. Greber. Kent, OH: Kent State University Press.
BAKER, RICHARD G., et al. 1992 'Patterns of Holocene Environmental Change in the Midwestern United States,' *Quaternary Research* 37:379–89.
BARKER, ALEX W., et al. 2002 'Mesoamerican Origin for an Obsidian Scraper from the Precolumbian Southeastern United States,' *American Antiquity* 67:103–08.
BARRETT, SAMUEL A. 1933 *Ancient Aztalan*. Bulletin 13. Milwaukee: Milwaukee Public Museum.
BELL, ROBERT E. 1972 *The Harlan Site, Ck-6, A Prehistoric Mound Centers in Cherokee County, Eastern Oklahoma*, Memoir 2. Oklahoma Anthropological Society.
BELOVICH, STEPHANIE J., AND DAVID S. BROSE 1992 'Late Woodland Fortifications in Northern Ohio: The Greenwood Village Site,' *Kirtlandia* 47:3–23.
BENSE, JUDITH A. 1994 *Archaeology of the Southeastern United States*. San Diego: Academic Press.
— 1998 'Santa Rosa-Swift Creek in Northwestern Florida,' in *A World Engraved: Archaeology of the Swift Creek Culture*, eds. M. Williams and D.T. Elliott, Tuscaloosa: University of Alabama Press.
BENTLEY, GILLIAN R., TONY GOLDBERG, AND GRAZYNA JASIENSKA 1993 'The Fertility of Agricultural and Non-Agricultural Traditional Societies,' *Population Studies* 47:269–81.
BEVERLEY, ROBERT 1947 [1705] *The History and Present State of Virginia*, ed. L.B. Wright. Chapel Hill: University of North Carolina Press.
BIRMINGHAM, ROBERT A., AND LESLIE E. EISENBERG 2000 *Indian Mounds of Wisconsin*. Madison: University of Wisconsin Press.
BLACK, GLENN A. 1967 *Angel Site: An Archaeological, Historical, and Ethnological Study*. 2 vols. Indianapolis: Indiana Historical Society.
BLANTON, DENNIS B. 1996 'Accounting for Submerged Mid-Holocene Archaeological Sites in the Southeast: A Case Study from the Chesapeake Bay Estuary, Virginia,' in *Archaeology of the Mid-Holocene Southeast*, eds. K.E. Sassaman and D.G. Anderson. Gainesville: University Press of Florida.
BLITZ, JOHN H. 1988 'Adoption of the Bow in Prehistoric North America,' *North American Archaeologist* 9:123–45.
— 1993 *Ancient Chiefdoms of the Tombigbee*. Tuscaloosa: University of Alabama Press.
BRACKENRIDGE, HENRY R. 1811 'Cantine Mounds, and the Monastery of La Trappe,' *Louisiana Gazette* January 9, p. 3.
— 1818 'On the Population and Tumuli of the Aborigines of North America,' *Transactions of the American Philosophical Society* 1:151–59.
BRAIN, JEFFREY P. 1988 *Tunica Archaeology*. Papers of the Peabody Museum of Archaeology and Ethnology 78. Cambridge: Harvard University.
BRASHLER, JANET G., et al. 2000 'Adaptive Strategies and Socioeconomic Systems in Northern Great Lakes Riverine Environments: The Late Woodland of Michigan,' in *Late Woodland Societies: Tradition and Transformation Across the Midcontinent*, eds. T.E. Emerson, D.L. McElrath, and A.C. Fortier. Lincoln: University of Nebraska Press.
BRAUN, DAVID P., JAMES B. GRIFFIN, AND PAUL F. TITTERINGTON

1982 *The Snyders Mounds and Five Other Mound Groups in Calhoun County, Illinois*. Technical Reports 13. Ann Arbor: Museum of Anthropology, University of Michigan.

BRIDGES, PATRICIA S., JOHN H. BLITZ, AND MARTIN C. SOLANO 2000 'Changes in Long Bone Diaphyseal Strength With Horticultural Intensification in West-Central Illinois,' *American Journal of Physical Anthropology* 112:217–38.

BROSE, DAVID S. 1985 'The Woodland Period,' in *Ancient Art of the American Woodland Indians*, by D.S. Brose, J.A. Brown, and D.W. Penney. New York: Harry N. Abrams.

— 1994 *The South Park Village Site and the Late Prehistoric Whittlesey Tradition of Northeast Ohio*. Monographs in World Archaeology 20. Madison, WI: Prehistory Press.

— 2000 'Late Prehistoric Societies of Northeastern Ohio and Adjacent Portions of the South Shore of Lake Erie: A Review,' in *Cultures Before Contact: The Late Prehistory of Ohio and Surrounding Regions*, ed. R.A. Genheimer. Columbus: Ohio Archaeological Council.

— 2001 'Penumbral Protohistory on Lake Erie's South Shore,' in *Societies in Eclipse*, eds. D.S. Brose, C.W. Cowan, and R.C. Mainfort Jr. Washington, DC: Smithsonian Institution Press.

BROSTER, JOHN B., AND MARK R. NORTON 1996 'Recent Paleoindian Research in Tennessee,' in *The Paleoindian and Early Archaic Southeast*, eds. D.G. Anderson and K.E. Sassaman. Tuscaloosa: University of Alabama Press.

BROWN, IAN 1981 'A Study of Stone Box Graves in Eastern North America,' *Tennessee Anthropologist* 6:1–16.

BROWN, JAMES A. 1967 *The Gentleman Farm Site*. Reports of Investigations 12. Springfield: Illinois State Museum.

— 1975 'Spiro Art and its Mortuary Contexts,' in *Death and the Afterlife in Pre-Columbian America*, ed. E.P. Benson. Washington, DC: Dumbarton Oaks Research Library and Collections.

— 1979 'Charnel Houses and Mortuary Crypts: Disposal of the Dead in the Middle Woodland Period,' in *Hopewell Archaeology*, eds. D.S. Brose and N.B. Greber. Kent, OH: Kent State University Press.

— 1981 'The Search for Rank in Prehistoric Burials,' in *The Archaeology of Death*, eds. R. Chapman, I. Kinnes, and K. Randsborg. Cambridge: Cambridge University Press.

— 1985a 'Long-Term Trends to Sedentism and the Emergence of Complexity in the American Midwest,' in *Prehistoric Hunter-Gatherers: The Emergence of Cultural Complexity*, eds. T. D. Price and J. A. Brown. Orlando: Academic Press.

— 1985b 'The Mississippian Period,' in *Ancient Art of the American Woodland Indians*, by D.S. Brose, J.A. Brown, and D.W. Penney. New York: Harry N. Abrams.

— 1996 *The Spiro Ceremonial Center*, 2 vols. Memoir 29. Ann Arbor: Museum of Anthropology, University of Michigan.

BROWN, JAMES A., AND ROBERT K. VIERRA 1983 'What Happened in the Middle Archaic? Introduction to an Ecological Approach to Koster Site Archaeology,' in *Archaic Hunters and Gatherers in the American Midwest*, eds. J.L. Phillips and J.A. Brown. New York: Academic Press.

BROWN, JAMES A., RICHARD A. KERBER, AND HOWARD D. WINTERS 1990 'Trade and the Evolution of Exchange Relations at the Beginning of the Mississippian Period,' in *The Mississippian Emergence*, ed. B.D. Smith. Washington, DC: Smithsonian Institution Press.

BROWN, JAMES A., AND ROBERT F. SASSO 2001 'Prelude to History on the Eastern Prairies,' in *Societies in Eclipse*, eds. D.S. Brose, C.W. Cowan, and R.C. Mainfort Jr. Washington, DC: Smithsonian Institution Press.

BUIKSTRA, JANE E. 1976 *Hopewell in the Lower Illinois Valley*. Scientific Papers 2. Evanston, IL: Northwestern University Archeological Program.

— 1981 'Mortuary Practices, Palaeodemography and Palaeopathology: A Case Study from the Koster Site (Illinois),' in *The Archaeology of Death*, eds. R. Chapman, I. Kinnes, and K. Randsborg, Cambridge: Cambridge University Press.

— 1992 'Diet and Disease in Late Prehistory,' in *Disease and Demography in the Americas*, eds. J.W. Verano and D.H. Ubelaker. Washington, DC: Smithsonian Institution Press.

BUIKSTRA, JANE E., AND LYNNE G. GOLDSTEIN 1973 *The Perrins Ledge Crematory*. Reports of Investigations 28. Springfield: Illinois State Museum.

BUIKSTRA, JANE E., AND SLOAN WILLIAMS 1991 'Tuberculosis in the Americas: Current Perspectives,' in *Human Paleopathology: Current Syntheses and Future Options*, eds. D.J. Ortner and A.C. Aufderheide, Washington, DC: Smithsonian Institution Press.

BULLINGTON, JILL 1988 'Middle Woodland Mound Structure: Social Implications and Regional Context,' in *The Archaic and Woodland Cemeteries at the Elizabeth Site in the Lower Illinois Valley*, eds. D.K. Charles, S.R. Leigh, and J.E. Buikstra. Research Series 7. Kampsville, IL: Center for American Archeology.

BUTLER, BRIAN M. 1979 'Hopewellian Contacts in Southern Middle Tennessee,' in *Hopewell Archaeology*, eds. D.S. Brose and N.B. Greber. Kent, OH: Kent State University Press.

— 1991 'Kincaid Revisited: The Mississippian Sequence in the Lower Ohio Valley,' in *Cahokia and the Hinterlands: Middle Mississippian Cultures of the Midwest*, eds. T.E. Emerson and R.B. Lewis. Urbana: University of Illinois Press.

BUTLER, BRIAN M., AND MARK J. WAGNER 2000 'Land Between the Rivers: The Late Woodland Period of Southernmost Illinois,' in *Late Woodland Societies: Tradition and Transformation Across the Midcontinent*, eds. T.E. Emerson, D.L. McElrath, and A.C. Fortier. Lincoln: University of Nebraska Press.

BUTLER, MARY 1939 *Three Archaeological Sites in Somerset County Pennsylvania*. Bulletin 753. Harrisburg: Pennsylvania Historical Commission.

CAMPBELL, KENNETH L., AND JAMES W. WOOD 1988 'Fertility in Traditional Societies,' in *Natural Human Fertility: Social and Biological Determinants*, eds. P. Diggory, M. Potts, and S. Teper. London: Macmillan.

CHAPMAN, B. JEFFERSON, AND JAMES M. ADOVASIO 1977 'Textile and Basketry Impressions from Icehouse Bottom, Tennessee,' *American Antiquity* 42:620–25.

CHAPMAN, CARL H. 1980 *The Archaeology of Missouri, II*. Columbia: University of Missouri Press.

CHARLES, DOUGLAS K. 1996 'Diachronic Regional Social Dynamics: Mortuary Sites in the Illinois Valley/American Bottom Region,' in *Regional Approaches to Mortuary Analysis*, ed. L.A. Beck. New York: Plenum.

CHARLES, DOUGLAS K., AND JANE E. BUIKSTRA 1983 'Archaic Mortuary Sites in the Central Mississippi Drainage: Distribution, Structure, and Behavioral Implications,' in *Archaic Hunters and Gatherers in the American Midwest*, eds. J.L. Phillips and J.A. Brown. New York: Academic Press.

CHARLES, DOUGLAS K., STEVEN R. LEIGH, AND DONALD G. ALBERTSON 1988 'Late Woodland and Unassignable Components,' in *The Archaic and Woodland Cemeteries at the Elizabeth Site in the Lower Illinois Valley*, eds. D.K. Charles, S.R. Leigh, and J.E. Buikstra. Research Series 7. Kampsville, IL: Center for American Archeology.

CLAUSEN, C.J., *et al.* 1979 'Little Salt Spring, Florida: A Unique Underwater Site,' *Science* 203:609–14.

CLAY R. BERLE 1983 'Pottery and Graveside Ritual in Kentucky Adena,' *Midcontinental Journal of Archaeology* 8:109–26.

— 1985 'Peter Village 164 Years Later: 1983 Excavations,' in *Woodland Period Research in Kentucky*, eds. D. Pollack, T. Sanders, and C. Hockensmith. Frankfort: Kentucky Heritage Council.

— 1987 'Circles and Ovals: Two Types of Adena Space,' *Southeastern Archaeology* 6:46–56.

COBB, CHARLES R. 2000 *From Quarry to Cornfield*. Tuscaloosa: University of Alabama Press.

COBB, CHARLES R., AND BRIAN M. BUTLER 2002 'The Vacant Quarter Revisited: Late Mississippian Abandonment of the Lower Ohio Valley,' *American Antiquity* 67:625–41.

COBB, CHARLES R., AND MELODY POPE 1998 'Sixteenth-Century Flintknapping Kits from the King Site, Georgia,' *Journal of Field Archaeology* 25:1–17.

CONNER, MICHAEL D. 1991 'Summary and Conclusions,' in *The Kuhlman Mound Group And Late Woodland Mortuary Behavior in the Mississippi River Valley of West-Central Illinois*, eds.

K.A. Atwell and M.D. Conner. Research Series 9. Kampsville: Center for American Archaeology.

CONNOLLY, ROBERT P. 1998 'Architectural Grammar Rules at the Fort Ancient Hilltop Enclosure,' in *Ancient Earthen Enclosures of the Eastern Woodlands*, eds. R.C. Mainfort Jr. and L.P. Sullivan. Gainesville, University Press of Florida.

CONRAD, LAWRENCE A. 1991 'The Middle Mississippian Cultures of the Central Illinois Valley,' in *Cahokia and the Hinterlands*, eds. T.E. Emerson and R.B. Lewis. Urbana: University of Illinois Press.

COOK, THOMAS G. 1976 *Koster: An Artifact Analysis of Two Archaic Phases in Westcentral Illinois*. Prehistoric Records 1. Evanston, IL: Northwestern University Archeological Program.

COUGHLIN, SEAN, AND MARK F. SEEMAN 1997 'Hopewell Settlements at the Liberty Earthworks, Ross County, Ohio, ' in *Ohio Hopewell Community Organization*, eds. W.S. Dancey and P.J. Pacheco. Kent, OH: Kent State University Press.

CRITES, GARY D. 1993 'Domesticated Sunflower in Fifth Millennium B.P. Temporal Context: New Evidence from Middle Tennessee,' *American Antiquity* 58:146–48.

CURRAN, MARY L. 1999 'Exploration, Colonization, and Settling In: The Bull Brook Phase, Antecedents, and Descendants,' in *The Archaeological Northeast*, eds. M.A. Levine, K.E. Sassaman, and M.S. Nassaney. Westport, CT: Bergin and Garvey.

CUSTER, JAY F., *et al.* 1995 'Data Recovery Excavations at the Slackwater Site (36LA207), Lancaster County, Pennsylvania,' *Pennsylvania Archaeologist* 65:19–112.

DAHL-JENSEN, *et al.* 1998 'Past Temperatures Directly from the Greenland Ice Sheet,' *Science* 282:268–71.

DANIEL, I. RANDOLPH JR. 1998 *Hardaway Revisited*. Tuscaloosa: University of Alabama Press.

DÉCIMA, ELENA B., AND DENA F. DINCAUZE 1998 'The Boston Back Bay Fish Weirs,' in *Hidden Dimensions: The Cultural Significance of Wetland Archaeology*, ed. K. Bernick. Vancouver: University of British Columbia Press.

DEJARNETTE, DAVID L., AND STEVE B. WIMBERLY 1941 *The Bessemer Site*. Museum Paper 17. University: Geological Survey of Alabama.

DELCOURT, PAUL A., HAZEL R. DELCOURT, AND ROGER T. SAUCIER 1999 'Late Quaternary Vegetation Dynamics in the Central Mississippi Valley,' in *Arkansas Archaeology*, eds. R.C. Mainfort Jr. and M.D. Jeter. Fayetteville: University of Arkansas Press.

DEPRATTER, CHESTER B. 1991 *Late Prehistoric and Early Historic Chiefdoms in the Southeastern United States*. New York: Garland.

DEPRATTER, CHESTER B., AND JAMES D. HOWARD 1981 'Evidence for a Sea Level Lowstand Between 4500 and 2400 Years BP on the Southeast Coast of the United States,' *Journal of Sedimentary Petrology* 51:1287–95.

DILLEHAY, TOM D. 1990 'Mapuche Ceremonial Landscape, Social Recruitment and Resource Rights,' *World Archaeology* 22:223–41.

— 1997 *Monte Verde: A Late Pleistocene Settlement in Chile*, vol. 2. Washington, DC: Smithsonian Institution Press.

DILLEHAY, TOM D., AND MARIO PINO 1997 'Radiocarbon Chronology,' In *Monte Verde: A Late Pleistocene Settlement in Chile*, vol. 2, ed. T.D. Dillehay. Washington, DC: Smithsonian Institution Press.

DINCAUZE, DENA F. 1993 'Pioneering in the Pleistocene: Large Paleoindian Sites in the Northeast,' in *Archaeology of Eastern North America: Papers in Honor of Stephen Williams*, ed. J.B. Stoltman. Archaeological Report 25. Jackson: Mississippi Department of Archives and History.

DOBYNS, HENRY F. 1983 *Their Number Become Thinned*. Knoxville: University of Tennessee Press.

DODD, CHRISTINE F. 1984 *Ontario Iroquois Tradition Longhouses*. Mercury Series 124. Ottawa: National Museum of Man.

DODD, CHRISTINE F. *et al.* 1990 'The Middle Ontario Iroquoian Stage,' in *The Archaeology of Southern Ontario to AD 1650*, eds. C.J. Ellis and N. Ferris. Occasional Publication 5. London: Ontario Archaeological Society.

DRAGOO, DON W., AND CHARLES F. WRAY 1964 'Hopewell Figurine Rediscovered,' *American Antiquity* 30:195–99.

DRISKELL, BOYCE N. 1996 'Stratified Late Pleistocene and Early Holocene Deposits at Dust Cave, Northwestern Alabama,' in *The Paleoindian and Early Archaic Southeast*, eds. D.G. Anderson and K.E. Sassaman. Tuscaloosa: University of Alabama Press.

DROOKER, PENELOPE B. 1997 *The View from Madisonville*. Memoirs 31. Ann Arbor: Museum of Anthropology, University of Michigan.

DROOKER, PENELOPE B., AND C. WESLEY COWAN 2001 'Transformation of the Fort Ancient Cultures of the Central Ohio Valley,' in *Societies in Eclipse*, eds. D.S. Brose, C.W. Cowan, and R.C. Mainfort Jr. Washington, DC: Smithsonian Institution Press.

DUNBAR, JAMES S., AND S. DAVID WEBB 1996 'Bone and Ivory Tools from Submerged Paleoindian Sites in Florida,' in *The Paleoindian and Early Archaic Southeast*, eds. D.G. Anderson and K.E. Sassaman. Tuscaloosa: University of Alabama Press.

DUNFORD, FREDERICK J. 1999 'Paleoenvironmental Context for the Middle Archaic Occupation of Cape Cod, Massachusetts,' in *The Archaeological Northeast*, eds. M.A. Levine, K.E. Sassaman, and M.S. Nassaney. Westport, CT: Bergin and Garvey.

DU PRATZ, A.S. LE PAGE 1972 [1774] *The History of Louisiana*. Baton Rouge, LA: Claitor's Publishing.

DYE, DAVID H. 1996 'Riverine Adaptation in the Midsouth,' in *Of Caves and Shell Mounds*, eds. K.C. Carstens and P.J. Watson. Tuscaloosa: University of Alabama Press.

EARLY, ANN M. 1993 'Hardman and Caddoan Saltmaking,' in *Caddoan Saltmakers in the Ouachita Valley*, ed. A.M. Early. Research Series 43. Fayetteville: Arkansas Archeological Survey.

— 2000 'The Caddos of the Trans-Mississippi South,' in *Indians of the Greater Southeast*, ed. B.G. McEwan. Gainesville: University Press of Florida.

EMERSON, E.F. 1957 'The Garden Beds Around Lake Michigan,' *The Michigan Archaeologist* 3:12–27.

EMERSON, THOMAS E. 1997 'Cahokian Elite Ideology and the Mississippian Cosmos,' in *Cahokia: Domination and Ideology in the Mississippian World*, eds. T.R. Pauketat and T.E. Emerson. Lincoln: University of Nebraska Press.

— 1999 'The Langford Tradition and the Process of Tribalization on the Middle Mississippian Borders,' *Midcontinental Journal of Archaeology* 24:3–56.

EMERSON, THOMAS E., AND DALE L. MCELRATH 1983 'A Settlement-Subsistence Model of the Terminal Late Archaic Adaptation in the American Bottom, Illinois,' in *Archaic Hunters and Gatherers in the American Midwest*, eds. J.L. Phillips and J.A. Brown. New York: Academic Press.

ERASMUS, CHARLES J. 1965 'Monument Building: Some Field Experiments,' *Southwestern Journal of Anthropology* 21:277–301.

ESAREY, DUANE 1986 'Red Ochre Mound Building and Marion Phase Associations: A Fulton County, Illinois Perspective,' in *Early Woodland Archaeology*, eds. K.B. Farnsworth and T.E. Emerson. Kampsville Seminars in Archeology 2. Kampsville, IL: Center for American Archeology.

— 2000 'The Late Woodland Maples Mills and Mossville Phase Sequence in the Central Illinois River Valley,' in *Late Woodland Societies: Tradition and Transformation Across the Midcontinent*, eds. T.E. Emerson, D.L. McElrath, and A.C. Fortier. Lincoln: University of Nebraska Press.

ESAREY, DUANE, AND SHARRON K. SANTURE 1990 'The Morton Site Oneota Component and the Bold Counselor Phase,' in *Archaeological Investigations at the Morton Village and Norris Farms 36 Cemetery*, eds. S.K. Santure, A.D., Harn, and D. Esarey. Reports of Investigations 45. Springfield: Illinois State Museum.

ESSENPREIS, PATRICIA S., AND MICHAEL E. MOSELEY 1984 'Fort Ancient: Citadel or Coliseum?,' *Field Museum of Natural History Bulletin* 55:5–10, 20–26.

FAIRBRIDGE, RHODES W. 1992 'Holocene Marine Coastal Evolution of the United States,' in *Quaternary Coasts of the United States: Marine and Lacustrine Systems*, eds. C.H. Fletcher III and J.F. Wehmiller. SEPM Special Publication 48. Tulsa, OK: Society of Sedimentary Geology.

FAULKNER, CHARLES H. 1996 'The Old Stone Fort Revisited: New Clues to an Old Mystery,' in *Mounds, Embankments, and Ceremonialism in the Midsouth*, eds. R.C. Mainfort and R. Walling. Research Series 46. Fayetteville: Arkansas Archeological Survey.

FENTON, JAMES P., AND RICHARD W. JEFFERIES 1991 'The Camargo Mound and Earthworks: Preliminary Findings,' in *The Human Landscape in Kentucky's Past: Site Structure and Settlement Patterns*, eds. C. Stout and C.K. Hensley. Frankfort: Kentucky Heritage Council.

FENTON, WILLIAM N. 1998 *The Great Law and the Longhouse*. Norman: University of Oklahoma Press.

FINLAYSON, WILLIAM D. 1985 *The 1975 and 1978 Rescue Excavations at the Draper Site: Introduction and Settlement Patterns*. Mercury Series Paper 130. Ottawa: National Museum of Man.

FLETCHER, ROBERT V., et al. 1996 'Serpent Mound: A Fort Ancient Icon?,' *Midcontinental Journal of Archaeology* 21:105–43.

FORD, JAMES A. 1963 *Hopewell Culture Burial Mounds Near Helena, Arkansas*. Anthropological Papers 50(1). New York: American Museum of Natural History.

FORD, JAMES A., AND GORDON R. WILLEY 1940 *Crooks Site, A Marksville Period Burial Mound in La Salle Parish, Louisiana*. Anthropological Study 3. New Orleans: Louisiana Geological Survey.

FORTIER, ANDREW C. 1983 'Settlement and Subsistence at the Go-Kart North Site: A Late Archaic Titterington Occupation in the American Bottom, Illinois,' in *Archaic Hunters and Gatherers in the American Midwest*, eds. J.L. Phillips and J.A. Brown. New York: Academic Press.

— 1989 'Community Plan and Feature Assemblage,' in *The Holding Site: A Hopewell Community in the American Bottom*. FAI-270 Site Reports 19. Urbana: University of Illinois Press.

FOSTER, J.W. 1873 *Pre-Historic Races of the United States of America*. Chicago: S.C. Griggs.

FOWKE, GERARD 1898 'Some Popular Errors in Regard to Mound Builders and Indians,' *Ohio Archaeological and Historical Publications* 2:380–403.

— 1902 *Archaeological History of Ohio*. Columbus: Ohio State Archaeological and Historical Society.

— 1928 'Archeological Investigations II,' in *44th Annual Report*. Washington, DC: Bureau of American Ethnology.

FOWLER, MELVIN L. 1959 *Summary Report of Modoc Rock Shelter 1952, 1953, 1955, 1956*. Report of Investigations 8. Springfield: Illinois State Museum.

— 1997 *The Cahokia Atlas: A Historical Atlas of Cahokia Archaeology*, rev. ed. Urbana: Illinois Transportation Archaeological Research Program, University of Illinois.

FOWLER, MELVIN L., et al. 1999 *The Mound 72 Area: Dedicated and Sacred Space in Early Cahokia*, Reports of Investigations 54. Springfield: Illinois State Museum.

FREEMAN, ANDREA K.L., EDWARD E. SMITH JR., AND KENNETH B. TANKERSLEY 1996 'A Stone's Throw from Kimmswick: Clovis Period Research in Kentucky,' in *The Paleoindian and Early Archaic Southeast*, eds. D.G. Anderson and K.E. Sassaman. Tuscaloosa: University of Alabama Press.

FRITZ, GAYLE J. 1990 'Multiple Pathways to Farming in Precontact Eastern North America,' *Journal of World Prehistory* 4:387–435.

— 1995 'New Dates and Data on Early Agriculture: The Legacy of Complex Hunter-Gatherers,' *Annals of the Missouri Botanical Garden* 82:3–15.

— 2000 'Native Farming Systems and Ecosystems in the Mississippi River Valley,' in *Imperfect Balance: Landscape Transformations in the Precolumbian Americas*, ed. D.L. Lentz. New York: Columbia University Press.

FUTATO, EUGENE M. 1996 'A Synopsis of Paleoindian and Early Archaic Research in Alabama,' in *The Paleoindian and Early Archaic Southeast*, eds. D.G. Anderson and K.E. Sassaman. Tuscaloosa: University of Alabama Press.

GALLAGHER, JAMES P., AND ROBERT F. SASSO 1987 'Investiga-

tions into Oneota Ridged Field Agriculture on the Northern Margin of the Prairie Peninsula,' *Plains Anthropologist* 32:141–51.

GARLAND, ELIZABETH B., AND SCOTT G. BELD 1999 'The Early Woodland: Ceramics, Domesticated Plants, and Burial Mounds Foretell the Shape of the Future,' in *Retrieving Michigan's Buried Past*, ed. J.R. Halsey. Bulletin 64. Bloomfield Hills, MI: Cranbrook Institute of Science.

GENHEIMER, ROBERT A. 1997 'Stubbs Cluster: Hopewellian Site Dynamics at a Forgotten Little Miami River Valley Settlement,' in *Ohio Hopewell Community Organization*, eds. W.S. Dancey and P.J. Pacheco. Kent, OH: Kent State University Press.

GIBSON, JON 1996 'Poverty Point and Greater Southeastern Prehistory: The Culture That Did Not Fit,' in *Archaeology of the Mid-Holocene Southeast*, eds. K.E. Sassaman and D.G. Anderson. Gainesville: University Press of Florida.

— 2000 *The Ancient Mounds of Poverty Point*. Gainesville: University of Florida Press.

GOLD, DEBRA L. 2000 '"Utmost Confusion" Reconsidered: Bioarchaeology and Secondary Burial in Late Prehistoric Interior Virginia,' in *Biological Studies of Life in the Age of Agriculture: A View from the Southeast*, ed. P.M. Lambert. Tuscaloosa: University of Alabama Press.

GOLDSTEIN, LYNNE G. 1980 *Mississippian Mortuary Practices: A Case Study of Two Cemeteries in the Lower Illinois Valley*. Scientific Papers 4. Evanston, IL: Northwestern University Archeological Program.

— 1995 'Landscapes and Mortuary Practices: A Case for Regional Perspectives,' in *Regional Approaches to Mortuary Analysis*, ed. L.A. Beck. New York: Plenum.

GOODYEAR, ALBERT C. 1999 'The Early Holocene Occupation of the Southeastern United States: A Geoarchaeological Summary,' in *Ice Age People of North America: Environments, Origins, and Adaptations*, eds. R. Bonnichsen and K.L. Turnmire. Corvallis: Oregon State University Press.

GRAHAM, RUSSELL W. 1986 'Plant-Animal Interactions and Pleistocene Extinctions,' In *Dynamics of Extinction*, ed. D. K. Elliott. New York: John Wiley.

GRAHAM, RUSSELL W., AND ERNEST L. LUNDELIUS JR. 1984 'Coevolutionary Disequilibrium and Pleistocene Extinctions,' in *Quaternary Extinctions: A Prehistoric Revolution*, eds. P.S. Martin and R.G. Klein. Tueson: University of Arizona Press.

GRAHAM, RUSSELL W., et al. 1981 'Kimmswick: A Clovis-Mastodon Association in Eastern Missouri,' *Science* 213: 1115–17.

GRAHAM, RUSSELL W., et al. 1996 'Spatial Response of Mammals to Late Quaternary Environmental Fluctuations,' *Science* 272:1601–06.

GREBER, N'OMI B. 1979 'A Comparative Study of Site Morphology and Burial Patterns at Edwin Harness Mound and Seip Mounds 1 and 2,' in *Hopewell Archaeology*, eds. D.S. Brose and N.B. Greber. Kent, OH: Kent State University Press.

— 1983 *Recent Excavations at the Edwin Harness Mound*. MCJA Special Paper 5. Kent, OH: Kent State University Press.

— 1997 'Two Geometric Enclosures in the Paint Creek Valley: An Estimate of Possible Changes in Community Patterns Through Time,' in *Ohio Hopewell Community Organization*, eds. W.S. Dancey and P.J. Pacheco. Kent, OH: Kent State University Press.

GREBER, N'OMI B., AND KATHARINE C. RUHL 1989 *The Hopewell Site: A Contemporary Analysis Based on the Work of Charles C. Willoughby*. Boulder: Westview Press.

GREEN, WILLIAM 1993 'A Prehistoric Frontier in the Prairie Peninsula: Late Woodland Upland Settlement and Subsistence Patterns,' *Illinois Archaeology* 5:201–14.

GRIFFIN, JAMES B. 1947 'The Spruce Run Earthworks: A Forgotten Adena Site in Delaware County, Ohio,' *Ohio State Archaeological and Historical Society Quarterly* 56:188–200.

— 1966 *The Fort Ancient Aspect*. Anthropological Papers 28. Ann Arbor: Museum of Anthropology, University of Michigan.

— 1967 'Eastern North American Archaeology: A Summary,' *Science* 156:175–91.

— 1978 'Late Prehistory of the Ohio Valley,' in *Handbook of*

*North American Indians: Northeast*, vol. 15, ed. B.G. Trigger. Washington, DC: Smithsonian Institution Press.

GRIFFIN, JAMES B., RICHARD E. FLANDERS, AND PAUL F. TITTERINGTON 1970 *The Burial Complexes of the Knight and Norton Mounds in Illinois and Michigan.* Memoir 2. Ann Arbor: Museum of Anthropology, University of Michigan.

GUCCIONE, MARGARET J., ROBERT H. LAFFERTY III, AND L. SCOTT CUMMINGS 1988 'Environmental Constraints of Human Settlement in an Evolving Holocene Alluvial System, the Lower Mississippi Valley,' *Geoarchaeology* 3:65–84.

GUTHRIE, R. DALE 2001 'Origin and Causes of the Mammoth Steppe: A Story of Cloud Cover, Woolly Mammoth Tooth Pits, Buckles, and Inside-Out Beringia,' *Quaternary Science Reviews* 20:549–74.

HALLY, DAVID J. 1993 'The Territorial Size of Mississippian Chiefdoms,' in *Archaeology of Eastern North America: Papers in Honor of Stephen Williams*, ed. J.B. Stoltman. Archaeological Report 25. Jackson: Mississippi Department of Archives and History.

HALLY, DAVID J., AND HYPATIA KELLY 1998 'The Nature of Mississippian Towns in Georgia: The King Site Example,' in *Mississippian Towns and Sacred Spaces*, eds. R.B. Lewis and C. Stout. Tuscaloosa: University of Alabama Press.

HALLY, DAVID J., AND JAMES L. RUDOLPH 1986 *Mississippi Period Archaeology of the Georgia Piedmont.* Laboratory of Archaeology Report 24. Athens: University of Georgia.

HALSEY, JOHN R. 1999 'Late Woodland Burial Practices,' in *Retrieving Michigan's Buried Past*, ed. J.R. Halsey. Bulletin 64. Bloomfield Hills, MI: Cranbrook Institute of Science.

HANTMAN, JEFFERY L. 1990 'Between Powhatan and Quirank: Reconstructing Monacan Culture and History in the Context of Jamestown,' *American Anthropologist* 92:676–90.

— 2001 'Monacan Archaeology of the Virginia Interior, AD 1400–1700,' in *Societies in Eclipse*, eds. D.S. Brose, C.W. Cowan, and R.C. Mainfort Jr. Washington, DC: Smithsonian Institution Press.

HARN, ALAN D. 1980 *The Prehistory of Dickson Mounds: The Dickson Excavation.* Reports of Investigations 35. Springfield: Illinois State Museum.

— 1994 *Variation in Mississippian Settlement Patterns: The Larson Settlement System in the Central Illinois River Valley.* Reports of Investigations 50. Springfield: Illinois State Museum.

HARRIOT, THOMAS 1972 [1590] *A Briefe and True Report of the New Found Land of Virginia.* New York: Dover.

HART, JOHN P. 1993 'Monongahela Subsistence-Settlement Change: The Late Prehistoric Period in the Lower Upper Ohio River Valley,' *Journal of World Prehistory* 7:71–120.

— 1999 'Dating Roundtop's Domesticates: Implications for Northeast Late Prehistory,' in *Current Northeast Paleoethnobotany*, ed. J.P. Hart. Bulletin 494. Albany: New York State Museum.

HART, JOHN P., AND C. MARGARET SCARRY 1999 'The Age of Common Beans (*Phaseolus vulgaris*) in the Northeastern United States,' *American Antiquity* 64:653–58.

HART, JOHN P., AND NANCY A. SIDELL 1997 'Additional Evidence for Early Cucurbit Use in the Northern Eastern Woodlands East of the Allegheny Front,' *American Antiquity* 62:523–37.

HIGGINS, MICHAEL J. 1990 *The Nochta Site: The Early, Middle, and Late Archaic Occupations (11-Ms-128).* FAI-270 Site Reports 21. Urbana: University of Illinois Press.

HINSDALE, W.B. 1924 'The Missaukee Preserve and Rifle River Forts,' *Papers of the Michigan Academy of Science, Arts, and Letters* 4:1–14.

HOFFMAN, CHARLES F. 1835 *A Winter in the West by a New Yorker.* 2nd ed. New York: Harper and Brothers.

HOLLINGER, R. ERIC 1995 'Residence Patterns and Oneota Cultural Dynamics,' in *Oneota Archaeology: Past, Present, and Future*, ed. W. Green. Report 20. Iowa City: Office of the State Archaeologist.

HOLMES, WILLIAM H. 1883 'Art in Shell of the Ancient Americans,' in *2nd Annual Report.* Washington, DC: Bureau of American Ethnology.

HOUSE, JOHN 1990 'Powell Canal: Baytown Period Adaptation on Bayou Macon, Southeast Arkansas,' in *The Mississippian*

*Emergence*, ed. B.D. Smith. Washington, DC: Smithsonian Institution Press.

HUDSON, CHARLES 1976 *The Southeastern Indians.* Knoxville: University of Tennessee Press.

HUTCHINSON, DALE L. 1996 'Brief Encounters: Tatham Mound and the Evidence for Spanish and Native American Confrontation,' *International Journal of Osteoarchaeology* 6:51–65.

HUTCHINSON, DALE L. *et al.* 2000 'Agricultural Melodies and Alternative Harmonies in Florida and Georgia,' in *Biological Studies of Life in the Age of Agriculture: A View from the Southeast*, ed. P.M. Lambert. Tuscaloosa: University of Alabama Press.

HUTCHINSON, DALE L. AND JEFFREY M. MITCHEM 1996 'The Weeki Wachee Mound, An Early Contact Period Mortuary Locality in Hernando County, West-Central Florida,' *Southeastern Archaeology* 15:47–65.

JACKSON, H. EDWIN 1998 'Little Spanish Fort: An Early Middle Woodland Enclosure in the Lower Yazoo Basin, Mississippi,' *Midcontinental Journal of Archaeology* 23:199–220.

JACKSON, H. EDWIN, AND SUSAN L. SCOTT 2001 'Archaic Faunal Utilization in the Louisiana Bottomlands,' *Southeastern Archaeology* 20:187–96.

JACKSON, STEPHEN T., *et al.* 2000 'Vegetation and Environment in Eastern North America During the Last Glacial Maximum,' *Quaternary Science Reviews* 19:489–508.

JACOBSON, GEORGE L. JR., THOMASON WEBB III, AND ERIC C. GRIMM 1987 'Patterns and Rates of Vegetation Change During the Deglaciation of Eastern North America,' in *North America and Adjacent Oceans During the Last Deglaciation*, ed. W. F. Ruddiman. Boulder, CO: The Geological Society of America.

JEFFERIES, RICHARD W. 1976 *The Tunacunnhee Site: Evidence of Hopewell Interaction in Northwest Georgia.* Anthropological Papers 1. Athens: Department of Anthropology, University of Georgia.

— 1983 'Middle Archaic – Late Archaic Transition in Southern Illinois: An Example from the Carrier Mills Archaeological District,' *American Archeology* 3:199–206.

— 1994 'The Swift Creek Site and Woodland Platform Mounds in the Southeastern United States,' in *Ocmulgee Archaeology 1936–1986*, ed. D.J. Hally. Athens: University of Georgia Press.

— 1995a 'Preliminary Assessment of Mississippian Settlement at the Croley-Evans Site (15KX24), Knox County, Kentucky,' in *Current Archaeological Research in Kentucky*, vol. 3, eds. J.F. Doershuk, C.A. Bergman, and D. Pollack. Frankfort: Kentucky Heritage Council.

— 1995b 'The Status of Archaic Period Research in the Midwestern United States,' *Archaeology of Eastern North America* 23:119–44.

— 1996a 'Hunters and Gatherers after the Ice Age,' in *Kentucky Archaeology*, ed. R.B. Lewis. Lexington: University of Kentucky Press.

— 1996b 'Middle Archaic Bone Pins: Evidence of Mid-Holocene Regional-Scale Social Groups in the Southern Midwest,' *American Antiquity* 62:464–87.

— 1996c 'The Emergence of Long-Distance Exchange Networks in the Southeastern United States,' in *Archaeology of the Mid-Holocene Southeast*, eds. K.E. Sassaman and D.G. Anderson. Gainesville: University Press of Florida.

JEFFERIES, RICHARD W., AND B. MARK LYNCH 1983 'Dimensions of Middle Archaic Cultural Adaptation at the Black Earth Site, Saline County, Illinois,' in *Archaic Hunters and Gatherers in the American Midwest*, eds. J.L. Phillips and J.A. Brown. New York: Academic Press.

JEFFERSON, THOMAS 1954 [1787] *Notes on the State of Virginia.* New York: W. W. Norton.

JESKE, JOHN A. 1927 *The Grand River Mound Group and Camp Site.* Bulletin 3(2). Milwaukee: Milwaukee Public Museum.

JOHANNESSEN, SISSEL 1984 'Paleoethnobotany,' in *American Bottom Archaeology*, eds. C.J. Bareis and J.W. Porter. Urbana: University of Illinois Press.

— 1993 'Farmers of the Late Woodland,' in *Foraging and Farming in the Eastern Woodlands*, ed. C.M. Scarry. Gainesville:

University Press of Florida.

JOHNSON, JAY K. 2000 'The Chickasaws,' in *Indians of the Greater Southeast*, ed. B.G. McEwan. Gainesville: University Press of Florida.

JOHNSON, JAY K., AND SAMUEL O. BROOKES 1989 'Benton Points, Turkey Tails, and Cache Blades: Middle Archaic Exchange in the Midsouth,' *Southeastern Archaeology* 8:134–45.

JOHNSON, JAY K., AND GEOFFREY R. LEHMANN 1996 'Sociopolitical Devolution in Northeast Mississippi and the Timing of the De Soto Entrada,' in *Bioarchaeology of Native American Adaptation in the Spanish Borderlands*, eds. B.J. Baker and L. Kealhofer. Gainesville: University Press of Florida.

JONES, DENNIS, AND CARL KUTTRUFF 1998 'Prehistoric Enclosures in Louisiana and the Marksville Site,' in *Ancient Earthen Enclosures of the Eastern Woodlands*, eds. R.C. Mainfort Jr. and L.P. Sullivan. Gainesville, University Press of Florida.

KATZENBERG, M. ANNE, *et al.* 1995 'Stable Isotope Evidence for Maize Horticulture and Paleodiet in Southern Ontario, Canada,' *American Antiquity* 60:335–50.

KELLAR, JAMES H. 1979 'The Mann Site and "Hopewell" in the Lower Wabash-Ohio Valley,' in *Hopewell Archaeology*, eds. D.S. Brose and N. Greber. Kent, OH: Kent State University Press.

KELLY, JOHN E. 1990a 'Range Site Community Patterns and the Mississippian Emergence,' in *The Mississippian Emergence*, ed. B.D. Smith. Washington, DC: Smithsonian Institution Press.

— 1990b 'The Emergence of Mississippian Culture in the American Bottom Region,' in *The Mississippian Emergence*, ed. B.D. Smith. Washington, DC: Smithsonian Institution Press.

KELLY, JOHN E., STEVEN J. OZUK, AND JOYCE A. WILLIAMS 1990 *The Range Site 2: The Emergent Mississippian Dohack and Range Phase Occupations*. Urbana: University of Illinois Press.

KELLY, LUCRETIA S. 1987 'Patrick Phase Faunal Remains,' in *The Range Site: Archaic Through Late Woodland Occupations*. Urbana: University of Illinois Press.

KIDDER, TRISTRAM 1992 'Coles Creek Period Social Organization and Evolution in Northeast Louisiana,' in *Lords of the Southeast: Social Inequality and the Native Elites of Southeastern North America*, eds. A.W. Barker and T.R. Pauketat. Archeological Papers 3. American Anthropological Association.

— 1998 'Mississippi Period Mound Groups and Communities in the Lower Mississippi Valley,' in *Mississippian Towns and Sacred Spaces*, eds. R.B. Lewis and C. Stout. Tuscaloosa: University of Alabama Press.

— 2002 'Mapping Poverty Point,' *American Antiquity* 67:89–101.

KIMBALL, LARRY R. 1996 'Early Archaic Settlement and Technology: Lessons from Tellico,' in *The Paleoindian and Early Archaic Southeast*, eds. D.G. Anderson and K.E. Sassaman. Tuscaloosa: University of Alabama Press.

KLEPINGER, LINDA, AND DALE R. HENNING 1976 'The Hatten Mound: A Two-Component Burial Site in Northeast Missouri,' *The Missouri Archaeologist* 37:92–170.

KNIGHT, VERNON J. JR. 1990 *Excavation of the Truncated Mound at the Walling Site: Middle Woodland Culture and Copena in the Tennessee Valley*. Report of Investigations 56. Tuscaloosa: Alabama State Museum of Natural History.

— 1998 'Moundville as a Diagrammatic Ceremonial Center,' in *Archaeology of the Moundville Chiefdom*, eds. V.J. Knight Jr. and V.P. Steponaitis. Washington, DC: Smithsonian Institution Press.

KNIGHT, VERNON J. JR., AND VINCAS P. STEPONAITIS 1998 'A New History of Moundville,' in *Archaeology of the Moundville Chiefdom*, eds. V.J. Knight Jr. and V.P. Steponaitis. Tuscaloosa: University of Alabama Press.

KNIGHT, VERNON J. JR., JAMES A. BROWN, AND GEORGE E. LANKFORD 2001 'On the Subject Matter of Southeastern Ceremonial Complex Art,' *Southeastern Archaeology* 20:129–41.

KONISBERG, LYLE W. 1985 'Demography and Mortuary Practice

at Seip Mound One,' *Midcontinental Journal of Archaeology* 10:123–48.

KRAUSE, RICHARD A. 1990 'The Death of the Sacred: Lessons from a Mississippian Mound in the Tennessee River Valley,' *Journal of Alabama Archaeology* 36:63–98.

KRECH, SHEPARD 1999 *The Ecological Indian: Myth and History*. New York: W. W. Norton.

KREISA, PAUL P. 1993 'Oneota Burial Patterns in Eastern Wisconsin,' *Midcontinental Journal of Archaeology* 18:35–60.

KROGMAN, WILTON M. 1931 'The Archaeology of the Chicago Area,' *Transactions of the Illinois State Academy of Science* 23:413–20.

KUHN, ROBERT D. AND MARTHA L. SEMPOWSKI 2001 'A New Approach to Dating the League of the Iroquois,' *American Antiquity* 66:301–14.

KULLEN, DOUGLAS 1994 'The Comstock Trace: A Huber Phase Earthwork and Habitation Site Near Joliet, Will County, Illinois,' *Midcontinental Journal of Archaeology* 19:3–38.

LANGFORD, GEORGE 1930 'The Fisher Mound and Village Site,' *Transactions of the Illinois State Academy of Science* 22:79–92.

LARSEN, CLARK S., REBECCA SHAVIT, AND MARK C. GRIFFIN 1991 'Dental Caries Evidence for Dietary Change: An Archaeological Context,' in *Advances in Dental Anthropology*, eds. M.A. Kelley and C.S. Larsen. New York: Willey-Liss.

LARSON, LEWIS H. JR. 1971 'Archaeological Implications of Social Stratification at the Etowah Site, Georgia,' *American Antiquity Memoir* 25:58–67.

LATHAM, INCREASE A. 1855 *The Antiquities of Wisconsin*. Smithsonian Contributions to Knowledge 7. Washington, DC: Smithsonian Institution.

LAWSON, JOHN 1709 *A New Voyage to Carolina*. London.

LEIGH, STEVEN R. 1988 'Comparative Analysis of the Elizabeth Middle Woodland Artifact Assemblage,' in *The Archaic and Woodland Cemeteries at the Elizabeth Site in the Lower Illinois Valley*, eds. D.K. Charles, S.R. Leigh, and J.E. Buikstra. Research Series 7. Kampsville, IL: Center for American Archeology.

LEIGH, STEVEN R., DOUGLAS K. CHARLES, AND DONALD G. ALBERTSON 1988 'Middle Woodland Component,' in *The Archaic and Woodland Cemeteries at the Elizabeth Site in the Lower Illinois Valley*, eds. D.K. Charles, S.R. Leigh, and J.E. Buikstra. Research Series 7. Kampsville, IL: Center for American Archeology.

LEPPER, BRADLEY T. 1996 'The Newark Earthworks and the Geometric Enclosures of the Scioto Valley: Connections and Conjectures,' in *A View from the Core: A Synthesis of Ohio Hopewell Archaeology*, ed. P.J. Pacheco. Columbus: Ohio Archaeological Council.

— 1998 'The Archaeology of the Newark Earthworks,' in *Ancient Earthen Enclosures of the Eastern Woodlands*, eds. R.C. Mainfort Jr. and L.P. Sullivan. Gainesville, University Press of Florida.

LEPPER, BRADLEY T. AND RICHARD YERKES 1997 'Hopewellian Occupations at the Northern Periphery of the Newark Earthworks,' in *Ohio Hopewell Community Organization*, eds. W. S. Dancey and P.J. Pacheco. Kent, OH: Kent State University Press.

LIMP, W. FREDERICK, AND VAN A. REIDHEAD 1979 'An Economic Evaluation of the Potential of Fish Utilization in Riverine Environments,' *American Antiquity* 44:70–78.

LITTLE, ELIZABETH A. 2002 'Kautantouwit's Legacy: Calibrated Dates on Prehistoric Maize in New England,' *American Antiquity* 67:109–18.

LOPINOT, NEAL H. 1991 'Archaeobotanical Remains,' in *The Archaeology of the Cahokia Mounds ICT-II: Biological Remains*. Illinois Cultural Resources Study 13. Springfield: Illinois Historic Preservation Agency.

MAINFORT, ROBERT C. JR. 1986 *Pinson Mounds: A Middle Woodland Ceremonial Center*. Research Series 7. Nashville: Division of Archaeology, Tennessee Department of Conservation.

— 2001 'The Late Prehistoric and Protohistoric Periods in the Central Mississippi Valley," in *Societies in Eclipse*, eds. D.S. Brose, C.W. Cowan, and R.C. Mainfort Jr. Washington, DC: Smithsonian Institution Press.

MAINFORT, ROBERT C., AND KENNETH C. CARSTENS 1987 'A Middle Woodland Embankment and Mound Complex in Western Kentucky,' *Southeastern Archaeology* 6:57–61.

MALLAM, R. CLARK 1976 *The Iowa Effigy Mound Manifestation: An Interpretive Model*. Report 9. Iowa City: Office of the State Archaeologist.

MANDRYK, CAROLE A.S., *et al.* 2001 'Late Quaternary Paleoenvironments of Northwestern North America: Implications for Inland Versus Coastal Migration Routes,' *Quaternary Science Reviews* 20:301–14.

MANN, DANIEL H., AND THOMAS D. HAMILTON 1995 'Late Pleistocene and Holocene Paleoenvironments of the North Pacific Coast,' *Quaternary Science Reviews* 14:449–71.

MARKMAN, CHARLES W. 1991 *Chicago Before History: The Prehistoric Archaeology of a Modern Metropolitan Area*. Studies in Illinois Archaeology 7. Springfield: Illinois Historic Preservation Agency.

MARTIN, PAUL S. 1973 'The Discovery of America,' *Science* 179:969–74.

MARTIN, PAUL S., AND CHRISTINE R. SZUTER 1999 'War Zones and Game Sinks in Lewis and Clark's West,' *Conservation Biology* 13:36–45.

MARQUARDT, WILLIAM H. 1985 'Complexity and Scale in the Study of Fisher-Gatherer-Hunters: An Example from the Eastern United States,' in *Prehistoric Hunter-Gatherers: The Emergence of Cultural Complexity*, eds. T.D. Price and J.A. Brown. Orlando: Academic Press.

— 2001 'The Emergence and Demise of the Calusa,' in *Societies in Eclipse*, eds. D.S. Brose, C.W. Cowan, and R.C. Mainfort Jr. Washington, DC: Smithsonian Institution Press.

MARQUARDT, WILLIAM H., AND PATTY JO WATSON 1983 'The Shell Mound Archaic of Western Kentucky,' in *Archaic Hunters and Gatherers in the American Midwest*, eds. J.L. Phillips and J.A. Brown. New York: Academic Press.

MCELRATH, DALE L., AND ANDREW C. FORTIER 2000 'The Early Late Woodland Occupation of the American Bottom,' in *Late Woodland Societies: Tradition and Transformation Across the Midcontinent*, eds. T.E. Emerson, D.L. McElrath, and A.C. Fortier. Lincoln: University of Nebraska Press.

MCGAHEY, SAMUEL O. 1996 'Paleoindian and Early Archaic Data from Mississippi,' in *The Paleoindian and Early Archaic Southeast*, eds. D.G. Anderson and K.E. Sassaman. Tuscaloosa: University of Alabama Press.

MCGIMSEY, CHARLES R., AND MICHAEL D. WIANT 1986 'The Woodland Occupations: Summary and Conclusion,' in *Woodland Period Occupations of the Napoleon Hollow Site in the Lower Illinois Valley*, eds. M.D. Wiant and C.R. McGimsey. Research Series 6. Kampsville, IL: Center for American Archeology.

MCKERN, WILLIAM C. 1931 *A Wisconsin Variant of the Hopewell Culture*. Bulletin 10(2). Milwaukee: Milwaukee Public Museum.

MCKUSICK, MARSHALL 1973 *The Grant Oneota Village*. Report 4. Iowa City: Office of the State Archaeologist.

MCMANAMON, FRANCIS P., JAMES W. BRADLEY, AND ANN L. MAGENNIS 1986 *The Indian Neck Ossuary*. Cultural Resources Management Study 17. Boston: North Atlantic Regional Office, National Park Service.

MELTZER, DAVID J. 1988 'Late Pleistocene Human Adaptations in Eastern North America,' *Journal of World Prehistory* 2:1–51.

— 1989 'Was Stone Exchanged Among Eastern North American Paleoindians?,' in *Eastern Paleoindian Lithic Resource Use*, eds. C.J. Ellis and J.C. Lothrop. Boulder, CO: Westview Press.

— 1993 *Search for the First Americans*. Washington, DC: Smithsonian Books.

— 1997 'Monte Verde and the Pleistocene Peopling of the Americas,' *Science* 276:754–55.

MELTZER, DAVID J., AND BRUCE D. SMITH 1986 'Paleoindian and Early Archaic Subsistence Strategies in Eastern North America,' in *Foraging, Collecting, and Harvesting: Archaic Period Subsistence and Settlement in the Eastern Woodlands*, ed. S.W. Neusius. Occasional Paper 6. Carbondale: Center for Archaeological Investigations, Southern Illinois University.

MELTZER, DAVID J., *et al.* 1997 'On the Pleistocene Antiquity of Monte Verde, Southern Chile,' *American Antiquity* 62:659–63.

MENSFORTH, ROBERT P. 1990 'Paleodemography of the Carlston Annis (Bt-5) Late Archaic Skeletal Population,' *American Journal of Physical Anthropology* 82:81–99.

MILANICH, JERALD T. 1994 *Archaeology of Precolumbian Florida*. Gainesville: University Press of Florida.

MILLS, WILLIAM C. 1907 'Explorations of the Edwin Harness Mound, Ohio,' *Archaeological and Historical Quarterly* 16:5–85.

— 1922 'Exploration of the Mound City Group,' *Certain Mounds and Village Sites in Ohio* 3:245–408.

MILNER, CLAIRE M., AND JOHN M. O'SHEA 1998 'The Socioeconomic Role of Late Woodland Enclosures in Northern Lower Michigan,' in *Ancient Earthen Enclosures of the Eastern Woodlands*, eds. R.C. Mainfort Jr. and L.P. Sullivan. Gainesville, University Press of Florida.

MILNER, GEORGE R. 1983 *The East St. Louis Stone Quarry Site Cemetery*. FAI-270 Site Reports 1. Urbana: University of Illinois Press.

— 1984 'Mississippian Sand Prairie Phase Mortuary Complex,' in *The Florence Street Site*. FAI-270 Site Reports 2. Urbana: University of Illinois Press.

— 1998 *The Cahokia Chiefdom: The Archaeology of a Mississippian Society*. Washington, DC: Smithsonian Institution Press.

— 1999 'Warfare in Prehistoric and Early Historic Eastern North America,' *Journal of Archaeological Research* 7:105–51.

MILNER, GEORGE R., AND RICHARD W. JEFFERIES 1987 'A Reevaluation of the WPA Excavation of the Robbins Mound in Boone County, Kentucky,' in *Current Archaeological Research in Kentucky: Volume 1*, ed. D. Pollack. Frankfort: Kentucky Heritage Council.

— 1998 'The Read Archaic Shell Midden in Kentucky,' *Southeastern Archaeology* 17:119–32.

MILNER, GEORGE R., AND SISSEL SCHROEDER 1992 'The Guy Smith Site and Stone-Box Graves: New Perspectives from Old Collections,' *Illinois Archaeology* 4:49–73.

MILNER, GEORGE R., EVE ANDERSON, AND VIRGINIA G. SMITH 1991 'Warfare in Late Prehistoric West-Central Illinois,' *American Antiquity* 56:581–603.

MILNER, GEORGE R., DOROTHY H. HUMPF, AND HENRY C. HARPENDING 1989 'Pattern Matching of Age-at-Death Distributions in Paleodemographic Analysis,' *American Journal of Physical Anthropology* 80:49–58.

MITCHIE, JAMES L. 1996 'The Taylor Site: An Early Occupation in Central South Carolina,' in *The Paleoindian and Early Archaic Southeast*, eds. D.G. Anderson and K.E. Sassaman. Tuscaloosa: University of Alabama Press.

MITCHEM, JEFFREY M. 1989 'Artifacts of Exploration: Archaeological Evidence from Florida,' in *First Encounters: Spanish Explorations in the Caribbean and the United States, 1492–1570*, eds. J.T. Milanich and S.Milbrath, Gainesville: University of Florida Press.

MOREY, DARCY F., AND MICHAEL D. WIANT 1992 'Early Holocene Domestic Dog Burials from the North American Midwest,' *Current Anthropology* 33:224–29.

MORGAN, RICHARD G. 1952 'Outline of Cultures in the Ohio Region,' in *Archeology of Eastern United States*, ed. J.B. Griffin. Chicago: University of Chicago Press.

MORSE, DAN F. 1990 'The Nodena Phase,' in *Towns and Temples Along the Mississippi*, eds. D.H. Dye and C.A. Cox. Tuscaloosa: University of Alabama Press.

MORSE, DAN F., AND PHYLLIS A. MORSE 1983 *Archaeology of the Central Mississippi Valley*. New York: Academic Press.

— (eds.) 1998 *The Lower Mississippi Valley Expeditions of Clarence Bloomfield Moore*. Tuscaloosa: University of Alabama Press.

MORSE, PHYLLIS A. 1990 'The Parkin Site and the Parkin Phase,' in *Towns and Temples Along the Mississippi*, eds. D.H. Dye and C.A. Cox. Tuscaloosa: University of Alabama Press.

MOSIMANN, J.E., AND P.S. MARTIN 1975 'Simulating Overkill by Paleoindians,' *American Scientist* 63:304–13.

MOULTON, GARY E. (ed.) 1986 *The Journals of the Lewis & Clark*

*Expedition*, vol. 2. Lincoln: University of Nebraska Press.
— (ed.) 1990 *The Journals of the Lewis & Clark Expedition*, vol. 6. Lincoln: University of Nebraska Press.
MULLER, JON 1986 *Archaeology of the Lower Ohio River Valley*. Orlando: Academic Press.
— 1997a *Mississippian Political Economy*. New York: Plenum.
— 1997b Native Eastern American Population Continuity and Stability,' in *Integrating Archaeological Demography: Multidisciplinary Approaches to Prehistoric Population*, ed. R.R. Paine. Occasional Paper 24. Carbondale: Center for Archaeological Investigations, Southern Illinois University.
NASS, JOHN P. JR., AND JOHN P. HART 2000 'Subsistence-Settlement Change During the Late Prehistoric Period in the Upper Ohio River Valley: New Models and Old Constructs' in *Cultures Before Contact: The Late Prehistory of Ohio and Surrounding Regions*, ed. R.A. Genheimer. Columbus: Ohio Archaeological Council.
NASS, JOHN P. JR., AND RICHARD W. YERKES 1995 'Social Differentiation in Mississippian and Fort Ancient Societies,' in *Mississippian Communities and Households*, eds. J.D. Rogers and B.D. Smith. Tuscaloosa: University of Alabama Press.
NASSANEY, MICHAEL S. 2000 'The Late Woodland Southeast,' in *Late Woodland Societies: Tradition and Transformation Across the Midcontinent*, eds. T.E. Emerson, D.L. McElrath, and A.C. Fortier. Lincoln: University of Nebraska Press.
NEUMANN, GEORG K., AND MELVIN L. FOWLER 1952 *Hopewellian Sites in the Lower Wabash Valley*. Scientific Papers 5(5). Springfield: Illinois State Museum.
NEUSIUS, SARAH W., *et al.* 1998 'Fortified Village or Mortuary Site? Exploring the Use of the Ripley Site,' in *Ancient Earthen Enclosures of the Eastern Woodlands*, eds. R.C. Mainfort Jr. and L.P. Sullivan. Gainesville: University Press of Florida.
NEWSOM, LEE A. 2002 'The Paleoethnobotany of the Archaic Mortuary Pond,' in *Windover: Multidisciplinary Investigations of an Early Archaic Florida Cemetery*, ed. G.H. Doran. Gainesville: University Press of Florida.
O'BRIEN, MICHAEL J. 2001 *Mississippian Community Organization: The Powers Phase in Southeastern Missouri*. New York: Plenum.
O'SHEA, JOHN M. 1988 'Social Organization and Mortuary Behavior in the Late Woodland Period in Michigan,' In *Interpretations of Culture Change in the Eastern Woodlands During the Late Woodland Period*, ed. R.W. Yerkes. Occasional Papers 3. Columbus: Department of Anthropology, Ohio State University.
O'STEEN, LISA D. 1996 'Paleoindian and Early Archaic Settlement Along the Oconee Drainage,' in *The Paleoindian and Early Archaic Southeast*, eds. D.G. Anderson and K.E. Sassaman. Tuscaloosa: University of Alabama Press.
OVERSTREET, DAVID F. 1997 'Oneota Prehistory and History,' *Wisconsin Archeologist* 78:250–96.
PACHECO, PAUL J. 1996 'Ohio Hopewell Regional Settlement Patterns,' in *A View from the Core: A Synthesis of Ohio Hopewell Archaeology*, ed. P.J. Pacheco. Columbus: Ohio Archaeological Council.
PAUKETAT, TIMOTHY R. 1994 *The Ascent of Chiefs: Cahokia and Mississippian Politics in Native North America*. Tuscaloosa: University of Alabama Press.
— 1998 *The Archaeology of Downtown Cahokia: The Tract 15A and Dunham Tract Excavations*. Studies in Archaeology 1. Urbana: Illinois Transportation Archaeological Research Program, University of Illinois.
PAYNE, CLAUDINE, AND JOHN F. SCARRY 1998 'Town Structure at the Edge of the Mississippian World,' in *Mississippian Towns and Sacred Spaces*, eds. R.B. Lewis and C. Stout. Tuscaloosa: University of Alabama Press.
PEEBLES, CHRISTOPHER S. 1971 'Moundville and Surrounding Sites: Some Structural Considerations of Mortuary Practices II,' *American Antiquity Memoir* 25: 68–91.
— 1983 'Moundville: Late Prehistoric Sociopolitical Organization in the Southeastern United States,' in *The Development of Political Organization in Native North America*, ed. E. Tooker. Washington, DC: American Ethnological Society.

PENNEY, DAVID W. 1985 'The Late Archaic Period,' in *Ancient Art of the American Woodland Indians*. New York: Harry N. Abrams.
PERINO, GREGORY H. 1971 'The Mississippian Component at the Schild Site (No. 4), Greene County, Illinois,' In *Mississippian Site Archaeology in Illinois*. Bulletin 8. Urbana: Illinois Archaeological Survey.
PETERSON, JAMES B., AND NANCY A. SIDELL 1996 'Mid-Holocene Evidence of *Cucurbita* sp. from Central Maine,' *American Antiquity* 61:685–98.
PHILLIPS, PHILIP 1970 *Archaeological Survey in the Lower Yazoo Basin, Mississippi, 1949–1955*. Papers 60. Cambridge: Peabody Museum of Archaeology and Ethnology, Harvard University.
PHILLIPS, PHILIP, AND JAMES A. BROWN 1978 *Pre-Columbian Shell Engravings From the Craig Mound at Spiro, Oklahoma*, Part 1. Cambridge: Peabody Museum Press.
PHILLIPS, PHILIP, JAMES A. FORD, AND JAMES B. GRIFFIN 1951 *Archaeological Survey in the Lower Mississippi Alluvial Valley, 1940–1947*. Papers 25. Cambridge: Peabody Museum of Archaeology and Ethnology, Harvard University.
PICKARD, WILLIAM H. 1996 '1990 Excavations at Capitolium Mound (33WN13), Marietta, Washington County, Ohio: A Working Evaluation,' in *A View from the Core: A Synthesis of Ohio Hopewell Archaeology*, ed. P.J. Pacheco. Columbus: Ohio Archaeological Council.
POLLACK, DAVID, AND A. GWYNN HENDERSON 2000a 'Insights into Fort Ancient Culture Change: A View From South of the Ohio River,' in *Cultures Before Contact: The Late Prehistory of Ohio and Surrounding Regions*, ed. R.A. Genheimer. Columbus: Ohio Archaeological Council.
— 2000b 'Late Woodland Cultures in Kentucky,' in *Late Woodland Societies: Tradition and Transformation Across the Midcontinent*, eds. T.E. Emerson, D.L. McElrath, and A.C. Fortier. Lincoln: University of Nebraska Press.
PORTER, JAMES W. 1974 *Cahokia Archaeology as Viewed from the Mitchell Site: A Satellite Community at AD 1150–1200*. PhD dissertation. Madison: Department of Anthropology, University of Wisconsin.
POTTER, STEPHEN R. 1993 *Commoners, Tribute, and Chiefs: The Development of Algonquian Culture in the Potomac Valley*. Charlottesville: University Press of Virginia.
POWELL, MARY L. 1991 'Endemic Treponematosis and Tuberculosis in the Prehistoric Southeastern United States: Biological Costs of Chronic Endemic Disease,' in *Human Paleopathology: Current Syntheses and Future Options*, eds. D.J. Ortner and A.C. Aufderheide, Washington, DC: Smithsonian Institution Press.
— 1996 'Health and Disease in the Green River Archaic,' in *Of Caves and Shell Mounds*, eds. K.C. Carstens and P.J. Watson. Tuscaloosa: University of Alabama Press.
— 1998 'Of Time and the River: Perspectives on Health During the Moundville Chiefdom,' in *Archaeology of the Moundville Chiefdom*, eds. V.J. Knight Jr. and V.P. Steponaitis. Tuscaloosa: University of Alabama Press.
PRICE, JAMES E. AND GREGORY L. FOX 1990 'Recent Investigations at Towosahgy State Historic Site,' *The Missouri Archaeologist* 51:1–71.
PRICE, JAMES E. AND JAMES B. GRIFFIN 1979 *The Snodgrass Site of the Powers Phase of Southeast Missouri*. Anthropological Papers 66. Ann Arbor: Museum of Anthropology, University of Michigan.
PRUFER, OLAF H. 1997 'Fort Hill 1964: New Data and Reflections on Hopewell Hilltop Enclosures in Southern Ohio,' in *Ohio Hopewell Community Organization*, eds. W.S. Dancey and P.J. Pacheco. Kent, OH: Kent State University Press.
PUTNAM, FREDERIC W. 1887 The Serpent Mound Saved. *Ohio Archaeological and Historical Quarterly* 1:187–90.
RAILEY, JIMMY A. 1984 *The Pyles Site (15MS228): A Newtown Village in Mason County, Kentucky*. Occasional Paper 1. Lexington, KY: W. S. Webb Archaeological Society.
RAMSDEN, PETER G. 1990 'The Hurons: Archaeology and Culture History,' in *The Archaeology of Southern Ontario to AD 1650*, eds. C.J. Ellis and N. Ferris. Occasional Publication 5. London: London Chapter, Ontario Archaeological Society.

REEDER, ROBERT L. 2000 'The Maramec Spring Phase,' in *Late Woodland Societies: Tradition and Transformation Across the Midcontinent*, eds. T.E. Emerson, D.L. McElrath, and A.C. Fortier. Lincoln: University of Nebraska Press.

RILEY, THOMAS J., *et al.* 1994 'Accelerator Mass Spectrometry (AMS) Dates Confirm Early *Zea Mays* in the Mississippi River Valley,' *American Antiquity* 59:490–98.

RINDOS, DAVID, AND SISSEL JOHANNESSEN 1991 'Human–Plant Interactions and Cultural Change in the American Bottom,' in *Cahokia and the Hinterlands: Middle Mississippian Cultures of the Midwest*, eds. T.E. Emerson and R.B. Lewis. Urbana: University of Illinois Press.

RIORDAN, ROBERT V. 1996 'The Enclosed Hilltops of Southern Ohio,' in *A View from the Core: A Synthesis of Ohio Hopewell Archaeology*, ed. P.J. Pacheco. Columbus: Ohio Archaeological Council.

— 1998 'Boundaries, Resistance, and Control: Enclosing the Hilltops in Middle Woodland Ohio,' in *Ancient Earthen Enclosures of the Eastern Woodlands*, eds. R.C. Mainfort Jr. and L.P. Sullivan. Gainesville, University Press of Florida.

RITCHIE, WILLIAM A. 1980 *The Archaeology of New York State*. rev. ed. Harrison, NY: Harbor Hill Books.

RODELL, RONALD L. 2000 'Patterns of Oneota Settlement Within the Middle Portion of the Upper Mississippi Valley,' in *Mounds, Modoc, and Mesoamerica: Papers in Honor of Melvin L. Fowler*, ed. S.R. Ahler. Scientific Papers 28. Springfield: Illinois State Museum.

ROLINGSON, MARTHA A. 1990 'Excavations of Mound S at the Toltec Mounds Site: Preliminary Report,' *The Arkansas Archeologist* 31:1–29.

— 1998 *Toltec Mounds and Plum Bayou Culture: Mound D Excavations*. Research Series 54. Fayetteville: Arkansas Archeological Survey.

ROUNTREE, HELEN C., AND E. RANDOLPH TURNER III 1998 'The Evolution of the Powhatan Paramount Chiefdom in Virginia,' in *Chiefdoms and Chieftaincy in the Americas*, ed. E.M. Redmond. Gainesville: University Press of Florida.

RUDOLPH, JAMES L. 1984 'Earthlodges and Platform Mounds: Changing Public Architecture in the Southeastern United States,' *Southeastern Archaeology* 3:33–45.

RUFF, CHRISTOPHER B. 1999 'Skeletal Structure and Behavioral Patterns of Prehistoric Great Basin Populations,' in *Prehistoric Lifeways in the Great Basin Wetlands: Bioarchaeological Reconstruction and Interpretation*, eds. B.E. Hemphill and C.S. Larsen. Salt Lake City: University of Utah Press.

RUSSO, MICHAEL 1996a 'Southeastern Archaic Mounds,' in *Archaeology of the Mid-Holocene Southeast*, eds. K.E. Sassaman and D.G. Anderson. Gainesville: University Press of Florida.

— 1996b 'Southeastern Mid-Holocene Coastal Settlements,' in *Archaeology of the Mid-Holocene Southeast*, eds. K.E. Sassaman and D.G. Anderson. Gainesville: University Press of Florida.

SALKIN, PHILIP H. 2000 'The Horicon and Kekoskee Phases: Cultural Complexity in the Late Woodland Stage in Southeastern Wisconsin,' in *Late Woodland Societies: Tradition and Transformation Across the Midcontinent*, eds. T.E. Emerson, D.L. McElrath, and A.C. Fortier. Lincoln: University of Nebraska Press.

SANTURE, SHARRON K. 1990 'Norris Farms 36: A Bold Counselor Phase Oneota Cemetery,' in *Archaeological Investigations at the Morton Village and Norris Farms 36 Cemetery*, eds. S.K. Santure, A.D. Harn, and D. Esarey. Reports of Investigations 45. Springfield: Illinois State Museum.

SANTURE, SHARRON K., AND DUANE ESAREY 1990 'Analysis of Artifacts from the Oneota Mortuary Component,' in *Archaeological Investigations at the Morton Village and Norris Farms 36 Cemetery*, eds. S.K. Santure, A.D. Harn, and D. Esarey. Reports of Investigations 45. Springfield: Illinois State Museum.

SASSAMAN, KENNETH E. 1993 *Early Pottery in the Southeast: Tradition and Innovation in Cooking Technology*. Tuscaloosa: University of Alabama Press.

— 1996 'Technological Innovations in Economic and Social Contexts,' in *Archaeology of the Mid-Holocene Southeast*, eds. K.E. Sassaman and D.G. Anderson. Gainesville: University Press of Florida.

— 1999 'A Southeastern Perspective on Soapstone Vessel Technology in the Northeast,' in *The Archaeological Northeast*, eds. M.A. Levine, K.E. Sassaman, and M.S. Nassaney. Westport, CT: Bergin and Garvey.

SASSAMAN, KENNETH E., AND R. JERALD LEDBETTER 1996 'Middle and Late Archaic Architecture,' in *Archaeology of the Mid-Holocene Southeast*, eds. K.E. Sassaman and D.G. Anderson. Gainesville: University Press of Florida.

SAUNDERS, JOE W., *et al.* 1997 'A Mound Complex in Louisiana at 5400–5000 Years Before the Present,' *Science* 277:1796–99.

SAUNDERS, JOE W., *et al.* 2001 'An Assessment of the Antiquity of the Lower Jackson Mound,' *Southeastern Archaeology* 20:67–77.

SCHNITGER, FRIEDRICH M. 1989 *Forgotten Kingdoms in Sumatra*. Oxford: Oxford University Press.

SCHOENINGER, MARGARET J., AND MARK R. SCHURR 1998 'Human Subsistence at Moundville: The Stable-Isotope Data,' in *Archaeology of the Moundville Chiefdom*, eds. V.J. Knight Jr. and V.P. Steponaitis. Tuscaloosa: University of Alabama Press.

SCHROEDER, SISSEL 1997 *Place, Productivity, and Politics: The Evolution of Cultural Complexity in the Cahokia Area*. PhD Dissertation. University Park: The Pennsylvania State University.

SCHROEDER, GERALD F. 1998 'Mississippian Towns in the Eastern Tennessee Valley,' in *Mississippian Towns and Sacred Spaces*, eds. R.B. Lewis and C. Stout. Tuscaloosa: University of Alabama Press.

SCHROEDL, GERALD F., C. CLIFFORD BOYD JR., AND R.P. STEPHEN DAVID JR. 1990 'Explaining Mississippian Origins in East Tennessee,' in *The Mississippian Emergence*, ed. B.D. Smith. Washington, DC: Smithsonian Institution Press.

SCHULDENREIN, JOSEPH 1996 'Geoarchaeology and the Mid-Holocene Landscape History of the Greater Southeast,' in *Archaeology of the Mid-Holocene Southeast*, eds. K.E. Sassaman and D.G. Anderson. Gainesville: University Press of Florida.

SEEMAN, MARK F. 1992 'The Bow and Arrow, the Intrusive Mound Complex, and a Late Woodland Jack's Reef Horizon in the Mid-Ohio Valley,' in *Cultural Variability in Context: Woodland Settlements of the Mid-Ohio Valley*, ed. M.F. Seeman. MCJA Special Paper 7. Kent, OH: Kent State University Press.

— 1995 'When Words are Not Enough: Hopewell Interregionalism and the Use of Material Symbols at the GE Mound,' in *Native American Interactions: Multiscalar Analyses and Interpretations in the Eastern Woodlands*, eds. M.S. Nassaney and K.E. Sassaman. Knoxville: University of Tennessee Press.

SEEMAN, MARK F., AND WILLIAM S. DANCEY 2000 'The Late Woodland Period in Southern Ohio: Basic Issues and Prospects,' in *Late Woodland Societies: Tradition and Transformation Across the Midcontinent*, eds. T.E. Emerson, D.L. McElrath, and A.C. Fortier. Lincoln: University of Nebraska Press.

SEVERINGHAUS, JEFFREY P. AND EDWARD J. BROOK 1999 'Abrupt Climate Change at the End of the Last Glacial Period Inferred from Trapped Air in Polar Ice,' *Science* 286:930–34.

SHARP, WILLIAM E. 1996 'Fort Ancient Farmers,' in *Kentucky Archaeology*, ed. R.B. Lewis. Lexington: University of Kentucky Press.

SHETRONE, H.C. 1925 'Exploration of the Wright Group of Prehistoric Earthworks,' *Certain Mounds and Village Sites in Ohio* 4:41–58.

— 1926 'Explorations of the Hopewell Group of Prehistoric Earthworks,' *Ohio Archaeological and Historical Publications* 35:5–227.

— 1951 *Primer of Ohio Archaeology: The Mound Builders and the Indians*. Columbus: Ohio State Archaeological and Historical Society.

SHOTT, MICHAEL J. 1989 'Technological Organization in Great Lakes Paleoindian Assemblages,' in *Eastern Paleoindian Lithic Resource Use*, eds. C.J. Ellis and J.C. Lothrop. Boulder,

CO: Westview Press.
— 1996 'Innovation and Selection in Prehistory: A Case Study from the American Bottom,' in *Stone Tools: Theoretical Insights into Human Prehistory*, ed. G.H. Odell. New York: Plenum Press.
SIMON, MARY L. 2000 'Regional Variations in Plant Use Strategies in the Midwest During the Late Woodland,' in *Late Woodland Societies: Tradition and Transformation Across the Midcontinent*, eds. T.E. Emerson, D.L. McElrath, and A.C. Fortier. Lincoln: University of Nebraska Press.
SMITH, BRUCE D. 1978 'Variation in Mississippian Settlement Patterns,' in *Mississippian Settlement Patterns*, ed. B.D. Smith. New York: Academic Press.
— 1986 'The Archaeology of the Southeastern United States: From Dalton to de Soto 10,500–500 BP,' *Advances in World Archaeology* 5:1–92.
— 1987 'The Economic Potential of *Chenopodium Berlandieri* in Prehistoric Eastern North America,' *Journal of Ethnobiology* 7:29–54.
— 1989 'Origins of Agriculture in Eastern North America,' *Science* 246:1566–71.
— 1992 'Hopewellian Farmers of Eastern North America,' in *Rivers of Change: Essays on Early Agriculture in Eastern North America*, by B.D. Smith. Washington, DC: Smithsonian Institution Press.
— 1995 *The Emergence of Agriculture*. New York: Scientific American Library.
SMITH, BUCKINGHAM (trans.) 1968 *Narratives of De Soto in the Conquest of Florida*. Gainesville: Palmetto Books.
SMITH, HARRIET M. 1969 'The Murdock Mound, Cahokia,' in *Explorations into Cahokia Archaeology*, ed. M.L. Fowler. Bulletin 7. Urbana: Illinois Archaeological Survey.
SMITH, MARIA O. 1997 'Osteological Indications of Warfare in the Archaic Period of the Western Tennessee Valley,' in *Troubled Times: Violence and Warfare in the Past*, eds. D.L. Martin and D.W. Frayer. Amsterdam: Gordon and Breach.
SMITH, MARVIN T. 1987 *Archaeology of Aboriginal Culture Change in the Interior Southeast*. Gainesville: University of Florida Press.
— 2000 *Coosa: The Rise and Fall of a Southeastern Mississippian Chiefdom*. Gainesville: University Press of Florida.
— 2001 'The Rise and Fall of Coosa, AD 1350–1700,' in *Societies in Eclipse*, eds. D.S. Brose, C.W. Cowan, and R.C. Mainfort Jr. Washington, DC: Smithsonian Institution Press.
SNOW, DEAN R. 1994 *The Iroquois*. Oxford: Blackwell.
— 1995 'Microchronology and Demographic Evidence Relating to the Size of Pre-Columbian North American Indian Populations,' *Science* 268:1601–04.
— 1996 'Mohawk Demography and the Effects of Exogenous Epidemics on American Indian Populations,' *Journal of Anthropological Archaeology* 15:160–82.
— 2001 'Evolution of the Mohawk Iroquois,' in *Societies in Eclipse*, eds. D.S. Brose, C.W. Cowan, and R.C. Mainfort Jr. Washington, DC: Smithsonian Institution Press.
SNYDER, JOHN F. 1962 [1895] 'A Group of Illinois Mounds,' in *John Francis Snyder: Selected Writings*, ed. C.C. Walton. Springfield: Illinois State Historical Society.
SONG, CHEUSOON A., KATHRYN A. JAKES, AND RICHARD W. YERKES 1996 'Seip Hopewell Textile Analysis and Cultural Implications,' *Midcontinental Journal of Archaeology* 21:247–65.
SQUIER, EPHRAIM G., AND EDWIN H. DAVIS 1848 *Ancient Monuments of the Mississippi Valley*. Contributions to Knowledge 1. Washington, DC: Smithsonian Institution.
STAFFORD, BARBARA D. 1985 'Summary,' in *Smiling Dan: Structure and Function at a Middle Woodland Settlement in the Illinois Valley*, eds. B.D. Stafford and M.B. Sant. Research Series 2. Kampsville, IL: Center for American Archeology.
STEADMAN, DAWNIE W. 2001 'Mississippians in Motion? A Population Genetic Analysis of Interregional Gene Flow in West-Central Illinois,' *American Journal of Physical Anthropology* 114:61–73.
STEPONAITIS, VINCAS P. 1998 'Population Trends at Moundville,' in *Archaeology of the Moundville Chiefdom*, eds. V.J. Knight Jr. and V.P. Steponaitis. Tuscaloosa: University of Alabama Press.

STEWART, R. MICHAEL 1995 'The Status of Woodland Prehistory in the Middle Atlantic Region,' *Archaeology of Eastern North America* 23:177–206.
STOLTMAN, JAMES B. 1979 'Middle Woodland Stage Communities of Southwestern Wisconsin,' in *Hopewell Archaeology*, eds. D.S. Brose and N.B. Greber. Kent, OH: Kent State University Press.
STOLTMAN, JAMES B., AND GEORGE W. CHRISTIANSEN 2000 'The Late Woodland Stage in the Driftless Area of the Upper Mississippi Valley,' in *Late Woodland Societies: Tradition and Transformation Across the Midcontinent*, eds. T.E. Emerson, D.L. McElrath, and A.C. Fortier. Lincoln: University of Nebraska Press.
STORCK, PETER L., AND ARTHUR E. SPEISS 1994 'The Significance of New Faunal Identifications Attributed to an Early Paleoindian (Gainey Complex) Occupation at the Udora Site, Ontario, Canada,' *American Antiquity* 59:121–42.
STOUT, CHARLES, AND R. BARRY LEWIS 1998 'Mississippian Towns in Kentucky,' in *Mississippian Towns and Sacred Spaces*, eds. R.B. Lewis and C. Stout. Tuscaloosa: University of Alabama Press.
STRIGHT, MELANIE J. 1990 'Archaeological Sites on the North American Continental Shelf,' in *Archaeological Geology of North America*, eds. N.P. Lasca and J. Donahue. Centennial Special Volume 4. Boulder, CO: Geological Society of America.
STYLES, BONNIE W. 1994 'The Value of Archaeological Faunal Remains for Paleodietary Reconstruction: A Case Study for the Midwestern United States,' in *Paleonutrition: The Diet and Health of Prehistoric Americans*, ed. K.D. Sobolik. Occasional Paper 22. Carbondale: Center for Archaeological Investigations, Southern Illinois University.
— 2000 'Late Woodland Faunal Exploitation in the Midwestern United States,' in *Late Woodland Societies: Tradition and Transformation Across the Midcontinent*, eds. T.E. Emerson, D.L. McElrath, and A.C. Fortier. Lincoln: University of Nebraska Press.
STYLES, BONNIE W., AND WALTER E. KLIPPEL 1996 'Mid-Holocene Faunal Exploitation in the Southeastern United States,' in *Archaeology of the Mid-Holocene Southeast*, eds. K.E. Sassaman and D.G. Anderson. Gainesville: University Press of Florida.
STYLES, BONNIE W., JAMES R. PURDUE, AND MONA L. COLBURN 1985 'Faunal Exploitation at the Smiling Dan Site,' in *Smiling Dan: Structure and Function at a Middle Woodland Settlement in the Illinois Valley*, eds. B.D. Stafford and M.B. Sant. Research Series 2. Kampsville, IL: Center for American Archeology.
SULLIVAN, LYNNE P. 1987 'The Mouse Creek Phase Household,' *Southeastern Archaeology* 6:16–29.
SWANTON, JOHN R. 1911 *Indian Tribes of the Lower Mississippi Valley and Adjacent Coast of the Gulf of Mexico*. Bulletin 43. Washington, DC: Bureau of American Ethnology.
— 1946 *The Indians of the Southeastern United States*. Bulletin 137. Washington, DC: Bureau of American Ethnology.
TANKERSLEY, KENNETH B. 1990 'Late Pleistocene Lithic Exploitation in the Midwest and Midsouth: Indiana, Ohio, and Kentucky,' in *Early Paleoindian Economies of Eastern North America*, eds. K.B. Tankersley and B.L. Isaac. Research in Economic Anthropology Supplement 5. Greenwich, CN: JAI Press.
TANKERSLEY, KENNETH B., AND JULIET E. MORROW 1993 'Clovis Procurement and Land-Use Patterns in the Confluence Region of the Mississippi, Missouri, and Illinois Rivers,' *Illinois Archaeology* 5:119–29.
TANNER, HELEN H. 1987 *Atlas of Great Lakes Indian History*. Norman: University of Oklahoma Press.
TAYLOR, K.C., *et al.* 1997 'The Holocene – Younger Dryas Transition Recorded at Summit, Greenland,' *Science* 278:825–27.
THOMAS, CYRUS 1894 *Report on the Mound Explorations of the Bureau of Ethnology*. 12th Annual Report. Washington, DC: Bureau of Ethnology.
THORNTON, RUSSELL 1987 *American Indian Holocaust and Survival: A Population History Since 1492*. Norman: University

of Oklahoma Press.

THWAITES, REUBEN G. 1896–1901 *The Jesuit Relations and Allied Documents: Travels and Explorations of the Jesuit Missionaries in New France 1610–1791*. 73 vols. Cleveland: Burrows Brothers.

TOTH, ALAN 1974 *Archaeology and Ceramics at the Marksville Site*. Anthropological Papers 56. Ann Arbor: Museum of Anthropology, University of Michigan.

UBELAKER, DOUGLAS H. 1974 *Reconstruction of Demographic Profiles from Ossuary Skeletal Samples*. Smithsonian Contributions to Anthropology 18. Washington, DC: Smithsonian Institution Press.

— 1988 'North American Indian Population Size, AD 1500 to 1985,' *American Journal of Physical Anthropology* 77:289–94.

VAN NEST, JULIANN, et al. 2001 'Sod Blocks in Illinois Hopewell Mounds,' *American Antiquity* 66:633–50.

VARNER, JOHN G., AND JEANNETTE J. VARNER (trans. and eds.) 1951 *The Florida of the Inca*. Austin: University of Texas Press.

VICKERY, KENT D. 1979 '"Reluctant" or "Avant-garde" Hopewell?: Suggestions of Middle Woodland Culture Change in East-Central Indiana and South-Central Ohio,' in *Hopewell Archaeology*, eds. D.S. Brose and N. Greber. Kent, OH: Kent State University Press.

WALTHALL, JOHN A. 1979 'Hopewell and the Southern Heartland,' in *Hopewell Archaeology*, eds. D.S. Brose and N.B. Greber. Kent, OH: Kent State University Press.

WARD, H. TRAWICK, AND R.P. STEPHEN DAVIS JR. 1993 *Indian Communities on the North Carolina Piedmont AD 1000–1700*. Monograph 2. Chapel Hill: Research Laboratories of Anthropology, University of North Carolina.

— 1999 *Time Before History*. Chapel Hill: University of North Carolina Press.

— 2001 'Tribes and Traders on the North Carolina Piedmont, AD 1000–1710,' in *Societies in Eclipse*, eds. D.S. Brose, C.W. Cowan, and R.C. Mainfort Jr. Washington, DC: Smithsonian Institution Press.

WARRICK, GARY A. 1984 *Reconstructing Ontario Iroquoian Village Organization*. Mercury Series 124. Ottawa: National Museum of Man.

— 2000 'The Precontact Iroquoian Occupation of Southern Ontario,' *Journal of World Prehistory* 14:415–46.

WASELKOV, GREGORY A., AND KATHRYN E.H. BRAUND (eds.) 1995 *William Bartram on the Southeastern Indians*. Lincoln: University of Nebraska Press.

WATSON, PATTY JO 1989 'Early Plant Cultivation in the Eastern Woodlands of North America,' in *Foraging and Farming: The Evolution of Plant Exploitation*, eds. D.R. Harris and G.C. Hillman. London: Unwin Hyman.

WEBB, CLARENCE H. 1977 *The Poverty Point Culture*. Geoscience and Man 17. Baton Rouge: School of Geoscience, Louisiana State University.

WEBB, S. DAVID, et al. 1984 'A *Bison Antiquus* Kill Site, Wacissa River, Jefferson County, Florida,' *American Antiquity* 49:384–92.

WEBB, WILLIAM S. 1939 *An Archaeological Survey of the Wheeler Basin on the Tennessee River in Northern Alabama*. Bulletin 122. Washington, DC: Bureau of American Ethnology, Smithsonian Institution.

— 1940 *The Wright Mounds*. Reports in Anthropology 5(1). Lexington: Department of Anthropology, University of Kentucky.

— 1941a *Mt. Horeb Earthworks and the Drake Mound*. Reports in Anthropology 5(2). Lexington: Department of Anthropology, University of Kentucky.

— 1941b *The Morgan Stone Mound*. Reports in Anthropology 5(3). Lexington: Department of Anthropology, University of Kentucky.

— 1942a *The C. and O. Mounds at Paintsville*. Reports in Anthropology 5(4). Lexington: Department of Anthropology, University of Kentucky.

— 1942b *The Robbins Mounds*. Reports in Anthropology 5(5).

Lexington: Department of Anthropology, University of Kentucky.

— 1943a *The Crigler Mounds and the Hartman Mound*. Reports in Anthropology 5(6). Lexington: Department of Anthropology, University of Kentucky.

— 1943b *The Riley Mound and the Landing Mound*. Reports in Anthropology 5(7). Lexington: Department of Anthropology, University of Kentucky.

— 1950 *The Read Shell Midden*. Reports in Anthropology 7(5). Lexington: Department of Anthropology, University of Kentucky.

WEBB, WILLIAM S., AND RAYMOND S. BABY 1957 *The Adena People No. 2*. Columbus: Ohio Historical Society.

WEBB, WILLIAM S., AND DAVID L. DEJARNETTE 1942 *An Archeological Survey of Pickwick Basin in the Adjacent Portions of the States of Alabama, Mississippi and Tennessee*. Bulletin 129. Washington, DC: Bureau of American Ethnology, Smithsonian Institution.

— 1948 *The Flint River Site, Ma*48*. Museum Paper 23. University: Alabama Museum of Natural History.

WEBB, WILLIAM S., AND WILLIAM G. HAAG 1940 *Cypress Creek Villages*. Reports in Anthropology 4(2). Lexington: Department of Anthropology, University of Kentucky.

WEBB, WILLIAM S., AND CHARLES E. SNOW 1945 *The Adena People*. Reports in Archaeology and Anthropology 6. Lexington: Department of Anthropology, University of Kentucky.

WEBSTER, DAVID 1981 'Late Pleistocene Extinction and Human Predation: A Critical Review,' in *Omnivorous Primates*, eds. R.S.O. Harding and G. Teleki. New York: Columbia University Press.

WELCH, PAUL D. 1998 'Outlying Sites Within the Moundville Chiefdom,' in *Archaeology of the Moundville Chiefdom*, eds. V.J. Knight Jr. and V.P. Steponaitis. Tuscaloosa: University of Alabama Press.

WESLER, KIT W. 2001 *Excavations at Wickliffe Mounds*. Tuscaloosa: University of Alabama Press.

WIANT, MICHAEL D. 1993 'Exploring Paleoindian Site Distribution in Illinois,' *Illinois Archaeology* 5:108–18.

WIDMER, RANDOLPH J. 1988 *The Evolution of the Calusa: A Nonagricultural Chiefdom on the Southwest Florida Coast*. Tuscaloosa: University of Alabama Press.

WILLIAMS, STEPHEN 1980 'Armorel: A Very Late Phase in the Lower Mississippi Valley,' *Southeastern Archaeological Conference Bulletin* 22:105–10.

WILLIAMS, STEPHEN, AND JEFFREY P. BRAIN 1983 *Excavations at the Lake George Site, Yazoo County, Mississippi, 1958–1960*. Papers of the Peabody Museum of Archaeology and Ethnology 74. Cambridge: Harvard University.

WILLOUGHBY, CHARLES C. 1919 'The Serpent Mound of Adams County, Ohio,' *American Anthropologist* 21:153–63.

WINTERS, HOWARD D. 1974 'Some Unusual Grave Goods from a Mississippian Burial Mound,' *Indian Notes* 10:34–46.

WINTHORP 1963 [1678] 'The Description, Culture, and Use of Maiz,' *Royal Society of London Philosophical Transactions*, vol. 12. New York: Johnson and Kraus Reprint Corporations.

WRIGHT, H.E. JR. 1992 'Patterns of Holocene Climatic Change in the Midwestern United States,' *Quaternary Research* 38:129–34.

WYMER, DEE ANNE 1997 'Paleoethnobotany in the Licking River Valley, Ohio: Implications for Understanding Ohio Hopewell,' in *Ohio Hopewell Community Organization*, eds. W.S. Dancey and P.J. Pacheco. Kent, OH: Kent State University Press.

YU, ZICHENG 2000 'Ecosystem Response to Late Glacial and Early Holocene Climate Oscillations in the Great Lakes Region of North America,' *Quaternary Science Reviews* 19:1723–47.

ZURELL, RICHARD L. 1999 'Earthwork Enclosure Sites in Michigan,' in *Retrieving Michigan's Buried Past*, ed. J.R. Halsey. Bulletin 64. Bloomfield Hills, MI: Cranbrook Institute of Science.

# Sources of Illustrations

## Color illustrations

I Postcard of shell mound at St Petersburg, Florida.
II Postcard of the Conus in the Mound Cemetery at Marietta, Ohio.
III The Saint Louis Art Museum. Eliza McMillan Trust.
IV Photo G. Milner.
V Photo G. Milner.
VI Photo © Richard Alexander Cooke III.
VII Photo G. Milner.
VIII Photo G. Milner.
IX Cahokia Mounds State Historic Site, painting by Lloyd K. Townsend.
X Photo Melvin L. Fowler.
XI Richard Schlecht, National Geographic Society Image Collection.
XII Cahokia Mounds Museum Society, photo by Art Grossmann
XIII Photo Dirk Bakker © 1985 The Detroit Institute of Arts/Ohio Historical Society.
XIV Photo Dirk Bakker © 1985 The Detroit Institute of Arts/Courtesy of the Frank H. McClung Museum, The University of Tennessee.
XV Photo Dirk Bakker © 1985 The Detroit Institute of Arts/Courtesy of the National Museum of the American Indian, Smithsonian Institution, New York.
XVI Photo Dirk Bakker © 1985 The Detroit Institute of Arts/The University of Arkansas Museum.
XVII Photo Dirk Bakker © 1985 The Detroit Institute of Arts/Courtesy of the U.S. National Park Service, Hopewell Culture National Historical Park.
XVIII Photo Dirk Bakker © 1985 The Detroit Institute of Arts/Ohio Historical Society.
XIX Photo Dirk Bakker © 1985 The Detroit Institute of Arts/Georgia Department of Natural Resources, Etowah Indian Mounds State Historic Site.
XX Photo Dirk Bakker © 1985 The Detroit Institute of Arts/Catalogue No. 448892, Department of Anthropology, Smithsonian Institution, New York.

## Black and white illustrations

*Title page*
Postcard of the Grave Creek mound, Moundsville, West Virginia.
1 Postcard of Monks Mound, Cahokia, Illinois.
2 Map T. Murtha.
3 Photo G. Milner.
4 Courtesy of the Alabama Museum of Natural History (3Mb5).
5 Courtesy of the Ohio Historical Society (P396, B1, F4, E8).
6 Courtesy of the Alabama Museum of Natural History (14Je14).
7 Photo T. M. Easterly, courtesy of the Missouri Historical Society, St. Louis.
8 Photo G. Milner.
9 Drawing R. Larson, courtesy of the Illinois State Museum.
10 Drawing G. Milner after Goodyear 1999: Figure 2b.
11 Map T. Murtha.
12 Courtesy of R. Graham and the Illinois State Museum.
13 Graph G. Milner.
14 Courtesy of the Frank H. McClung Museum, The University of Tennessee.
15 Courtesy of the Illinois State Museum (AR985).
16 Postcard of mound at New Smyrna, Florida.

17 Drawing M. Lorenz.
18 Drawing G. Milner after neg. 3667, the W. S. Webb Museum of Anthropology, University of Kentucky.
19 Drawing G. Milner after Webb and DeJarnette 1948: Figure 21a.
20 Courtesy of the W. S. Webb Museum of Anthropology, University of Kentucky (4467).
21 Courtesy of the Center for Archaeological Investigations, Southern Illinois University, and R. Jefferies.
22 Courtesy of the W. S. Webb Museum of Anthropology, University of Kentucky (4201).
23 Drawing T. Gatlin, reprinted by permission of Southern Illinois University Press, Center for Archaeological Investigations, © 1987 by the Board of Trustees, Southern Illinois University.
24 Courtesy of the Louisiana Ancient Mounds Heritage Area and Trails Advisory Commission.
25 Courtesy of the Louisiana Division of Archaeology.
26 Drawing J. Cooper after photo by R. Jefferies.
27 Courtesy of the Louisiana Ancient Mounds Heritage Area and Trails Advisory Commission.
28 Photo J. Saunders.
29 Drawing G. Milner after Penney 1985: Plate 24.
30 Photo M. Schwadron, courtesy of M. Russo and the U.S. National Park Service.
31 Courtesy of the Illinois State Museum.
32 Map T. Murtha.
33 Courtesy of the Ohio Historical Society (P396, B1, F1, E3).
34 Drawing S. Hammerstedt after Webb 1942a: Figure 14.
35 Courtesy of the W. S. Webb Museum of Anthropology, University of Kentucky (5622).
36 Courtesy of the W. S. Webb Museum of Anthropology, University of Kentucky (4699).
37 Courtesy of the W. S. Webb Museum of Anthropology, University of Kentucky (4629).
38 Drawing J. Cooper.
39 Photo W. Clarke, courtesy of the Cleveland Museum of Natural History and N. Greber.
40 Courtesy of the Cleveland Museum of Natural History.
41 Photo G. Milner.
42 Photo C. Carr and A. Lydecker, courtesy of C. Carr and the Ohio Historical Society.
43 Courtesy of the Ohio Historical Society (P396, B3, F6, E4).
44 Courtesy of the Ohio Historical Society (P396, B3, F6, E6).
45 Drawing S. Hammerstedt after Buikstra 1976: Figure 2.
46 Drawing G. Milner.
47 Drawing S. Hammerstedt after McKern 1931: Figure 15.
48 Courtesy of the Alabama Museum of Natural History (1Ma49).
49 Courtesy of R. Jefferies and D. Hally.
50 Photo G. Milner.
51 Courtesy of the Ohio Historical Society (P396, B4, F2, E6).
52 Drawing S. Hammerstedt after Webb 1941a: Figures 5 and 11.
53 Courtesy of the W. S. Webb Museum of Anthropology, University of Kentucky (3190).
54 Photo G. Milner.
55 Postcard of the Newark earthwork complex, Ohio.
56 Courtesy of the Ohio Historical Society (P396, B4, F2, E3).
57 Courtesy of the Ohio Historical Society (P129, B1, F28).
58 Drawing S. Hammerstedt after Baby and Langlois 1979: Figures 4.3 and 4.4.
59 Peabody Museum, Harvard University, Photo N27081.
60 Photo G. Milner (Field Museum of Natural History, Illinois, 56784, 56797).

61 Photo © The Field Museum, Illinois neg. CSA39671.
62 Graph G. Milner.
63 Drawing J. Cooper after Brose 1985: Plate 48.
64 Photo G. Milner.
65 Drawing J. Cooper after the Ohio Historical Society (P396, B6, F1, E7).
66 Courtesy of the W. S. Webb Museum of Anthropology, University of Kentucky (2263).
67 Photo Dirk Bakker © 1985 The Detroit Institute of Arts/Permission of the University of Michigan Museum of Anthropology.
68 Courtesy of the W. S. Webb Museum of Anthropology, University of Kentucky (2092).
69 Courtesy of the Illinois Transportation Archaeological Research Program, University of Illinois.
70 Courtesy of Wisconsin Historical Society (WHi-2385).
71 Drawing M. Hampshire, courtesy of the U.S. National Park Service.
72 Courtesy of Wisconsin Historical Society (WHi-2389).
73 Drawing S. Hammerstedt after Birmingham and Eisenberg 2000: Figure 5.9.
74 Courtesy of Wisconsin Historical Society (WHi-2386).
75 Drawing S. Hammerstedt after Rolingson 1998: Figure 1.
76 Courtesy of the Arkansas Archeological Survey (TOL C440/19).
77 Courtesy of the Illinois Transportation Archaeological Research Program, University of Illinois.
78 Drawing S. Hammerstedt after Kelly *et al.* 1990: Figure 2.19.
79 Drawing G. Milner after Kelly 1987: Plate 40.
80 Drawing T. Gatlin, reprinted by permission of Southern Illinois University Press, Center for Archaeological Investigations, © 1987 by the Board of Trustees, Southern Illinois University.
81 Map T. Murtha.
82 Courtesy of the Alabama Museum of Natural History (25Ja180).
83 Courtesy of the Alabama Museum of Natural History (47Je14).
84 Drawing S. Hammerstedt after Blitz 1993: Figures 11 and 13.
85 Drawing S. Hammerstedt after National Museum of Natural History field notes.
86 Courtesy of the Oklahoma Archaeological Survey.
87 Courtesy of the National Museum of the American Indian, Smithsonian Institution, New York. Photo Werner Forman.
88 Courtesy of the Illinois State Museum.
89 Computer image E. Schroeder, courtesy of the Illinois State Museum.
90 Photo G. Milner.
91 Taken from Holmes 1883: Plate 58 (facing page 282).
92 Photo by Dirk Bakker © 1985 The Detroit Institute of Arts/Courtesy of the University of Alabama Museums.
93 Taken from Holmes 1883: Plate 70 (facing page 297).
94 Photo G. Milner (Field Museum of Natural History, Illinois, 55500).
95 Drawing J. Cooper after Brown 1985b: Figure 19.

96 Drawing J. Cooper after an Illinois Transportation Archaeological Research Program photo.
97 Photo Dirk Bakker © 1985 The Detroit Institute of Arts/From the Collections of the Saint Louis Science Center.
98 Courtesy of the W. S. Webb Museum of Anthropology, University of Kentucky (7109).
99 Drawing J. Cooper.
100 Courtesy of the Illinois Transportation Archaeological Research Program, University of Illinois.
101 Courtesy of the Alabama Museum of Natural History (2890).
102 Courtesy of the Center for Archaeological Investigations, Southern Illinois University, and J. Porter.
103 Courtesy of R. Diehl.
104 Courtesy of the Alabama Museum of Natural History (3896).
105 Drawing S. Hammerstedt after O'Brien 2001: Figure 5.8, and Price and Griffin 1979: Figure 12.
106 Courtesy of the Illinois Transportation Archaeological Research Program, University of Illinois.
107 Drawing M. Lorenz after Swanton 1946: Plate 73.1.
108 Courtesy of the Illinois State Museum and M. Fowler.
109 Photo G. Milner.
110 Courtesy of the Illinois Transportation Archaeological Research Program, University of Illinois.
111 Drawing G. Milner (Illinois State Museum specimens).
112 Photo G. Milner (Field Museum of Natural History, Illinois, 50717).
113 Photo G. Milner.
114 Photo G. Milner.
115 Courtesy of the W. S. Webb Museum of Anthropology, University of Kentucky (7285).
116 Photo G. Milner.
117 Painting M. Pate, Newnan, GA, courtesy of the artist and the Southeast Archeological Center, U.S. National Park Service.
118 Photo G. Milner; Matson Museum of Anthropology, Pennsylvania State University.
119 Courtesy of the Illinois State Museum.
120 Photo G. Milner.
121 Drawing G. Milner after Santure and Esarey 1990: Figure 10.4.
122 Photo D. Snow.
123 Photo D. Snow.
124 Drawing G. McKay, courtesy of D. Snow.
125 Courtesy of Dover Publications, Harriot 1972 [1590]: 67.
126 Courtesy of the Arkansas Archeological Survey (PAR-93 946060).
127 Courtesy of Claitor's Publishing Division, Du Pratz 1972 [1790]: 338.
128 Drawing G. Milner after Smith 2000: Plate 2d.
129 Courtesy of the Illinois State Museum.
130 Painting R. Lindeaux, courtesy of the Woolaroc Museum, Bartlesville, Oklahoma.
131 Postcard of mounds at St. Paul, Minnesota.

# Index